THE JENA SYSTEM, 1804–5: LOGIC AND METAPHYSICS

G. W. F. HEGEL

Translation edited by John W. Burbidge and George di Giovanni
With an introduction and explanatory notes by H. S. Harris

Translated into English for the first time in this edition, *The Jena System, 1804–5: Logic and Metaphysics* is an essential text in the study of the development of Hegel's thought. It is the climax of Hegel's efforts to construct a neutral theory of the categories of finite cognition ("logic") as the necessary bridge to the theory of infinite, or philosophical, cognition ("metaphysics").

As he worked on the Jena system, Hegel's understanding of the nature of logic and its connection with metaphysics underwent changes crucial to his later system. As a result, logic acquired a new and expanded significance for him. This text is thus the key to an understanding of the works of Hegel's maturity, and to their relation to the major works of Schelling and Fichte that preceded them.

Scholars from the universities of Guelph, Lethbridge, McGill, McMaster, Toronto, Trent, and York have prepared this translation, a work of critical analysis in its own right. The introduction by H. S. Harris adds a concrete dimension to Hegel's abstract categories, showing how, in developing these categories, Hegel was even at this early date thinking deeply about the structure and life of society.

JOHN W. BURBIDGE is a member of the Department of Philosophy, Trent University.

GEORGE DI GIOVANNI is a member of the Department of Philosophy, McGill University.

H. S. HARRIS is a member of the Department of Philosophy, Glendon College, York University, and author of several books on Hegel.

McGILL-QUEEN'S STUDIES IN THE HISTORY OF IDEAS

G. W. F. HEGEL
THE JENA SYSTEM, 1804–5:
LOGIC AND METAPHYSICS

Translation edited by
John W. Burbidge and George di Giovanni

Introduction and
explanatory notes by H. S. Harris

McGill-Queen's University Press
Kingston and Montreal

© McGill-Queen's University Press 1986
ISBN 0–7735–1011–7
Legal deposit 2nd quarter 1986
Bibliothèque nationale du Québec
Printed in Canada

The translation of Hegel's text is from G. W. F. Hegel, *Gesammelte Werke*, volume 7, *Jenaer Systementwürfe II*, edited by Rolf-P. Horstmann and Johann Heinrich Trede and published by Felix Meiner Verlag, Hamburg, 1971. By permission of the Rheinisch-Westfälischen Akademie der Wissenschaften in Düsseldorf.

This book has been published with the help of a grant from the Canadian Federation for the Humanities, using funds provided by the Social Sciences and Humanities Research Council of Canada.

Canadian Cataloguing in Publication Data

Hegel, Georg Wilhelm Friedrich, 1776–1831.
The Jena system, 1804–5
Translation of: Jenaer Systementwürfe II.
Bibliography: p.
Includes index.
ISBN 0–7735–1011–7
1. Logic. 2. Metaphysics. I. Burbidge, John, 1936–
II. Di Giovanni, George, 1935–   III. Title.
B2944.J42E5 1986   193   c85–099954–5

Contents

THE JENA SYSTEM, 1804–5: LOGIC AND METAPHYSICS

METAPHYSICS 131

Preface to the Translation

At the 1978 meeting of the Hegel Society of America, held at Pennsylvania State University, John Burbidge called together all the members in attendance from Ontario and Quebec and suggested that the group meet regularly somewhere in Toronto to discuss issues of common interest. He also suggested that, as a catalyst for discussion, the group undertake a common project, such as the translation of a Hegelian text. H. S. Harris proposed the Jena Logic as a suitable candidate. Both Burbidge's idea and Harris's specific proposal were accepted, and a meeting that was to be the first of a long series was soon called at Trinity College in the University of Toronto. In the early stages the group was able to work from a draft prepared by André Dekker. Subsequently, those named below undertook in turn to provide preliminary translations, which were then submitted for discussion and revision to the group as a whole. Burbidge, Donogho, di Giovanni, Harris, Pfohl, and Schmitz formed a core group that provided continuity. Peter Preuss contributed valuable editorial comments from a distance.

At first the group had no intention of ever publishing the results of its work. Over the years, however, as the group became more cohesive and was drawn more and more into the problems of interpreting and translating an early Hegelian text, its members slowly came to appreciate the complexity and the value of the project they had undertaken. They decided at one point to extend the translation to include the Metaphysics, too, and to see to it that the translation would eventually be published. The Logic and Metaphysics represent, in effect, half of Hegel's 1804–5 system. The group chose not to tackle the third and largest part, the Philosophy of Nature, because its translation would require specialized knowledge that none of the members has and also because it is removed from the interests of all of them. The final text was edited by Burbidge and di Giovanni, and the index prepared by Pfohl.

The text we used was that edited by R.-P. Horstmann and J. H. Trede in volume seven (1971) of the critical edition of Hegel's work, which will be referred to as CE. The bracketed numbers in our text indicate the beginning of the pages in the critical edition. We have not felt bound by the German editors' decisions, however, and have frequently preferred the original manuscript to their emendations. We have on occasion incorporated suggestions from two previous editions, that of H. Ehrenberg and H. Link (*Hegels erstes System*) and that of G. Lasson (*Jenenser Logik, Metaphysik und Naturphilosophie*). Most of our emendations involve punctuation (locating the comma that demarcates the range of a subordinate clause; introducing semi-colons into run-on sentences, and so forth), providing auxiliary verbs where only an infinitive or participle is present, and variations in grammatical suffixes and pronominal genders. At many points we compared our proposals with the French translation of D. Souche-Dagues, *Logique et Métaphysique, Iéna 1804–1805*. Unfortunately, the Italian translation of F. Chiereghin et al., *Logica e metafisica di Jena*, appeared too late to be of use to us in the translation.

The manuscript proper is a good copy (or *reine Schrift*) prepared by Hegel himself. In the first part minor amendments appear, indicating that Hegel made editorial revisions on a later reading. From the beginning of 'The Syllogism,' however, there is less evidence of careful revision, and in the sections on the syllogism and proportion we find a number of comments entered in the margin and extensive underlining, which suggests that Hegel used this material either for lectures or in preparing a later manuscript.

Hegel's numbering of the sections follows no consistent convention, and in the Metaphysics it becomes quite confused. The major sections are numbered: I. Cognition as System of First Principles; B. Metaphysics of Objectivity; C. Metaphysics of Subjectivity. The subsections of I are labelled A, B, and C; those of B as I, B, C; and those of C as I, II, III. We have left these numberings in the text, but the table of contents is structured on the underlying principles. We have indicated the relative level of the titles of the various sections by means of typography.

Some pages of the original manuscript are missing. Hegel used large sheets, folded in four, and numbered each set of four. Missing are sheets 1 to 3, the inner half of sheet 6, all of sheet 7, and the inner half of sheet 39.

Although a good copy, the manuscript is written in a language that is just as cumbersome and obscure as only Hegel (and especially the younger Hegel) would use. In our translation we have endeavoured to get to the meaning of Hegel's text and render it in a language that, while faithful to the original, yet retains as little as possible of its cumbersomeness. Any translation is first of all appropriation. It can therefore make the text much more accessible by clarifying it in the very process of translating it. That task in part resolves itself into the development of certain conventions, and the most important of the conventions we adopted are summarized in the glossary. Some must be noted here, however, because of their especially broad application:

— To distinguish *formelle, ideelle,* and *reelle* from *formale, ideale,* and *reale,* we use with the English "formal," "ideal," and "real" the subscript $_2$ (for example, "formal$_2$") to indicate the German form that has two *l*s.

— The article *ein* used with a neuter adjective or participle we translate "something . . ."; *das* with an adjective is translated "what is. . . ." For example, *ein gesetztes*: "something posited"; *das gesetzte*: "what is posited."

— In German the gender of a pronoun frequently allows a precise reference to the appropriate noun. In our translation we have often substituted nouns for pronouns when the reference is clear in German but would become problematic in English if the pronoun were kept.

— Occasionally, where a root is common to several different German words used in the same discussion, we have included the originals. We have done the same where our translation has had to deviate from conventions to clarify meaning.

— We have used parentheses as punctuation, along with frequent dashes and semi-colons, to bring some order into the long, intricate sentences of Hegel. Square brackets, however, indicate insertions either by the German editors or by the translators.

The translators express their appreciation to the provost of Trinity College, Professor F. K. Hare, who most graciously provided facilities for our use and encouraged us with our venture. They also wish to acknowledge grants from Trent University and McGill University that helped to defray some of the costs of the translation and of the preparation of the final manuscript.

Lorraine Code
William Carruthers
Martin Donogho
Henry S. Harris
Helga Hunter
Kem Luther

Lee Manchester
Jeff Mitscherling
David Pfohl
Kenneth Schmitz
Donald Stewart

JOHN BURBIDGE
Trent University

GEORGE DI GIOVANNI
McGill University

Preface to the Commentary

In writing the Introduction and headnotes to our translation I have found the much more ambitious commentary provided by the Italian translators very helpful. This translation, *Logica e metafisica di Jena*, edited by F. Chiereghin and others, came to our notice too late to be of assistance in the making of our own, English version. But the commentary (which is about twice as long as the translated text) deserves the attention of all readers who can use it. Chiereghin and his collaborators have traced both the earlier and the later evolution of the main categories of the present work.

My own aim here is much humbler—and rather different. The best summary and analysis of Hegel's argument in its own terms that I was able to give when this translation was still in its infancy will be found in my *Night Thoughts*, chapter 8.[1] So instead of repeating that, I have here tried to interpret the structure and goals of Hegel's logical construction in terms of the "real philosophy" that it was designed to lead to—and especially in terms of the "First Philosophy of Spirit,"[2] which Hegel had only recently composed and clearly intended to revise as the climax of the manual that he was here trying to write. It will be clear to any careful reader that the theory of social consciousness that forms the main thread of my interpretation is not the only concern in Hegel's mind. Indeed, the student of the text may even be tempted to think at some stages that this concern is not in

1. *Hegel's Development II: Night Thoughts (Jena 1801–6)*, hereinafter referred to as *Night Thoughts*.
2. In *Gesammelte Werke*, VI, 268–331; and in Harris and Knox, trans. and eds., *System of Ethical Life and First Philosophy of Spirit*, pp. 205–50.

Hegel's mind at all. I have, however, focused attention on the way in which the argument of the Logic and Metaphysics is exemplified in social experience because I believe that this is the best way to show how Hegel's project arose from (and is related to) the earlier projects and problems of Kant and Hegel.[3] The manuscript here translated is the earliest formulation of Hegel's conception of "pure thinking" that has survived. But because the projects of the later *Phenomenology* and *Science of Logic* are united in a single undertaking in this Logic and Metaphysics, Hegel's own determination to develop logical theory from a neutral standpoint does not obscure his preoccupation with the more "subjective" logic of Kant and Fichte. I have relied on this generally evident preoccupation to justify my own reading of the whole argument in terms of the emergence of consciousness (or singular subjectivity) in the social substance.[4]

H. S. HARRIS
Glendon College
York University

3. If we forget about Kant's "deduction of the categories" and Fichte's "self-positing of the Ego," then the affinities of Hegel's work with the *Parmenides* of Plato, with Aristotle's theology, and with the Cartesian tradition may lead us to agree with Michael Rosen, in *Hegel's Dialectic and Its Criticism*, that the short answer to the question "What is living in the logic of Hegel?" is "Nothing" (p. 179).

4. Even the Italian commentators could perhaps learn from my few pages to concentrate their attention on Leibniz, rather than Spinoza, as Hegel's philosopher of "substance" in the present text.

H. S. Harris

General Introduction

On 29 September 1804 (just a month or so after his thirty-fourth birthday) Hegel appealed to Goethe to see to it that he was not passed over when certain other licensed private teachers (*Privatdozenten*) of philosophy at the University of Jena were promoted to the rank of professor. At that time he had been teaching philosophy at Jena for three years and he was the senior *Privatdozent* in the field. Also, since Schelling's departure to Wurzburg in the spring of 1803 Hegel had been for more than a year the principal representative at Jena of the kind of natural philosophy that he knew Goethe was anxious to foster. He had some right, therefore, to count on Goethe's support, and he duly received it.[1]

In his appeal to Goethe Hegel dismissed his own published work as unworthy of the great man's attention.[2] But he did think fit to mention to Goethe the manuscript that he was currently working on: "the purpose of a work that I hope to complete this winter for my

---

1. But the promotion, when it came, still brought him no salary—it took Goethe another year to procure the tiniest pittance for him (a mere one hundred dollars)—so his financial situation, which was already very straitened, soon became critical.

2. His *published* essays, being mainly technical philosophical criticism and polemic, were not likely to interest Goethe much. But he no doubt expressed himself in this way because, ever since the departure of Schelling, he had been expounding his philosophical system in quite a different way. As the reader will soon see for himself, the "purely scientific treatment of philosophy" that Hegel was willing to lay before Goethe as soon as it was ready was just as technical as the *Difference* essay or *Faith and Knowledge* or the essay on *Natural Law*. (And we should remember that we only know definitely which of the major essays in the *Critical Journal* of 1801–3 [*Gesammelte Werke*, Band IV] were Hegel's because he had to submit a curriculum vitae, including a list of publications, before his promotion could be approved.)

lectures—a purely scientific treatment of philosophy—will allow me to lay it before your excellency, if you will kindly permit me to do that."[3]

From the evidence of the handwriting we can say with considerable security that the Logic and Metaphysics here translated formed the first part of this "purely scientific treatment of philosophy." Some of it was recopied from earlier drafts—for Hegel had been lecturing on logic and metaphysics regularly, and he had been announcing the imminent publication of a textbook ever since his second semester. But the *structure* into which the older material was incorporated was itself new. After two years spent in the elaboration of a four-part system in terms of a number of fundamental dichotomies and antitheses established by Schelling, Hegel began, in October 1803, to articulate his thought in terms of the great triad of logic, nature, and spirit that is familiar to students of the Berlin *Encyclopaedia*. The treatise that he mentions to Goethe was to be articulated in this way. But we can see from the manuscript as we have it that he did not finish it; and from the subsequent lecture announcements and the surviving manuscripts of the system in its next state we can infer that it was precisely a revolution in his concept of logic that caused him to abandon our manuscript about half-way through the Philosophy of Nature.[4]

To reconstruct the early evolution of Hegel's conception of philosophical logic is not easy, because the evidence is very fragmentary and inadequate. Any reconstruction must contain much that is hypothetical and some elements that are mere conjecture. But certain basic facts are clear enough to be relatively uncontroversial; and it is important for the reader of this first surviving version of Hegel's logic to be familiar with them because the mature logic (which anglophone readers first met in the pages of Stirling's *Secret of Hegel* in 1865) only began to emerge as a result of the revolution in Hegel's thought that caused him to abandon our manuscript unfinished. What we have here is the final form of his *early* logic. A preliminary account of how the

---

3. *Briefe von und an Hegel*, ed. Hoffmeister and Flechsig, 1, 85.
4. We have not translated the incomplete Philosophy of Nature. A short note about it appears at the end of our translation of the Logic and Metaphysics.

The next phase in the evolution of Hegel's logic itself does not survive in the manuscripts. But we have both lecture announcements *about* the new logic (no longer "Logic and Metaphysics") and the new logical structure of the "real philosophy" (the Philosophy of Nature and Spirit of 1805, which does survive) as evidence for the revolution in Hegel's logical theory.

early concept of logic differs from the later one is therefore essential, even though it has to be somewhat schematic, and some rather conjectural statements about its evolution must be asserted dogmatically.[5]

"Logic," in the essays that Hegel thought unworthy of Goethe's notice, is "the extended science of the Idea as such."[6] "Idealism" is a synonym for logic in this more general sense. The "Idea of reason" in its "extended" form in human experience and in the sciences requires to be collected and organized into systematic coherence. The collecting is a "critical" task, since the elements cannot be organized just as we find them. Thus, "transcendental philosophy" (another synonym for "idealism, or logic") has two great branches: critical theory and speculation.[7] When Hegel gave courses under the traditional title "Logic and Metaphysics," he used these more specific terms for the two branches of "idealism, or logic," generally. In this narrower usage logic is *critical* idealism, the necessary preamble to speculative metaphysics properly so called. Our manuscript is divided in this way. Logic is distinguished here as a preparatory or introductory study for philosophy proper. The *systematic* exposition of philosophy begins only with "metaphysics." When Hegel himself gave systematic survey courses, he either dispensed with the critical preamble altogether or supplied only a minimal version or substitute for it. So what he called logic in these systematic courses was (at least in the main) metaphysics according to the technical division of the two topics in our present manuscript.[8]

5. The story can be found in full detail in Harris, *Night Thoughts*; see pp. 22–73, 200–206, 226–37, and chap. 8.

6. This definition actually comes from Hegel's draft for the first lecture of his *Introduction to Philosophy* (Oct. 1801). The text will be found in *Gesammelte Werke*, v, 259–65. But see also Harris and Cerf, trans. and eds., *The Difference between Fichte's and Schelling's System of Philosophy*, pp. 89–117.

7. The identity of philosophy with "idealism, or logic" (and the resultant possibility of its reduction to logic in the narrow, or "critical" sense) is clearly explained in Cerf and Harris, trans. and eds., *Faith and Knowledge*, p. 68. For Hegel's use of "transcendental philosophy" in this sense see especially the announcement of the "System of Speculative Philosophy" for the winter semester of 1803–4 (*Hegel-Studien* 4: 54; *Night Thoughts*, pp. 228–29n).

8. It is clear, for instance, that the lost "Logic" of the "System of Speculative Philosophy" of 1803–4 was in the main a metaphysical theory of "Substance" (see the retrospective summary of the argument at the beginning of the surviving "Philosophy of Spirit," in Harris and Knox, trans. and eds., *System of Ethical Life and First Philosophy of Spirit*, p. 205. The fragments of the introductory lecture for the "Delineatio" of 1803 (*Gesammelte Werke*, v, 365–69; see Harris, *Night Thoughts*, pp. 200–202) show that critical

Logic—both in the broad, speculative sense and in the narrow, critical sense—was an innovation introduced into the "transcendental idealism" of Schelling's identity philosophy by Hegel himself. He insisted that the critical approach to the "absolute identity" must be "objective," in the sense of being neutrally applicable both to thinking subjects and to the objects of thought.[9] Thus the logic of his first course on logic and metaphysics began with the theory of the "finite categories" taken in this logically neutral or objective sense. This approach was critical, first, in the obvious sense that it was founded upon a critique of the "subjective formalism" of Kant (whose categories are the *forms of subjective manifestation* for a problematic absolute object, the "thing in itself"). But secondly—and much more importantly—Hegel's logic was critical in its own internal method. It proceeds dialectically, or (to use the language of Plato's *Republic*) by the "destruction of hypotheses." In the first phase the categories are brought forth one by one, only to be "nullified" in their relation to the absolute.

From Hegel's essay *The Difference between Fichte's and Schelling's System of Philosophy* (1801) we can reliably infer that the finite categories that were here engulfed in the absolute must have included Kant's first three triads but not the final triad of modality, for in that essay Hegel dismisses the categories of modality as principles of "the nonidentity of subject and object."[10] We can also infer from this passage that these nine categories were not the only ones treated in his first course; and we know that Kant did not treat them in the proper order, "just as they come forth from reason." But what this proper order was we cannot say. The Logic of 1804 proceeds from the triad of quality to that of quantity and arrives finally at the categories of relation. But Hegel's insistence in 1801 that "we must always keep before our eyes the archetype that it [understanding] copies" might

---

logic was replaced (at least in that instance) by a discussion of the cultural "need of philosophy." In the Berlin *Encyclopaedia*, by contrast, the systematic exposition of the need of philosophy (in the *Phenomenology of Spirit*) was replaced by something more nearly akin to the critical logic of the early Jena years. (This comparison helps us to recognize that the introduction to the *Encyclopaedia* is only a pedagogical expedient.)

9. See *Gesammelte Werke*, v, 271–72, for Hegel's programmatic outline for this course. The slightly abbreviated quotation by Rosenkranz is translated in Cerf and Harris, *Faith and Knowledge*, pp. 9–10, and the omissions are made good in Harris, *Night Thoughts*, pp. 36–37.

10. *Gesammelte Werke*, IV, 6; Harris and Cerf, *Difference*, p. 80.

be taken to imply that the "dynamic" categories, and particularly the category of "substance and accident" (which is called in the *Difference* essay "the true relation of speculation"),[11] came first. Schelling had already inverted the order of the dynamic and the "mathematical" categories (in the deduction offered in the *System of Transcendental Idealism*).[12] It was Fichte who was the first to begin from the categories of quality,[13] as Hegel does in 1804 (and always thereafter). Hegel was consciously proud of his logic as a novelty in 1801, but it seems altogether probable that he would follow Schelling's lead at that stage. The model offered by Fichte would more naturally have attracted Hegel's serious attention when he adopted the new phenomenological approach (through the concept of "consciousness") in 1803.[14] According to the *Difference* essay, the "negative absolute" in which the finite categories of our intuitive spatio-temporal experience are nullified is the understanding itself. So the second phase of the logic of 1801 was the theory of finite intelligence in its active construction of concepts, judgments, and syllogisms.[15]

This construction is engulfed, in its turn, in the "true infinite of reason." What Hegel calls "the speculative theory of the syllogism" leads us in 1801 to a metaphysics that was apparently an exposition of the "Idea of philosophy" combined with a critique of the systematic forms that it has assumed (dogmatic, transcendental, idealistic, realistic, and sceptical) during its history.[16] From the Idea of philosophy

11. *Gesammelte Werke*, IV, 33; Harris and Cerf, *Difference*, p. 166.

12. F. W. J. Schelling, *System des Transcendentalen Idealismus*, in *Sämmtliche Werke*, I, iii, 467ff., 505ff.; Heath, trans., pp. 103–12, 134–54.

13. J. G. Fichte, *Grundlage der gesammten Wissenschaftslehre* (1794), in *Sämtliche Werke*, I, 125ff.; Heath and Lachs, trans., pp. 122ff.

14. The view taken in *Night Thoughts* (pp. 42–43) that the order in 1801 was probably the same as that of 1804 now seems to me less probable because of these antecedent models, to which my attention was drawn by the commentaries of Chiereghin and Moretta in the Italian translation.

15. In *Night Thoughts* (pp. 43–52) I have shown how this part of the program can be interpreted in terms of the reconstruction of Kant that Hegel offers us in *Faith and Knowledge*. But Werner Hartkopf has rightly pointed to the "mechanism of intelligence" in Schelling's *System of Transcendental Idealism* as a probable model for Hegel's logical theory (*Kontinuität und Diskontinuität in Hegels Jenaer Anfängen*, esp. pp. 254–55).

16. Hegel's first course broke up early and he retired to his study to write a textbook before he attempted to teach the subject again. So it is quite possible that the first project for metaphysics never existed in written-out form at all. We know that the first textbook draft contained a *systema reflexionis* (logic) and a *systema rationis* (metaphysics); but how these two systems were related either to one another or to the earlier and

Hegel's version of the identity system moved to "real philosophy," or the theory of "the universe." This differed from the "philosophy of nature," which succeeds metaphysics in our manuscript, because it embraced the whole of finite reality. The philosophy of finite spirit was itself one of the two parallel aspects of the "absolute identity." It was also *higher* than the theory of physical nature because it dealt with the practical *reconstruction* of identity as the intuition of *ethical* nature. But it was itself *part* of nature as a whole; so the relation of spirit and nature was more positive and direct than that which exists in the tripartite system to which our Logic and Metaphysics belongs. In the earlier system it is only the theory of absolute (or free) spirit that stands apart as the "resumption into unity" of the whole extension of "idealism, or logic."[17]

We do not know how the *systema reflexionis et rationis* of 1802 was organized. It seems possible (for example) that the cyclic parallel treatment of Cartesian, Spinozist, and Leibnizian themes that is to be found both in the Logic and in the Metaphysics of 1804 had its origin here. For this cyclic parallel can be viewed as a reflection of the historical treatment of metaphysics projected in 1801. But this is mere speculation (and unless more of the manuscripts are found, it can never be any more than that). What we know for certain is that as soon as Schelling left Jena (so that Hegel was obligated to lecture on the identity philosophy as a whole), the Kantian conception of a moral *opposition* between nature and spirit began to take on greater significance in Hegel's mind. At the same time the theme of *consciousness* as the discursive medium of experience became the focal topic of his philosophical system. In the pure abstraction of logic this theme appears as the concept of "cognition." The task of logic generally is to

---

later versions of Logic and Metaphysics is not certain. (Parts of this first textbook may survive in our text, and even the basic pattern of our text may go back to 1802. But Hegel continued to employ the critical-historical approach to metaphysics too. So there is no solid ground even for conjectures here.)

17. This emphasis on the contrast between the finite world (nature, and finite spirit, subjective and objective) and the infinite (transcendental philosophy and absolute spirit) is maintained in the system of 1805, but is there successfully conciliated with the triadic structure of 1803–4. The conciliation thus achieved remains valid in Hegel's maturity; and for that reason the *Phenomenology*—as the final instrument of this conciliation—remains essential to the encyclopaedic synthesis. (It supplies the mature form of the critical survey of the Idea in its "extension"; this is what is "resumed" in the mature theory of absolute spirit.)

construct the concept of "absolute cognition": "The Idea of cognition is the first Idea of metaphysics."[18]

The fragments dealing with Hegel's logic and metaphysics in this first year after Schelling's departure are rather exiguous. We have a draft for two "notes" that were probably part of the continually evolving textbook, and the summary outline for a discussion of metaphysics that would have occupied several lectures. The two notes are also concerned with the foundation stone of metaphysics; the remarkable thing about this stage in Hegel's logical reflections is that the starting-point of metaphysics is taken to be a unitary principle. Instead of beginning (as our Metaphysics does, in 1804) with a "system of principles," the Metaphysics of 1803 apparently began with a "fundamental proposition." We do not know for certain what this basic thesis about philosophical cognition was; but the most plausible inference from the evidence that we have suggests that it was a formulation of the "principle of ground."[19] In any case this proposition with which metaphysics began was also the terminus of philosophical speculation. Thus, the ideal of philosophy as a self-grounding circle was perfectly realized.

The ideal of this perfect circularity, however, creates a problem. For it is now hard to see how the initial approach to this closed circle of speculative knowledge can be a *logical* one. The comprehension of one's time and of its "need of philosophy" seems now to be the only natural path to the discovery of this absolute beginning (and end) of metaphysics.

This is the solution that Hegel eventually adopted in the "system of science," which combined the "science of the experience of consciousness" with the "science of logic." But before he could be satisfied with that solution, he had to find a way of resolving all of the *logical* content of his critical logic into the unitary science of speculative logic (which is this circular metaphysics under its *general* name). In 1804 the Metaphysics begins with a system of principles and proceeds to

18. *Gesammelte Werke*, VII, 341. This sketch for lecturing on or writing up the topic of metaphysics cannot be dated at all precisely because of its brevity. But it must be later than April 1803, and it does not fit into the plan for *our* manuscript, which was certainly clear in Hegel's mind before September 1804. (Someone, however, did insert it into our manuscript at a more or less appropriate point.)

19. See the "Zwei Anmerkungen" in *Gesammelte Werke*, VII, 343–47; the discussion in *Night Thoughts*, 226–37, depends heavily on the interpretation proposed by J. H. Trede (*Hegel-Studien* 7: 160–65).

deal with the Kantian "Ideas of reason" (which are the topic of the Metaphysics outline of 1803–4). But at the climax of the very first phase of the Logic we are already faced with the true infinite. Admittedly, the true infinite is introduced at this point only by anticipation: in the Logic it actually functions only negatively. Thus the essentially critical (or dialectical)[20] character of logic in the narrow sense is preserved. But the very fact that the true infinite can legitimately be introduced so early in the discussion shows how easy the move to a *completely speculative* conception of logic and metaphysics has now become.

In order that this speculative conversion may occur, critical logic must lose its *externally* reflective character, that is, its dependence upon the *contingent* consciousness of a particular thinker. Even as the logic of understanding (which is what we find in the first phase of the present manuscript), logic must be the work of *absolute* reflection. This implies that the problem of how the historically contingent consciousness of the rational animal is to overcome its contingency and arrive at the absolute standpoint of "pure thought" must be consigned to a different science. The "need of philosophy" and the evolution of consciousness to the point where this need is *absolutely* comprehended—that is, the point where it is comprehended as the self-sufficient goal of rational cognition, or as the very *concept* of cognition—must become the object of quite a different logical science, the science of *time*, and of our "experience of consciousness" in time.

The logic of our manuscript is ready for this conversion. Since we know that Hegel had already experimented with a *historical* approach to his "system," it is no surprise to learn that in the semester following his promotion Hegel announced a course on his system as a whole but actually gave one on "Logic."[21] And we find also among our manuscript remains, at the very moment of this change, the earliest scraps that are demonstrably connected with the project of the *Phenomenology.*[22]

---

20. In all his Jena writings, but especially in this manuscript, Hegel uses the noun and adjective "dialectic," "dialectical," to refer to an essentially negative, destructive process, phase, or method. The process is *progressive* because the overthrow of each thought-hypothesis (or the breakdown of a real institution) indicates or leads us to its replacement.

21. The announcement for summer 1805 is in *Hegel-Studien* 4: 54. We know about the actual course because we have the list of the students who enrolled in it (ibid., 62).

22. Rosenkranz, in *Georg Wilhelm Friedrich Hegels Leben*, p. 202, considered that

It is likely that the course on logic in summer 1805 dealt with phenomenology and speculative logic together. We know that once the manuscript of the *Phenomenology* existed, Hegel used it in his course on "Speculative Philosophy or Logic" (summer 1806, the last course that he actually gave at Jena); and he even included the topic "Phenomenology of Spirit" separately in the announcement for winter 1806–7 (when he actually gave no classes because the military and political crisis coincided with, and contributed to, his own personal crisis, and forced him to abandon his first academic career). In the summer course of 1806 the speculative logic was dealt with only briefly at the end of a much fuller treatment of (at least some parts of) the *Phenomenology*.[23]

Possibly Hegel's new speculative logic was still only a skeleton when he left Jena. For his most urgent task was to work out the application of the new *logical* method to his "real philosophy." He lectured on this steadily in 1805 and 1806, and the manuscript—which has come down to us—shows that the whole system was reorganized in accordance with the fully developed pattern of what is called in the work of Hegel's maturity "subjective logic." Every stage—from the basic theory of space and time onwards—is conceived as an evolution from "concept" through "judgment" to "syllogism."

This whole task of reorganizing the "real philosophy" was achieved after the abandonment of our manuscript (in which the philosophy of nature is organized in quite a different way). But K. W. G. Kastner (who attended the class for which our manuscript was written, before passing on to Heidelberg as professor of chemistry the next year) wrote to Schelling in March 1806 that "according to the Jena lecture-list Hegel's system is appearing at Easter, and as I have heard tell it is in four volumes at one time."[24] Kastner misunderstood the lecture-list (which announced only the "System of Science," meaning phen-

---

Hegel conceived this project as early as 1804. But the rightful assignment of our present manuscript to that period makes his hypothesis rather implausible. The earliest fragment that can plausibly be interpreted as part of such a project is a sketch dealing with the clash of divine and human law (*Gesammelte Werke*, IX, 437). This was written on the back of one of the drafts for Hegel's letter to Voss (May 1805).

23. The course announcements are in *Hegel-Studien* 4: 54–55; for the content of the 1806 course on "Logic and Metaphysics or Speculative Philosophy" we have the testimony of Gabler, who took it (ibid., 71).

24. G. Nicolin, ed., *Hegel in Berichten seiner Zeitgenossen*, report 43.

omenology and logic together). But either Hegel himself or someone
close to him had obviously said or written that the system would be
in four parts and that it would appear soon. Had it not been for the
battle of Jena (and the imminent arrival of an illegitimate child),
Kastner's forecast might have been fulfilled within a year or two. In
actual fact it took Hegel ten more years to complete the Logic, and
he never did produce the "real philosophy" in a proper book form
at all.

From this bird's-eye view of the evolution of Hegel's logic we can
see that there is indeed, as J. Heinrichs suspected, a close relation
between the Logic of 1804 and the program of the *Phenomenology*.[25]
But the relation is both closer and more distant than he believed. The
whole system that the Logic of 1804 is designed to introduce was
conceived and structured phenomenologically (that is, as a logical
evolution of consciousness). It is therefore right to look for the principle of consciousness in the Jena Logic from the very beginning.
"Consciousness," or the subject-object opposition, appears there as the
principle of "reflection"; and in the brief analyses of each stage of the
argument that are offered here as aids to the user of this translation,
I have tried to show how the dialectic of subject and object in consciousness can provide a key to difficult transitions.[26]

But Heinrichs' claim that the pattern of the Logic and Metaphysics
of 1804 can be directly mapped on to the *Phenomenology* of 1807 is
highly dubious, since the *Phenomenology* of 1807, although itself an
introduction and first part to the system of philosophy, repeats the
whole sytem of 1803–5 (not just that introduction and first part that
the Logic and Metaphysics was to be). A mapping of this kind may
still be possible, because of the internal mirroring that can be observed
in properly selected "wholes" within Hegel's system. The Logic and
Metaphysics is one such whole, and it does share with the *Phenomenology* the peculiarity of being both an introduction and a first part.
But the problem of the relationship between them must be ap-

---

25. *Die Logik der "Phänomenologie des Geistes."*
26. This is a novelty in the analyses offered here as compared with the more detailed
examination of the argument in *Night Thoughts*, chap. 8. I was well aware of the phenomenological character of the system when I wrote that chapter, but I was more struck
then by the continuity of the 1804 Logic with the logic program of 1801—which requires
that the initial evolution of the categories should be objective or neutral. I think now
that *both* emphases are present. But the reader must decide for himself which of them
is predominant, or how they are equilibrated.

proached cautiously; and the very different structure and goals of the systems that they introduce must be kept firmly in mind.[27] With that preliminary caveat the reader can be left to study the texts for himself. Certainly the close affinity between this text and the great book that emerged only two years later is one of the most compelling reasons why we should study it with passionate care and attention.

27. This is difficult because very little of Hegel's discussion of the *goal* of the system in 1803–5 survives. But it seems clear that a *complete system* whose discursive principle is phenomenological aims at *scientia intuitiva*, or "absolute intuition." The goal of a *systematic phenomenological introduction*, on the other hand, is the system itself as *discursive* science (or cognition).

THE JENA SYSTEM, 1804–5: LOGIC AND METAPHYSICS

.

of quantity – unity
plurality
totality

of quality – reality
negation

Logic *limitation*

I / Simple Connection

A / QUALITY

Hegel's manuscript originally consisted of 102 doubly folded sheets that he numbered himself. The most serious lacuna in what survives arises from the loss of the first three of these sheets. The inner half of sheet 6 and the whole of sheet 7 are also missing. For this reason the reconstruction of the first part of the argument, and even our conception of its formal articulation into sections and subsections, is somewhat hypothetical. The very title "Simple Connection" is a conjecture. Hegel may (for instance) have called the whole section "Quality" and begun the use of subheadings only when "Quantity" emerges from this initially undifferentiated unity. In the translation, however, we follow the articulation proposed by the editors of our German text.

Later on, Hegel refers back to this first section as "the logic of understanding."[1] He apparently began with the three categories of quality in Kant's table: reality, negation, and limitation (but perhaps he called negation "ideality"). Kant began *his* deduction of the "mathematical" categories—with which "Simple Connection" is plainly concerned—with the triad of quantity. It was Fichte who first began with the triad of quality. Fichte is certainly in Hegel's eye as a critical target here; but this should not cause us to overlook the fact that he is also the obvious inspiration and first model for this logic of consciousness.

---

1. See CE 175, l. 3, below. Hence, when he tells us here that the independent subsistence (*Fürsichseyn*) of terms is the "general principle of the logic of understanding," he is speaking of the basic hypothesis of natural consciousness, according to which everything exists on its own account and is "simply connected" with everything else.

Near the beginning of the Metaphysics (see CE 129, below) Hegel says, "the Logic began with unity itself as the self-equivalent." This "unity or being" (CE 154–55) is certainly not the mathematical unit (which we shall meet later on under "Quantity"). There may—as the Italian commentators think—be an implicit reference to the "first hypothesis" of the *Parmenides*.[2] But it is probably safer not to look beyond the fundamental tenet of the understanding as formulated by Bishop Butler: "Everything is what it is, and not another thing." This is the fundamental hypothesis of the logic of understanding (and we should notice how it involves both reality and negation). The view that whatever is real is self-identical and has only "simple" (that is, external) connections with everything else is plainly quite inadequate for the fundamental "connections" of physical forces and the philosophical connection between consciousness and its world.[3]

At the point where our manuscript starts, Hegel has reached the third moment of quality—the logical "totality" of the triad in the category of limit. The fragmentary text begins in the midst of a discussion of the "construction" of consciousness in Fichte's theory. Hegel argues that this construction only shows that our sense consciousness is a "limit" that arises because two opposed "forces" have arrived at an equilibrium. A *conceptual* limit of this kind is quite different from the limiting *boundary* between two physical objects that lie next to each other; and even the "force" of gravity that holds those two objects in place on the earth beneath them is again a limit of this conceptual kind, for it logically involves the *inward character* of the earth and of the objects thus held in place.

The "unity" of which Hegel is speaking in the first complete sentence is apparently the unity of the self, or of cognitive consciousness conceived in a Kantian "formal" way. The "highest unity" will then be the Fichtean Ego, within which all finite knowers subsist, and "the multiplicity" will be the objects of consciousness, including the other selves. The unity with which *transcendental* logic begins is the being of the finite self and its finite world. This self moves from its *possible* connection with everything to the *necessary* "proportion"

2. See Chiereghin's discussion in *Logica e metafisica*, p. 231. The suggestion of Moretto (ibid., p. 266, n. 4)—that the general progression of the Logic as it moves from the indeterminacy of simple connection to the determinate concreteness of proportion owes something to the progression in the *Philebus* from the *apeiron* through *peras* and *mikton* to *aitia*—also deserves serious consideration. Certainly the inspiration of Hegel's "objective logic" is more Platonic than Aristotelian.

3. We can also get some idea of what Hegel sought to show in his discussion of reality and ideality (or negation) from the retrospective summaries below (CE 5–7). Compare Harris, *Night Thoughts*, pp. 347–49.

of philosophical *cognition*. The proper explication of this highest unity is the theme of this Logic and Metaphysics. When it reaches its climax, this phenomenological theory of absolute cognition is one long search for the right solution of Fichte's problem about the conscious *reality* of the Ego.

[. . . the opposites . . .] are beings [. . .]. One of the opposites is necessarily the unity itself; but just for that reason this unity is not the absolute one, and since at the same time it is not simply to be as an opposite, but also to be in itself, it follows that, as unity of itself and of its opposite, it can be only limit; for as unity of both it would itself cease to be an opposite. Thus the so-called construction of the idea out of the opposed *activities*, of the *ideal₂* and *real₂* ones, as unity of both, has produced nothing but the limit. The ideal₂ activity has simply the same meaning as the unity; the double meaning of this unity determines itself as the unity of the antithesis because, as unity of itself and of the real₂ activity (that is, the multiplicity), it still remains outside itself as a non-unified unity and the multiplicity remains over against it; so that each such unity of opposites—as a moment of the whole and also as the whole, the highest idea itself as well—remains nothing but limit. The decision whether the unity is just limit or absolute unity depends directly upon whether, outside of or after the unity, what are posited in it as one are still self-subsistent beings. In the concept of limit itself the unity and multiplicity, or the reality and negation, still subsist on their own acount, and their principle, as the general principle of the logic of understanding, is recognized as not self-subsistent, because it is truly sublated and is not just something that is to be sublated. Just for that reason the construction out of opposed activities that is called idealism is itself [4] nothing other than the logic of understanding, inasmuch as the steps of the construction arise within this principle; and this idealism remains this logic too, inasmuch as the result of its absolute syllogism is that the ideal₂ activity, the unity (which as beginning is altogether indeterminate and equivocal as to whether it is true unity or unity as quality), is only the latter, for the absolute unification remains just an *ought*, that is, a beyond over against the unity of the limit; and the two[4] fall asunder.

The same occurs with the construction of matter out of *opposed forces*, the forces of *attraction* and *repulsion*, in which the former signifies the (differentiated) unity and the latter the (differentiated) multi-

---

4. *Trans.*: That is, the absolute unity as a beyond and the unity of the limit.

plicity. Like the opposed unity and multiplicity, these forces are as opposites nothing in themselves; but because they are set forth as forces, they are fixed as self-subsistent, as absolute qualities. Considered on their own account in this way, however, they turn out to be completely equal: insofar as there is attractive force, there is repulsive force; there is no distinction between them at all, save that of direction. But each of the opposed directions can be regarded equally well as an effect of attractive or as an effect of repulsive force; for direction is the empty connection, which is determined by anything fixed. The opposition of the directions is nothing but a completely empty opposition; but that through which the directions are truly distinguished—a posited point—would already be the oneness of them both, in which all opposition and the directions themselves are dissolved; apart from this their being-dissolved they are nothing—that is, they have no reality at all. Matter is nothing but that one[ness], or its absolute equilibrium, in which the directions are neither opposed nor even forces, and apart from which they have just as little being. But they are after all posited as beings on their own account, and the differentiation of matter is supposed to be a resolution into these *entia rationis*; in other words, these forces are supposed to emerge from the equilibrium that sublates them and to have a being apart from it. However, the differentiation of matter is essentially just this: that matter, the equilibrium itself, remains equal to itself; the differentiation cannot [be] a differentiation of the force of attraction and that of repulsion, [5] for that would be a sublating of matter itself. This differentiation would consist of a more of the *one* and a less of the other; but they have significance simply as connected with each other, as opposed directions: to the extent that one went beyond the other, to that extent it would itself cease to be. In their equilibrium, however, both are just as sublated within their distinction, but they are to have being not as sublated but rather as qualities or as subsisting on their own account; and that they should be so is clear because, apart from the equilibrium, their being one, they should yet have being. Therefore, this equilibrium is not itself the true unity because a oneness of those things which have being essentially, on their own account, is just their nothingness; so it is not matter, not a true reality that has been posited, but only a limit, the nothingness of the opposites *and* their being.

2 / In the limit the nothingness of reality and negation is posited, as well as their being apart from this nothingness; *in this way quality itself*

is realized in the limit; for the limit so expresses the concept of quality as the being *per se* of the determinacies, that in it both determinacies, each on its own account, are posited as indifferent to each other, as subsisting apart from each other. At the same time each, in accordance with its content, expresses not determinacy in general (as it does in the concept) but rather determinacy as determinate, as reality and negation; in other words, with respect to each [each expresses] what it would be only in the antithesis or in connection with the other; this connection with the other (being taken back into itself and because as relation it is only external to it) [is] now itself posited with respect to it;[5] the one, itself the nothingness of the qualities, the other, their being.

This indifferent subsistence of the nothingness and of the being of the qualities, however, does not exhaust the *and* of the limit; that is, the limit is not just this one side of reality, [the side] of the being *per se* of the qualities contained in it—the limit derives from the [6] negation, and the latter is only reality's being-external-to-the-limit—but also the connection with it; through this connection the limit in the form of connection is equal to its content. The one side of the content is the reality, the being or subsistence of the determinacies; in this way its determinacies—the being and the nothingness of the qualities—subsist. The other side is their nothingness, and in this way they are related, yet they are nothing in the connection; no matter how the being of the qualities might be posited alone and their nothingness posited as falling outside of being, it would not be a nothingness that is so connected with the being that both subsist. The connection of the nothingness of the qualities with their subsistence, however, is one that excludes this being—that is, [it is] not an undifferentiated subsistence of both but a negation that is connected with itself. In this self-connection, however, or in this positive connection, [the negation] sublates not being as such but only being in self-connection, that is, a *negative* connection. The limit is true quality only insofar as it is self-connection, and it is this only as negation, which negates the other only in connection with itself. In this way the limit is now synthesis as well, unity in which both subsist at the same time, or real quality. But the quality that must become limit has itself, by the same token, become the contrary of itself; its concept is the being *per se* of the

---

5. *Trans.*: The reference for "it" is ambiguous. It could be "connection" or it could be "each determinacy."

determinacies. Since that gets expressed which in truth is posited in the negation, the quality becomes limit; it remains the concept of itself, namely, a negation connecting with itself [and] excluding reality from itself. But this quality no longer is the concept of quality, for negation in its connecting only with itself is connected with that which it excludes. For quality is not absolutely on its own account, but it is on its own account only insofar as [something] else is not. The concept of quality, however, is this: to be only equal to itself, without respect to an other. In the limit, quality becomes what it is according to its absolute essence, what according to its concept (posited essence), however, it is not to be, and into which at the same time its concept must pass, in that the latter is posited as what it is to be; the limit is thereby the totality or true reality, which, [when] compared with its concept, contains its dialectic as well, because the concept sublates itself therein in such a manner that it has become its own contrary. [7] As its concept, quality is the reality out of which it has come to be the contrary of itself, negation; and out of this it has come to be the contrary of the contrary of itself, and has thus come to be itself again as totality. This totality is itself quality and at the same time the concept of quality; but the concept both comes forth from the contrary of quality and expresses it in itself, and hence, in that at the same time it has in itself an other than it is, it has become the contrary of quality. The limit, as the totality, as this negation which excludes itself [as] an other in its connecting with itself, [and] thereby is connected with an other (the subsistence), posits that which was our necessary reflection upon quality, namely, that the determinacy that is on its own account, which the quality is to be, is not; [that is,] it is not a truly unrelated determinacy but in its self-connection it connects itself negatively with an other; in other words, this limit is called *quantity*.

B / QUANTITY

The upshot of the argument of "Quality" is that the concept of quality as limit is a proper concept—that is, it is a unity of opposites. The concept of quality is every quality potentially and no quality actually. It is the limit to which all qualities are equally referred; and as such it is an absolutely unitary consciousness. The unitary consciousness that is the limit is thus the concept of "quantity"—the *self-moving point* that generates the *line* that Hegel calls *mens* in the Dissertation of 1801 (*On the Orbits of the Planets*). The whole mass of qualitative contents is "outside" it and exists for it as a positive *field*, patterned in accordance with any discriminations that the qualitative mass offers. Thus, there is the extended world (as a "positive unity") on one side; and the "negative unity" of the self that quantifies it on the other. They are radically opposed, but they also belong to the same whole (the "world" proper).

Since the world of quality is itself the world of consciousness, its manifold variety is *within* consciousness as *sequentially* unified. This temporal unification is a perpetual flowing. Consciousness is a continual emptying for refilling.

The world of the self is now a "heap or collection of impressions." It is *Allheit*, or "allness."[6] The self is not the all; but it is what makes everything into one heap. In thus comprehending its world quantitatively, the self is the *total* concept of quantity: it is a "quantum."

In this headnote we have again concentrated our attention on the transcendental *idealist* aspect of the logical dialectic. But the argument is *objective* throughout; that is to say, it has a transcendental *realist* application as well. The "one" and the "many ones" are not just conscious subjects but physical centres of attraction and repulsion—the thought-elements that are needed for the construction of a *dynamic* physical theory (compare the way that the fragmentary discussion of "Quantum" begins). This transcendental-realist concern is what makes the doctrine of the 1801 Dissertation relevant.

a / Numerical One

1 / Quantity according to its concept is immediately a negating self-connection. What this negation excludes from itself is the subsistence of the qualities as distinguished, the being-many. This simple unity, connecting purely with itself, which excludes every many from itself [or] negates them with respect to itself, is the *numerical one*; unity as self-equivalence in general passes over into the *one, one* self-equivalent [8] in virtue of the fact that unity contains in it this reflection expressed: that it excludes the many. It is negative unity. This absolute limit is indifferently posited both as excluding the many and (*qua* self-connection) on its own account, not a negating of the many, but, in its negating of them, a connecting only with itself, that is, a being

---

6. We have translated *Allheit* in this literal way in order to avoid confusion with the Hegelian concept of "totality," which is a more organic category altogether. When Hegel writes, "the limit is ... the totality [*Totalität*] or true reality, which ... simultaneously contains its dialectic" (CE 16, ll. 28–30), it is essential for the reader to be able to distinguish between this dynamic *Totalität* and the Kantian formal concept that Hegel calls *Allheit*. What he calls *Totalität* here is the first appearance of "true infinity"— compare CE 29 below.

negated or being excluded of the many in such a way that negating
as the totality of quality is reflected into itself and does not go outside,
and thereby has precisely the form of the absolutely qualitative. Here
the true significance becomes clear of how quality, having become
limit or quantity, is totality: it is totality in that its concept, determinacy
as connection of determinacy with itself, has returned into itself; not
just determinacy connecting with itself but determinacy as it has come
to be the contrary of itself and from this has again come to be itself,
and, as this its-having-come-to-be-its-contrary-and-again-itself, is not
something bygone but, as this movement, constitutes the content of
quality as of a totality. Quality, which thus as totality expresses within
itself this its-having-become-other [than itself], is just on that account—in that it itself is—at the same time the other of itself; the
concept is only this: the quality itself, its connections with itself;[7] the
real concept, or the totality, however, [is] quality's having become itself
from its being other, or [the fact] that in its being other it is itself.
This quality's being-other-than-itself is the side of its antithesis, the
determinacy of quality, or its content, a negative connection; for quality itself is simple connection only with itself. However, in this content
the real concept is at the same time this: the quality itself; and this
quality in respect to this content opposed to quality is this: that the
content, the negative connection connected only with itself, is not for
example a force, a unity differentiated from the other, but is, as a
sublatedness of the other, equal to itself, or a numerical *one*.
2 / That which is excluded from the numerical *one* is multiplicity in
general, the being of qualities, which, however, since they are posited
only as self-connections without negation, comes together into unity,
is equal to itself, being, [9] the *positive*, [and is] thus the many returned
into itself which thereby ceases to be many, and is only the possibility
of distinguishing, *extension*, which, equal to itself, at the same time is
not the negative equality of the point, because nothing negative is
posited [with respect] to it. This unity gets this determinacy of a
positive only through its antithesis to the negative or numerical unity;
the latter is excluded from it, but it is thereby also only the concept
of this negatedness of the posited distinction; with respect to the unity
this negatedness does not express itself as a negating. The quality of

---

7. *Trans.*: The original has only a comma here, so that the succeeding nouns may
be in apposition to "[quality]" and "connection." In our interpretation there is a contrast
between "concept" and "the real concept."

negation has hereby determined itself as negative unity, that of reality or position as positive unity; this determining is nothing other than that quality as real concept has gained a content, while it itself has come to be the form. Since the numerical *one* determined[8] itself as limit through the antithesis of both absolute qualities, and is only as the unity of these yet (as being on its own account, as the totality) is their sublatedness, then the numerical *one* determines them in such a way that the limit on its own account is their concept, or quantity, with the result that they themselves become their concept and are only as opposed to the concept of quantity. This concept is negative *one*; the qualities are nothing but positive *one*. In other words, since the concept is connected with itself, so the qualities are connected with themselves and therein become self-equivalence. And because they are an excluded self-equivalence, whereas the first is the negative self-equivalence, they are the positive. But in this way again only a required, not an actual distinction is posited; for the antithesis of positive-and-negative[9] expresses nothing but absolute opposition— but only as a requirement, which, however, is not only posited with respect to the members, but [is] unity as that which both have in common. This common unity of both is the same positive unity as the possibility of multiplicity that was previously opposed to the negative unity, which, however, has been shown to be that rather in which both members are equal. In this positive unity positive-and-negative is itself opposed, but on their own account they do not have any significance, and they express nothing but this: that the one is not the other, or that they exclude each other, thus [are] both numerical *ones*; in other words, what is posited in truth is a multiplicity of numerical *ones*. [10]

b / Multiplicity of Numerical Ones

1 / Negative unity is exclusive and posits itself as being on its own account against the other, but in this excluding it is immediately connected with the other; if what is excluded is conceived as multiplicity,

8. *Trans.*: Reading *bestimmt* rather than *bestimmte*. (Hegel himself made such a correction on the next line.)

9. *Trans.*: Hyphens are used to indicate that the definite article is singular and not plural. Compare l. 23 below, where a singular verb is governed by the phrase "positive and negative," straining the sense in English.

then negative unity itself is immediately a many as well; for however many the many is, so many times is it negated by the unity; such a manifold negating, or such a manifold, is the unity itself; and[10] negative unity is rather its contrary, positive unity, and as such, multiplicity, which, being internally differentiated, is posited as an aggregate of numerical *ones*.

2 / This aggregate of the distinguished *ones* is reciprocally exclusive; their connection, positive unity, their common, quiescent medium or their subsisting is an out and out negative connecting, an absolute fleeing, a mutual repulsion of all parts, or the equilibrium of the nothing, a unity without distinction, with respect to which even the distinction of positive and negative unity disappears.

N[ote] / The invincibility of being fortifies itself even more through the form which it gives to itself as negative being, as numerical *one*; being as such appears on its own account as empty, at least, and in need of an other; but the numerical *one* appears absolutely on its own account in that it excludes from itself the other of which being is in need, and is posited absolutely, without lack and as something indestructible. But because it is negative unity, it is determinacy and sublates itself by passing over into its contrary; the negative is simply connected with an other, and as this connection it is the other of itself; in other words, it is ideal$_2$, it is sublated. The mere simplicity of the *one* is itself the nothing, but its negating simplicity is supposed precisely to preserve its self-equivalence in that it excludes otherness from itself; but in this excluding it is itself one with the otherness [11] and sublates itself. This self-equivalence is the absolute quantity or that which quantity is in truth, that is, its own sublatedness, and similarly that which absolute quality is, that is, just the sublatedness of quality, the self-equivalent.

c / Allness[11]

1 / This self-equivalence, however, is itself determined by [the fact] that it is absolute quantity, or that it springs from the multiplicity of the numerical *one*; it is not posited on its own account but as the

10. *Trans.*: Hegel first wrote "instead of the negative unity it is." He deleted the preposition "instead" and changed the case of the noun to the nominative but did not delete the pronoun "it." We have assumed that this should have been done to complete the emendation.

11. *In the ms margin*: A distinction of the *one* and the many which is also no distinction, or a connecting of the one and the many, which is also their unconnectedness.

nothing of this determinate multiplicity. As the *one* that has passed into its contrary, the multiple *one*, and therefore is identical with it, it is *allness*.

2 / However, this allness is not the absolute equivalence but determines[12] the equivalence of this one and the many, of negative and positive unity. It is only their being sublated; insofar as they themselves are, in other words, it is conditioned through them. But since it is their unity, it is, only insofar as it excludes their being from itself, and it is itself quantity, a negative unity that is the being equivalent of the *one* and the many and [that] has excluded from itself their being not equivalent or their being on their own account. There is hereby posited a connectedness of the *one* and the many and, excluded from it, an unconnectedness of the *one* and the many.

This allness is the totality of quantity; its concept is the negative unity which itself, as multitude of the many, becomes another, and as allness becomes itself again. But here in its totality, quantity in general has itself become an other than it is, and in its return into itself it has passed over into its contrary. Quantity itself, or its concept, was the simple negative unity which excludes multiplicity; [12] quantity reflected into itself, its real concept, is negative unity, which is itself the unity of negative and positive unity, and likewise has excluded them both. What amounts to the same thing, quantity is a limited positive unity, for as the unity of both unities it is the possibility of multiplicity, which is posited in it as sublated; their unity is thus equivalence in the sense of commonality. It is limited commonality or extension, for apart from it [the unity is] also the unconnectedness of both unities. This real quantity is *one* quantity or . . .

c / QUANTUM

The transition from "Quantity" to "Quantum" is missing because the inner half of sheet 6 is lost; and most of the first two moments of the argument are missing also, because sheet 7 is lost. So the reconstruction of the argument is necessarily hypothetical, and the inserted subtitle is a conjecture. Because of a later reference back to this point, however, we can be fairly certain that the first moment of "Quantum" was "A Whole and Its Parts" (see CE 62, below). Conceptual wholeness is not the wholeness of a heap that can be dissipated into *separate* parts, but is cumulative in an *intensive* way (like tem-

---

12. *Trans.*: Following the punctuation of the ms rather than the emendation of the CE.

perature). In what remains to us from the main argument of this stage Hegel is mainly concerned with the application of this concept to the objective world. But his primary concern with the conscious self is evident from the "dialectic of quantum," which survives in its integrity.

At the beginning of sheet 8 we are near the end of the second moment of "Quantum." Probably we ought to call this second moment "Continuous and Discrete Magnitude."[13] The review at the beginning of the third moment shows that the argument here was that every degree is a *distinct* quantum (as the self is a new and different self in every moment of sensory consciousness), although it can only be determined as this quantum by reference to all the other quanta that lie behind it or beyond it (just as the self must retain its own past and project its own future). "Number" is the conceptual model of this real infinity (and the self is the zero point between two bad infinities, but also the *one* that occupies every place in the numerical sequence).

The "bad infinity" of quantum is the topic of the dialectical third moment. The infinite appears as this "absolute contradiction" (the self is both zero and one and is neither of them "truly"). Hegel needs to resort to a long note (or a series of notes) at this point because in the first place he wants to put his discussion of the "bad" infinite into the context of the "good" infinite (the "absolute essence," which properly belongs to metaphysics); and secondly (in the sub-notes, marked αα, 2, 3, and 4) he wants to state his conception of the methodology of the infinitesimal calculus. As opposed to the theory of consciousness, this is "the externality of quantum." We should note two things: first, that (in section αα) consciousness is clearly identified as *die Sache selbst*; and secondly, that Hegel does not attack mathematics—he only criticizes loose and illogical ways of describing what we do when we perform the logical operations of differentiation, integration, and so on. It is essential to the progress of Hegel's own argument that mathematical calculus should be accepted as valid and that its validity should *not* be implicitly undermined by the way that we talk about it. (Hegel's concrete illustrations in this note throw valuable light on the argument of the previous sections; and the theory of motion as the primitive datum of "dynamic physics"—in sub-note 4—shows that his philosophy of nature should be studied as a kind of proto relativity theory).

At the end of the long note Hegel returns to the main argument of the "dialectic of quantum" and sums it up. The concept of quantum has shown

13. But perhaps the first two moments were to be called "Degree" and "Number." Since the third moment has no heading except a marginal addition, Hegel seems not to have come to a final decision about category headings for "Quantum."

itself to be "infinity." Thus, the way that this category applies to the conscious self—with the explicit rejection of "degrees of consciousness" and the implicit rejection of "immortality" as a bad infinite—is peculiarly important. Consciousness—as *die Sache selbst*—is "true infinity."

... [it sublates][14] itself in the simplicity of force. But the need for a distinction of magnitude remains, in order to determine it[15] as a quantum—that is, to posit with respect to it a diversity that would not be a diversity of itself. The degree of simple force expresses as magnitude simply its connection with something else; and at the same time, as intensity, the degree is to express force as pure self-connection, as it is absolute for itself or simple within itself. The degree is to dispense with the absolute multitude of atomism as much as with this: that the diversity of matter be merely external and a diversity of figure and thereby of external placement, and be separation of the atoms through diverse empty spaces. Dynamic physics, alternatively, wants to cognize this diversity not as something external but as something in and of itself in matter. We have shown above that it is self-contradictory to explain, on the basis of a diverse relationship of forces over against each other, the diversity that is to be comprehended; there is nothing left but to posit *one* force in [13] a diversity of degree. Because it is a magnitude, however, the degree is so far from sublating multitude and externality that that is rather what it essentially is. A larger or smaller multitude of mass = heat = etc. particles transformed into a higher or lower intensity of mass or heat, etc., sublates, to be sure, the semblance of atomic multiplicity in what appears to be mass or heat; but if this [multiplicity] now has actually to be expressed as a determinate magnitude, then this can only happen through connection with numbers. Admittedly the fortieth, the hundredth, etc., degree still does not express a multiplicity with respect to the degree itself but with its simplicity; however, this diversity has significance simply and solely in relation to another. This determinate intensity is not this at all, if it is not this for something external; and it is simply not at all what it would be for itself—what it is to be as dynamic. The simple itself (for instance, the speed, the specific weight, heat, etc.)

14. *Trans.*: The verb particle *auf*, which alone remains, suggests that the verb was *aufheben*.

15. *Trans.*: The gender of the pronoun suggests that it could refer either to "force" or to "magnitude."

escapes the determination of magnitude; and insofar as it is in general determined as magnitude, it is posited as a manifold, as something external. This is how the form of simplicity of magnitude, or of intensive magnitude, does not wrestle it away from. . . .

. . . [*continu*]*ous magnitude*; conversely, the many *ones* of the division, posited as the essential for which the connection is the external, [are] a *discrete magnitude*. The continuous magnitude has posited its limit wholly outside itself, not with respect to itself as an external [limit]; in order to be quantum on its own account it must necessarily posit itself as essentially limited, or as internally divided in an absolute way, in other words, as a determinate aggregate of self-distinguishing negative unities. Only *number* is the realized quantum, in which it expresses itself as what it is; degree, just as much as a continuous magnitude, must[16] [14] resort to number in order to be determined as quantum. In quantum connectedness in general is numerical *one* and the many are connected in the same way; in number this concept of quantum is not the form of something else, but the many are each of them a numerical *one*; and the whole [is one] too, since the numerical *one*[17] has in it the double sense of being negative and exclusive yet, as unity, of being at the same time positive unity, in other words, the connection of the many numerical *ones*. The part of this whole is in this [way] completely determined through itself, because it is numerical *one* and equal with the form of the whole, which itself is *one*, but not identical with its content, through which it is quantum.

3[18] / Quantum sublates itself not only insofar as it is connected with itself or is the unity of a whole and the parts, but also insofar as, excluding [this], it is on its own account the connectedness of the *one* and the many, outside of which there would be the unconnectedness of the *one* and the many.

Concerning the relationship of the whole and the parts it has been shown[19] that in truth the whole as *one* and the parts as many *ones* fall asunder and are not connected. Quantum only is as an excluding from itself; what is thus excluded would be the unconnectedness of the *one* with the many *ones*. But in it indeed the *one* and the many

16. *Trans.*: The ms has a plural verb here.
17. *In the margin*: absolute measure.
18. *In the margin*: *Dialectic of quantum*.
19. *Trans.*: In the lost parts of the original.

ones are indifferent to each other: it is thus equal to what it negates from itself and is in truth non-excluding. Particularly as number, quantum should posit limit or otherness as self-subsisting [*an sich selbst seiend*]; however, it is manifest that number has no limit but is equal to what is excluded. What is here excluded (with which it is equal) is the unconnectedness of the *one* and the many. When quantum is formally considered as what it should be but is not ([that is as] something limited) and what is excluded likewise only as something equal to it, then only what is formal is posited: the requirement that what is limited or negative shall make itself equal to what is excluded, to which it is equal. Or rather the following has been posited: that what is negative posits [itself] as equal to that which it negates from itself, to that which [15] it posits as absolutely unequal to itself. In it indeed what was previously considered as indifferently falling asunder is by the same token the positing of itself as equal to that to which it posits itself as absolutely unequal. Number as numerical *one* is positive unity, which connects the many *ones*; but because as negative unity number posits itself as equal to the many *ones*, it posits itself as equal to them only as unequal to them, that is, as positive unity. Number is quantum only as negative *one*, as a determinate aggregate of the *ones* that it comprehends within itself; but in these, number does not have a limit either, for as *ones* they are likewise unity, a connection of numerical *ones*. Hence, in that it connects a determinate aggregate—whereby alone it is quantum—number posits itself in fact only as an indeterminate aggregate; for the connected *ones* are indeed a unity that is equal to itself, or not limited; in this way as well [they are] as something limited, equal to what is not limited. Quantum posits itself as equal to what it excludes from itself, and so in truth it does not exclude it. Insofar as quantum is considered as a self-subsisting being from which an other is excluded, to this extent it has [*ist an ihm selbst*] positive unity or non-limitation, not-excludedness. Going out beyond the limit *ad infinitum* and dividing inwardly *in infinitum* is one and the same for each, so that the limit or determinacy posited in it is no limit, no determinacy; in quantum the absolute contradiction or infinity is posited.

N[ote] 1 / The result of the dialectic of quantum is that *quantitative* distinction, insofar as it is a strictly external, accidental one without this necessary reflection, [is] a limitation that is in fact no limitation; for an absolutely external limit has thereby no relation with that of which it ought to be the limitation [*denn eine absolut aüssere ist darum nicht an dem, und für das, dessen Begräntzung sie seyn soll*]. But just for this reason *it may seem therefore, as if this form of a merely quantitative distinction* correctly expresses the way *in which differentiation in general* occurs *in connection with* [16] *the absolute* or in itself—namely, as an external differentiation not affecting the essence itself in any way. Since the absolute essence is thus that in which differentiation *is* simply sublated, we should avoid making it seem as if the distinctions themselves were outside the essence and their sublating took place outside it as well—as if the essence itself were just the sublatedness and not just as absolutely the being and sublating of the antithesis. The antithesis is in general the qualitative. Since nothing is outside the absolute, the antithesis itself is absolute, and only because it is absolute does it sublate itself in itself. In the repose of its sublatedness the absolute is just as absolutely the movement of the being or the sublating of the absolute antithesis. The absolute being of the antithesis, or, if one likes, the being of the antithesis in the absolute essence itself, is so far from making it into a mutually external, indifferent subsistence of its moments that it is simply and solely this *in which the antithesis sublates itself*—that is, it is through this that the antithesis *is neither quantitative nor external*. But the determinacy of the absolute essence considered singularly cannot be cognized any better through the more or less of one or the other moment, the predominance of what is called the one or the other factor. For what is here isolated only is because it is essentially in this determinate state, or because the determinate state is posited as having being in the absolute essence itself. Since the essence is something real, or the unity of opposites, these are immediately of equal magnitude. They have no significance except insofar as they are opposed to each other; and this they are essentially. In other words, there is no quantitative distinction with respect to them. If there were any, what they are essentially as determinate would be something external for them. By the same token the opposites would not be absolutely with respect to themselves—that is, [they would not be] sublating the determinacy itself—if the determinacy were an absolute, external, quantitative one, even to the extent that it is on its own account. Strictly only what is accidental to the determinacy would be on its own account, while their sublatedness would be outside them.

If the antithesis only sublates itself beause it is in itself and is not quantitative or external, then the antithesis in general—let it occur with whatever particular determination there may be—is a true determinacy only as a qualitative one; [17] and insight into the nature of a determinate Thing [*Sache*] lies only in becoming *cognizant* of its determinacy as a determinacy in itself, *not as an accidental, that is, quantitative one. The determinacy of quantum* is one not *posited* through the Thing *itself, or it is not such a one as is in the Thing itself*. Because the quantum expresses the determinacy of the Thing itself only externally, it is only the *sign* of the determinacy of the Thing itself (which can be designated by this quantum, but just as well by another one).

We consider this externality of quantum as it appears in its diverse aspects.

αα / The determinacy of quantum as a limit of the many is no determinacy whatever of the Thing itself; its concept is not affected thereby. The realization of the concept is an otherness that is posited with respect to it and through itself, one in which [the concept] remains what it is, that is, one that is just as absolutely sublated within it. The other[ness] of its quantum indeed leaves the concept what it is, but it is not otherness posited with respect to it, and therefore its sublatedness is not for and through the concept itself either; in other words, the concept is simply sameness, only the sameness of something dead. Therefore no becoming other, be it of space or time or mass or heat, colour, etc., or of sensibility, irritability, etc., or of subjectivity and objectivity, etc., is posited, be they posited as great or small as you will, and in both cases either extensively or intensively. The limit of quantum is something that does not touch them at all and which, where it is determined, can just as well be either drawn closer or removed further. The Thing *does not disappear in the absolutely small* any *more than it goes* beyond *itself in the absolutely large*; the disappearance does not become intelligible by increase or decrease because it is of the essence of magnitude that it be not a determinacy of the Thing itself. "The disappearing of consciousness as of a force having a determinate degree, as resulting from a gradual diminution of this faculty of apperception,"[20] is an empty [18] thought which in the first place introduces into the essence of spirit the determination of magnitude (that is, the determination that a determinacy be absolutely external to it), whereas its essence is rather that no determinacy be external but be simply sublated within it, and so the diminution is to pass into a disappearing of consciousness. Of course, the sublating of

---

20. *Trans.*: This is not a direct quotation, but a plain echo of Kant's refutation of Mendelssohn's doctrine of immortality; see *Critique of Pure Reason*, B 413–15.

magnitude would indeed sublate that to which it is ascribed, if [magnitude] were essential to it; but it is of the nature of magnitude to be accidental, an excluding which in truth however does not exclude, a limit which in truth however is no limit. The disappearance of what is here intrinsically accidental to a magnitude is so far from resulting in the disappearance of that with respect to which it was posited that now this last rather comes forth purely as what it truly is in itself. *Only consciousness having no degree is true consciousness*. This is at the same time the true meaning of *the disappearing magnitudes of analysis*; the infinitely small is not to be nothing, and yet is no longer to have magnitude. After this concept had been in use a hundred years, it was made into a prize essay topic[21] whether it actually has a meaning, and we can see that the answers given have not come clear. In the infinitely small the magnitude in truth totally disappears; the infinitely small is not just something relatively small in the way that Wolf (*Anfangsgründe der Algebra* §6) explicates the matter: that in measuring a mountain a grain of sand blown away from the top by the wind makes it lower in fact, but considering the mountain's magnitude no account need be taken of it. The issue is not whether something relatively very small can be left out of account; that can be satisfied by an imprecise determination of the magnitude, be the imprecision as small as you like. But in spite of the small bit that is left out of account, the determination made in the use of infinitesimal calculus is absolutely precise. In other words, when one lets a posited magnitude within a system of magnitudes disappear absolutely, just for that reason the concept of what is to be determined comes forth purely as[22] an absolute ratio, which is all we want to know, not the determinate magnitudes. Therefore [19] the unchangeable magnitudes, which do not just express how they are in a ratio but how they are on their own account outside of this ratio, fall away completely; the products in which the ratio of the factors likewise disappears set themselves up as sums, etc. The differentials are semblances of differentiations in magnitude that are forthwith sublated again; they are used where a system of reciprocally determining moments has been duplicated for the purpose of expressing it as an equivalence of diverse moments. In the duplication one moment appears in diverse magnitudes; but conceptually these

---

21. *Trans.*: In 1784 Lagrange set a prize question for award in 1786: "Une théorie claire et précise de ce qu'on appelle Infinie en Mathématique."

22. *In the margin*: 2 Absc[issae].

two diverse magnitudes are completely the same, and since the diversity has been presented as a differential, nothing occurs but the elimination of the diverse magnitudes and the establishment of the concept. Similarly, in order to express that the subtangent of a curved line is completely determined by the abscissa and ordinate that it belongs to, the abscissa and ordinate are doubled, so that the determinacy of this single moment is expressed by the others as an equivalence of two ratios of the subtangent to the ordinate. In the determination thus arrived at there is no magnitude omitted whereby it would become imprecise, but the diversity of magnitude, the duality of ordinate and abscissa, is totally nullified, and hence the determination is a pure connection through its ratio, not through its magnitudes as such or through them as concepts. This duplication is the same as the one employed by *Euclid* [to prove] his simple propositions that in a triangle the rest is fully determined by three elements (if there is a line among them, not only as to the ratio but also as to determinate magnitudes; if there is no line, and so only the angles— that is, the pure ratio of the lines—are posited, just the ratios of the lines alone). The superimposition of the two triangles is the disappearing of the differential, that is to say, not of them as a magnitude— for they [are] not of diverse magnitudes—but [the differential] of their quite formal duality. The disappearing of the differential, alternatively, is a disappearing of a magnitude; but this differentiation is just as much only a semblance of a diversity as is the duality of the triangles, for in the ratio [20] it is only the concept that is involved. The need for this division of a system lies in the task of mathematics, which is to treat the moments of a closed system as beings on their own account or as quanta. A system of moments is a unity of opposites, which are nothing apart from this opposition, apart from this ratio. They do not as it were still have a remainder with respect to each other, through which they would be on their own account; but they so match one another as it were that, since they are in fact presented as a system in their opposition or as unity, they sublate themselves. Thus the system as a whole that nullifies itself in its moments—as it must—is the presentation of an equation reduced to zero. But the moments as quanta are to set themselves forth as subsisting; and their *unity* in the system is thereby transformed into *equivalence*. The system as a whole is within itself a duality of itself, which is posited as one. The unity of the opposites is indeed each of these opposites, and as thus set forth it falls apart into an equivalence of its doubled being, or of its being in general. For, as has been shown with regard to quality,[23] reality is a doubling of unity; or unity *is* only as unity and multiplicity, which are both the same, or [unity] itself. Now, the system—which, if it is a system, posited in the form of unity, reduces itself to zero—comes to be an equivalence of diverse [terms]; and the positing of the differential of the moments is a form of doubling for the sake of expressing as an equation the determinacy of the moments by means of the whole, and so by means of each other. Because each single moment as differential acquires the semblance of a diversified magnitude, therefore, since the two wholes are the same in essence (that is, in their internal ratio of moments), an equivalence of ratios can be posited in which there are the moments as magnitudes. However, this determination of magnitudes disappears because it has no significance in connection with the internal ratios, which is the essential determinacy of the moment with respect to itself, not as the external quantitative determinacy but rather as its concept. And what results is determination as a determination within this [21] internal ratio. In this ratio the moments do not have magnitude on their own account but purely and simply a magnitude as ratio; and what is determined is not their magnitude as [the magnitude] of singulars, but only their ratio to each other. In other words, the moment is in truth sublated as quantum in the diminution *ad infinitum*, and it has a magnitude only within the system, an absolutely relative one, or one that is determined with respect to itself by the whole. In this way, the hypotenuse as a $= \sqrt{(b^2 + c^2)}$ and the ordinate as, for instance, $y = \sqrt{(px)}$, etc., are set forth as they are in themselves, namely not as a line apart from the right-angled [triangle] or apart from the determinate curved line, etc., which is what they are simply as quanta, but as being essentially hypotenuse, ordinate, etc.

The limit of the meaning and usage of "disappearing magnitude" also results from this nature that it has. Just as, in the example of the doubled abscissa used above, only the one abscissa in the abscissa itself disappears, while the abscissa as such simply remains, so it is in general the case that the internal ratio and its moments remain simply as such. If the abscissa (for instance of the ellipse, taking its start in the centre) disappears, then the ordinate becomes equal to the small axis, and we can just as well say if we like that the abscissa equals zero as that it equals the large axis. But this is pointless; the ratio of abscissa and

23. *Trans.*: In the lost parts of the original.

ordinate has in truth been sublated, and only its formal expression is left over. But wherever the ordinate remains as ordinate, the abscissa remains; and their determinate ratio to each other remains the same in their decrease *ad infinitum*, by which it is not at all affected. To let them become equal in the absolute diminution does not mean to decrease them or to sublate them as magnitude, but to destroy them as what they are essentially, or to destroy their concept. Thereby their ratio and the whole system is sublated; and from this result, the same, or any determinate case of it, simply cannot again arise. *Therefore* it is an absolute misuse of "disappearance" when even Newton makes arc, sine, and versed sine[24] equal to each other in the infinitely small; doing this means sublating not their magnitude but these [functions] themselves and their system. [22] To put the one determinacy in place of the others on the basis of this disappearance, then, while supposing that the system and its ratios nevertheless remain, must be taken as a complete misunderstanding.

2 / It has been shown *that* the quantum as limit of the many is inde-terminate in itself and *how* this external accidental determination be-comes a determinacy of the Thing itself through its annihilation as a quantum in differential calculus. Moreover, this is just what will be necessary with respect to things as systems of moments; in other words, the opposition of the moments is not to be considered as this external, quantitative opposition but as opposition as it is in itself—that is, as qualitative opposition, or as determinacy. The quantitative differen-tiation of the moment of a thing does not affect the concept of the moment or the concept of the thing; but the thing is only the system of its moments, and these only are what they are in relation[25] to each other, and the thing itself is this relation; in that the singular moment changes, it changes its relationship to the others; the whole relation, the thing itself, becomes something else. And it is in truth not a change of the moment that takes place; rather, the life cycle of the Thing itself is expressed since the moment is not on its own account, and its change is wholly determined solely by its relationship, by the being it has in the Thing itself. But this concept of the moment is precisely what the diversity as quantitative does not affect: the determinacy as it is within the Thing itself, or as it is in itself. And the rise and fall on the ladder of degree or of extensive magnitude is only to be re-

24. *Trans.*: Versed sine = 1 minus the cosine in a unit circle.
25. *Trans.*: "Relationship," "relation," and "ratio" all translate *Verhältnis*.

garded as an external indicator. The differentiation of the internal ratio turns the differentiation of the quantum as one of that sort[26] into something quite other than [what] it expresses.

In the number system itself this diversity is expressed as a diverse mode of considering the numbers vis-à-vis one another; the numbers are, on their own account, pure quanta, but in their reciprocal relations they get posited in a qualitative way. Addition is the purely quantitative change in which the diversity displays itself as one accruing merely from outside; it lets the diversity stand on its own account rather than as a determinacy that in truth is only a moment in a system. Precisely through its merely seeming to be on its own account, whereby it is absolutely an aggregate or a diversity, the quantum is not on its own account; [it is] something external, [23] arbitrary. The ratio of the numbers expresses them as [they] are in their determinacy vis-à-vis another—that is, as they are in themselves; but the numbers themselves do not determine anything about this ratio, which is an entirely external one, or indeed a quantum; on the contrary, the numbers with respect to themselves also become ratios: 8 and 9 are 2^3 and 3^2 respectively; each number is equal to itself, and its limit is at the same time an internal relation, the relation of a concept that produces itself, whereby the limitation expresses its law with respect to itself; the addition of 1 to 8 transforms 2^3 into 3^2, which the addition of 1 to another number does not do; in other words, the quantitative change does not express the change that occurs in a number as a system that is set forth with respect to itself.

This very diversity between a merely quantitative distinction and the change of the Thing itself will become clearer through the example of the temperature of water. The mere rise and fall on the heat scale lets cold take the place of heat, its direct opposite. With the temperature of water, though, the whole quantitative distinction becomes a quite superficial one that of itself in no way indicates what has changed in the Thing itself. A decrease in temperature of 30° from 80° Fahrenheit exhibits a change in the volume of the water, namely a decrease; but a further decrease in the temperature does not diminish the volume of the water: the temperature being lowered to 32°, the volume increases and the water passes from the liquid,[27]

26. *Trans.*: The reference here is either to "indicator" or to "relation/ratio."

27. *Trans.*: "Liquid, fluid" = *tropfbar flüssigen*; "gaseous" = *elastisch flüssigen* (cf. p. 25, l. 4).

fluid [state] into the solid one; and snow, changed by pouring water
of a very high temperature on it, maintains the same degree of temperature; similarly, the temperature of the boiling point resists change,
although, in contrast, the water takes on a gaseous form. Thus the
determinacies of temperature, as set forth quantitatively, articulate
nothing but indicators of the change in the Thing, not the change
itself. The qualitative interrupts the quantitative scale altogether; and
the change in the Thing itself or in the internal relation, the change
in temperature as it really takes place in water, is quite different from
temperature as an *ens rationis* that on its own account is supposed to
be purely simple and in this self-equivalence would be capable only
of a quantitative progression. In the same way the quantitative [aspect]
of the [24] change posits temperature as self-equivalent in its progression; but as this abstraction of the self-equivalent, the change
becomes precisely something external to temperature, even as this
externally posited, self-equivalent change contradicts all along this
[fact]: that temperature is not this self-equivalent [*ens rationis*] but just
a moment in a relationship; it is its consequent internal change, now
inhibiting, now accelerating, that even-measured progression. If the
abscissa expresses the congruent quantum of change, then the actual
temperature will always be an ordinate, whose change, *qua* quantum,
relates to the abscissa but whose absolute determinacy is posited by
the nature of the curved line to which it belongs, and which alone
remains always self-identical; once again it is the merely quantitative
[and] external that changes.

3 / The quantitative expresses [itself] contingently as the *one* in the
same way as it does in its multiplicity—as that which is indeterminate
in itself or as determinacy. In the form of numerical *one*, negative
unity is posited as it is in itself, and number is its external, arbitrary
composition. But as a determinacy quantum has a content whose
determinacy it is. In pure quantum, numerical *one* is unity itself, and
thereby an indeterminate [one]; and thus it exists in that it is referred
to a quality, as determinacy posited externally with respect to it. The
one, the scale, is in itself quite indeterminate, and it is as absolutely
impossible to indicate the highest or the lowest degree for an intensive
magnitude as it is to indicate what is largest or smallest for an extensive
one; for since the *one* is unity, what is posited as *one* is itself a manifold,
and capable of decrease as well as of increase. In other words, as
negative *one* the *one* is essentially equal to what it excludes; as pure
one it is equal to the many; so it is not at all a pure *one* but is a

requirement whose satisfaction in and of itself is impossible. Although with regard to degree, which has the form of something simple, a first seems even more likely to be able to present itself, this is illusory; for just as the extensive is absolutely divisible in itself, so the intensive is absolutely confinable from outside. Degree is just as essentially a magnitude as what is extensive; just for that reason the smallest magnitude of degree is still not something simple but is posited as an [25] external connection. This expanse is itself strictly a manifold, something divisible in itself, contingent and susceptible of being made both smaller and bigger. Belief in the possibility of a smallest degree or a smallest extensive magnitude, [that is,] of magnitude as an absolute scale, has quite likely arisen because magnitude itself can be nullified as such entirely, and if the nullifying is not understood [*aufgefasst*], then the nullified magnitude is still taken for a magnitude.

4 / Little as the determination of magnitude expresses the determinacy as it is in the Thing or in itself, even less is [it] capable of expressing it as a diversified determination of opposed qualities. Opposed qualities of this kind simply cannot emerge from their absolutely qualitative connection and equality; or, insofar as they are distinguished and determined as magnitudes, they are incommensurable through and through; for it is of their essence to be opposed to one another. Thus, for instance, the time and space of absolute motion are simply equivalent to one another, [or] the same absolute relationship is expressed as time and as space; the velocity is their absolute relation to one another, and the magnitude is expressed in both according to the nature of this relation. The velocity is these [temporal and spatial] moments posited as absolutely one; but insofar as they express their antithesis (time being the square root, but space the square), this is not a determination of the magnitude of time as such and of space as such; rather it is their determinacy as it is in itself, or as space over against time and time over against space, each of them only in connection with the other. But when each is posited on its own account, then time and space as one determinate magnitude are the root and the square of a determinate quantum; and if 9 space quanta are traversed in 3 time quanta, these magnitudes, 9 spaces and 3 times, are totally incommensurable. One hundred and thirty-five feet are neither greater nor less than 3 seconds, any more than the distance of a fixed star is; but if the foot [is taken] as the arbitrary space unit, and the second as the equally [26] arbitrary time unit, and motion [is defined] as free fall towards the surface of the earth, then the 135

feet are perfectly equal to the first 3 seconds. In other words, the velocity of this fall in these 3 seconds is a magnitude that in time expresses itself as 3 seconds, in the space traversed as 135 feet; again, on its own account the magnitude is contingent. That the body traverses some 15 feet in 1 second is just an indication of the fact that the motion gets posited as a fall on the surface of the earth; the expression of magnitude, however, in the way it is expressed as a peculiarly simple magnitude diversified with respect to time and space, is grounded in the absolute unity in motion of time and space, which as distinct are absolutely opposed moments and express this their determinacy or their essence (that is, their being in relation) in such a way that the one is a root, the other a square.

Likewise, attractive and repulsive forces are simply equal to one another; neither [is] greater than the other; neither has a significance except within their oneness—that is, within their sublated state. One never exceeds the other. In other words, when they are distinguished and expressed as magnitudes and diversely determined, then they are totally incommensurable; and it can no more be said that a time is larger than a space than it can be said that what is called an attractive force is larger than what is called a repulsive force. They can no more emerge from their equilibrium than unity and multiplicity, which is what they essentially are. The pull that appears as coherence, separability, and the displacability of the parts comes readily to mind when one talks of greater or lesser attractive force. But coherence has no antithesis in the repulsive force; it is posited as a pure quality, and its magnitude is compared not with the magnitude of repulsive force but with greater or lesser coherence. For that reason it is not coherence that is meant when one speaks of an attractive force that is greater or smaller, stronger or weaker than the repulsive force. Since matter [is] the absolute equilibrium of attraction and repulsion, which is nothing but [the equilibrium] of the differentiated unity and the [27] differentiated multiplicity, they are purely ideal$_2$, pure *entia rationis*, determinacies that, sublated in and of themselves, have no reality. Neither can appear as singular; they are the moments of the cognition of matter. But matter is precisely in the totality of cognition the moment of their oneness (that is to say, their non-being), and this oneness is the first reality; the very differentiation of matter always remains in that one[ness], and if it were a separation, a diversity of attraction and repulsion, matter itself would be dissolved. The quantitative is something quite external, not an analysis of the one, or an internal ratio. The attempt, which absolutely contradicts the concept of the quantitative, to conceive the quantitative as an internal ratio, as a relation within the Thing itself, in such a way that it is as this relation to remain quantitative, has made the difference in magnitude of matter into a dissociation of its ideal$_2$ moments. Specific gravity has as its moments only what is real$_2$, weight, and what is ideal$_2$, volume. Its quantum, however, is purely a diversified quantum of the simple, of extension, or of the absolutely communal, of the self-equivalent; and what has been thus posited as externally determined is nothing but the simple oneness of both these moments, specific gravity itself.

The same is the case with the dissociation of centrifugal and centripetal force. Both of these so-called forces are nothing in and of themselves: the centripetal force is essentially nothing but the appearance of the restoration of the sublated unity; it has no antithesis at all with respect to a centrifugal force, [that is,] to a self-sustaining [*für sich selbstseyenden*]^{28} sublating of this unity; and the way of demonstrating it as a self-sustaining force borders on absurdity. Where they are to be distinguished, these forces simply show themselves to be always equally great, so that it is always immaterial whether the magnitude of an appearance be determined through the so-called centripetal or centrifugal force. It is always the simple that is determined as quantum, and this simple is motion, not its magnitude as a result of the diverse magnitude of differentiated forces. Where one is taken to be greater than the other, as in the conception of greater speed of motion in the proximity of the sun or the earth and a lesser speed at a distance from the sun or the earth, it is completely immaterial whether the one or the other is posited greater at a given position; that is, both forces will always [be]^{29} equally great; [28] for just as the one has been posited as greater, so also must the other be increased. The same is the case with the diversity of the two forces posited in order to account for [*begreifen*] the diverse rates of pendular motion at diverse latitudes; what is posited as in truth diverse is one and the same: [it is] motion, greater in one place, less in another, not two types of forces, one greater than the other, both entirely incommensurable. We shall come back to this topic later on.

The way in which this applies to the diversified magnitude of sensibility and irritability over against each other follows from what has

28. *Trans.*: Compare with the *für sich* in "in and of themselves."
29. *Trans.*: CE proposes "both forces are always posited equally great."

been said so far: these also only rise and fall in common; their equilibrium is not disturbed; their common magnitude is not a sum that maintains itself and that they would apportion unequally between themselves should each deviate from its normal degree, the one going down, the other going up. As opposed they are absolute determinacies, which cease *ipso facto* to be magnitudes over against each other; the determination of magnitudes affects only what they have in common, what is simple; that is, [it affects] them insofar as they are not distinguished. In other words, it is not their relation over against each other; insofar as the simple, conceived as relation, is posited, it is something internal and ceases to be capable of determination as a magnitude altogether. Sensibility is self-connection, in the same way as attractive force is, while repulsion and irritability, thought of as negative connection, are each a differentiated unity.

3^{30} / As a connection of unity with multiplicity, which is limited—that is, excludes from itself the unconnectedness of unity with multiplicity—quantum posits itself in the extensive magnitude as what it is according to its concept. But regarding this magnitude it has been shown that, because it displays the connected multiplicity with respect to itself, it posits itself in truth as equivalent to the unconnected multiplicity, and, instead of being limited, is unlimited. What it excludes it rather has with respect to itself; it is no longer in our reflection that the other is excluded from it to make the magnitude accord with its concept, but this exclusion is in the concept itself. For this reason the absolute contradiction, infinity, has in truth been posited with respect to it. [29]

D / INFINITY

Infinity is not one of the categories of simple connection as such. Rather, it is a *meta*-category, for it is the total context of the dialectical movement that has brought simple connection to the recognition of "absolute contradiction." That Hegel emphasizes, as soon as this context has become explicit, that it was already implicit in every step of the dialectical progress we have made

---

30. *Trans.*: If this were part of the note(s), it would be 5. If it were a new section of the main discussion, it would be 4. But all that Hegel does here is to sum up the argument of section 3 above (the "dialectic of quantum"). Thus his 3 *can* be interpreted as an indicator ("3 continued") that he is now returning to the main flow of the argument.

implies that logic is properly a speculative science. For the recognition of "true infinity" belongs at this climactic moment of "Simple Connection" precisely because this recognition transforms the dialectic of external reflection into a dialectic that is internally necessary to the concepts themselves. From this point onwards we know that concepts are *constituted* by their internal relationship. (Hegel draws attention to this transition in his last sentence about quantum—see CE 28.) But in that case, if the true infinite was implicit from the first, then the simplicity of simple connection was always a dialectical illusion, and what was taken to be a dialectic of external reflection was always, properly speaking, an internal dialectic. Thus simple connection as the *first* stage of logic "sublates" itself when it is forced to recognize that it was *not* the first moment at all. The "infinite contradiction" was properly the *first* moment (as it will be the last).

Hegel's argument continues quite "objectively." But *logical* objectivity is not *opposed* to "subjectivity." It is important to grasp the *subjective* aspect of what it might be better to call this *neutrality*. The reflective self, which knows itself to be external precisely because it is a quantum (it is born and dies, but the world abides) has to recognize itself as the infinite contradiction because it is the fount of logical necessity and truth. *That* the world abides is a *truth* of its own cognition.

"The world" is both internal and external to consciousness as understanding (that is, as simple connection). This contradiction means that consciousness is itself the infinite. Hegel gives us a preliminary discussion of this thesis as the *fourth* moment of "Simple Connection" because it cannot be spelled out in the next stage of logic proper. The whole argument of the Logic and Metaphysics is required to spell it out in detail. In giving "Simple Connection" a fourth moment, Hegel is showing us the place of simple connection (a *first* moment, which will also be the *last* one) in the general theory of logic as a speculative science. This contradiction of what simple connection itself is "forced to recognize" (according to the preceding paragraph) is deliberate. *Both* ways of stating the position are valid.

The logic of quality began—according to Hegel's summary—with consciousness as a *pure* aggregate of qualities. Its purity was revealed by its permanence in the sensory flux. This negative unity both is and is not identical with the consciousness of the present moment. Hence it embraces a bad infinite both spatially and temporally; but also, by definition, that infinity transcends and embraces it likewise. From this springs Kant's "unreasoning astonishment" over the starry heavens (as a positive infinite) and the sceptical confidence of von Haller that no mere created spirit can penetrate to the core of living nature (the core is precisely the *emptiness* of rational consciousness itself).

The genuine infinity of consciousness is comprehensive self-consciousness. Self-consciousness is mediated initially through the consciousness of another consciousness. Here consciousness becomes objectively aware of what it is. Only through seeing myself in another can I *see* what I am. With this step we shall pass from simple connection to "relationship." But in logic as the theoretical evolution of consciousness, this step is not made through a struggle for independence but through the recognition that consciousness is a social continuum, that our transcendent world is the world of our community, that as conscious beings we are moments of the social substance; and this recognition matures slowly and goes through many phases ("the proof, not the *one* substance itself, is this absolute reflection").

The self only exists as consciousness, however, by excluding the world and asserting its independence of it; and the continuum of consciousness exists only because selves exist. So the existence of self-consciousness is not simple connection but relationship.

1 / Simple connection is realized in quantum in that its concept, quality, as limit (the mutual exclusion of determinacies) became the contrary of itself in allness. That is, it became the connecting of the determinacies; and from this contrary it returned to itself. As this totality it is quantum, namely allness recapitulated under limit, a connecting of unity and multiplicity that is simultaneously connected with a non-connecting of unity and multiplicity and excludes this from itself. But therein precisely it is with respect to itself absolute contradiction, infinity, and thus has its genuine realization here. Since simple connection is in truth infinity, each of its moments in which it displays itself is itself infinity and is quality and quantity as well as quantum. In other words, simple connection becomes infinity because it reflects itself into itself and only then posits itself as what it is according to its essence, whereas previously the dialectical in its moments was just our reflection. That in their essence the moments contradict themselves is now posited as a reflection of simple connection into itself, as absolutely dialectical essence, as infinity. But it is only purely and of itself as its own concept that this infinity is genuinely what it is, not as it appears with respect to the determinacy of its moments. Quality, quantity, and quantum are quality or simple connection; each has as its essence the concept of this whole sphere, and, because this concept

of the whole sphere has been cognized truly as infinity, each is itself infinite. But just for that reason this exposition of infinity is an impure one. *With respect to* a determinacy that is posited as permanent, this infinity (which we want to call bad infinity) can only express the striving to be itself; it cannot express itself in truth, for its essence is the absolute sublating of determinacy, the contradiction that determinacy, so far as it is, is not, and so far as it is not, is. This contradiction is the true reality of determinacy [30]—for the essence of determinacy is to nullify itself—and just for that reason it is, as immediate, true ideality.

a / Infinity *with respect to* quality—that is, with respect to the simple concept of connection or of determinacy as purely self-connecting— is to let the quality subsist as such and at the same time to display in it its contrary: the connection with another, that is, the multiplicity. Infinity is therefore an aggregate of qualities and, indeed, a pure aggregate, one that is not connected with the qualities themselves at all; that is, it is not a qualitative but an indeterminate aggregate of qualities, which is thus an infinite aggregate because it is simultaneously pure determinacy as quality and pure indeterminacy. Quality is posited as multiplicity or, compared with others in the form of limit, as excluding, and therefore as numerical *one*; the aggregate is an infinite aggregate of *ones*, and these qualities are self-connecting determinacies.

b / When posited with respect to quantity, infinity, as allness, is at the same time both subsisting and quantum; that is, [it is] in the form of its opposite: limit. But subsisting as allness, the self-equivalent connection—that is, the pure unity that is to be as such and the pure unity of quality, of which there is an infinite aggregate—can be posited too.[31] In that it is limited or becomes a determinate quantum, it is at the same time to be pure unity; the limit, which is an inequality or a negation, must have been surpassed. This sublating of the limit or the re-established unity must once again be limited. What has been posited is simply the contradiction that there be a limit and the pure unity, and that both be connected to each other and yet be not sublated. This is bad infinity, and just an alternation of the positing and

---

31. *Trans.*: The ms has only a comma here. Ehrenberg and Link introduce a semicolon after "quantum," making the next clause subordinate to what follows. CE puts a semicolon here (after "posited too"). We have followed CE.

sublating of the limit and of the self-equivalent unity. Because there is immediately in each of them the requirement of the other, both continue *in infinitum*.

The contradiction that bad infinity expresses, both that of infinite aggregate and that of infinite expansion, stays within the acknowledgment of itself; there is indeed a contradiction, but not *the* contradiction, that is, infinity itself. Both get as far as the requirement that the two alternating members be sublated, but the requirement is as far as they go. A limit is [31] posited; thus, the pure unity is sublated. The pure unity is re-established, and thus the limit is sublated. So, too, in the infinite aggregate beyond every determinacy there is another, and beyond that yet another again. The subsistence of the many qualities as of the many quanta has simply the "beyond" of a unity that has not been taken up into them and that would sublate the subsistence if it were so taken up. In order to subsist, the aggregate is not allowed to take up this beyond into itself, but just as little can it free itself from it and cease to go beyond itself. The determinacies or limits seem to preserve themselves because they posit the unity outside themselves as a beyond; but because this beyondness of unity is necessary for their preservation or subsistence, they are essentially connected with it; and their exclusion of it, or their own preservation, is in truth a oneness with it—in other words, what is posited is true infinity or absolute contradiction.

N[ote] / This bad infinity is the third [moment] to bad reality and bad ideality; these two come to themselves or are reflected within it, but still in the form of bad reality, or in such a way that bad reality and ideality subsist in it. Bad reality stays at the concept of quality as a posited, solely self-connecting determinacy; bad ideality likewise stays at the concept of quantity, the exclusion of the limit; and bad infinity connects these concepts with each other in just this way, in that it allows them both to subsist. Bad reality remains in that it is surpassed— that is, in that ideality is posited with respect to it; and ideality is just this surpassing, a negating outside of which the negated still subsists, or (what comes to the same thing) pure unity, for which the necessity of limiting sets in as well. Or, because bad infinity stays at the concept of simple connection only, it is itself only the limit, the *and* of self-connecting and other-connecting, with the reflection thereon that these two connections are as much self-positing as they are self-excluding— a formal return of the simple connection into itself, in which it only goes over to negation because it leaves reality behind; and thereby also [32] [it is] reality because it goes over to negation.[32] In other words, in that it comes to unity from the quantum of the determinate aggregate, it has that behind it; and in that it comes to quantum from unity, it likewise has unity as a beyond. Thus [it is] nothing but the movement of the *and* of the limit, through which it goes only from one to the other; [it] can stay at neither but, because each is affected by the *and*, is driven on through it to the other again. For absolute infinity [is], by contrast, the absolute *and*, the absolute return of simple connection into itself, or the simple immediate sublating of the opposites with repect to themselves.

Bad infinity is the last step to which the incapacity to unify and sublate the antithesis in an absolute way proceeds, in that it merely sets up the requirement of this sublation and contents itself with displaying the requirement instead of meeting it. It reckons itself to be at the end because in intuition it passes beyond the limited and falls into an unreasoning astonishment in the face of what is im-measurable and countless, whether it be the stars, or multifaceted organizations, or because in its return from intuition it salvages [its] activity, as pure unity over against the limited, in an infinite progress. In both, the incapacity is without presence: in the former it enlarges the positive quantum that has being, recognizing it as limited, and in passing beyond it arrives only at the requirement of the sublatedness of its limitation; alternatively, in the sublating of the quantum it again arrives at only the empty nothing and the requirement once more that nothing be filled. It has both of them, the bounded and the void lying outside each other—one as the "beyond" of the other. Let it posit no matter how many bounded [things], it still has a void outside in which nothing bounded is as yet posited; through its enlargement it still does not bring unboundedness into the bounded itself. In the latter case that incapacity is likewise without presence, in that it en-larges the negative [33] quantum; the negation is simply just negation of this determinate, or the absolute negation is precisely that emptiness itself of which the absolute aggregate of determinacy is the opposite. Because this negation, emptiness, or freedom has been made into the

32. *Trans.*: We follow Ehrenberg and Link by simply inserting "it is." Lasson and CE substitute "negation" for "reality" on p. 32; CE substitutes "reality" for "negation" here. Our reading appears to be confirmed by the following sentence.

positive, we have here the converse of the previous requirement: in the former case the filling of the empty, the being of the bounded within the nothing that is still at hand, is required; in the latter, the being of the empty and the sublatedness of the bounded that is always still at hand. Because this emptiness is on its own account, there is thus only the empty possibility that the bounded that is at hand outside the ideal$_2$ activity can be taken up. The sublatedness is the infinite progress, that is, a sublatedness that is simply not realized; and the sublimity of this activity is just as devoid of reason as the sublimity of that being, and is content in the same way with the display of the unmet requirement.

2 / Genuine infinity is the realized requirement that the determinacy sublate itself: $a - A = 0$. It is not a series that always has its completion in some other yet always has this other outside itself. Rather, the other is in the determinate itself; it is a contradiction, absolute on its own account: and this is the true essence of the determinacy. In other words, [it is] not [the case] that a term of the antithesis is on its own account, but that it only is within its opposite or that only the absolute antithesis is, while the opposite, since it only is within its opposite, annihilates itself therein, and annihilates this other as much as itself. The absolute antithesis, infinity, is this absolute reflection into itself of the determinate that is an other than itself (that is, not an other in general against which it would be indifferent on its own account, but its immediate contrary), and as that, it is itself. This alone is the true nature of the finite: that it is infinite, that it sublates itself in its being. The determinate has as such no other essence than this absolute un-rest: not to be what it is. It is not nothing, because it is the other itself, and this other, being just as much the contrary of itself, is again the first. For nothing, or emptiness, is equivalent to pure being, which is just this emptiness; and both of them immediately have with respect to them the antithesis of the something, or of the determinate, and just for that reason they are not the true essence but themselves [34] terms of the antithesis. Nothing or being, emptiness in general, only is as the contrary of itself, as determinacy; and this last is just the other of itself or nothing. Infinity as this absolute contradiction is thereby the sole reality of the determinate and is not a "beyond", but simple connection, pure absolute movement, being-outside-itself within being-within-itself. As the determinate is one with its opposite and both are not, so likewise their non-being or their otherness only is in

the connection with them, and it is in the same way the immediate contrary of itself or their being: each of them posits itself just as immediately as it sublates itself.

Infinity is [to be found] within this immediacy of otherness and the otherness of this other, or of being the first again, the immediacy of the *duplex negatio* that is once more *affirmatio*, simple connection that in its absolute inequality is self-equivalent. For the unequal, or the other, is just as much the other of itself immediately as it is an other according to its essence. The simple and infinity, or the absolute antithesis, make no antithesis save this very one that they are absolutely connected, and insofar as they are opposed, they are by the same token absolutely one. There can be no talk of the going forth of the absolute out of itself; for only this can appear as a going forth: that the antithesis is, yet the antithesis cannot pause at its being; rather, its essence is the absolute unrest of sublating itself. Its being would be its terms, but these essentially are only as connected with each other—that is, they are not on their own account; they are only as sublated. What they are on their own account is: not to be on their own account. If the absolute antithesis is separated from unity, then the latter is on its own account just as the former is outside itself, but in this case the antithesis itself has only changed its expression, and the simple, which [is then] not infinite, is indeed a determinacy but quite remote from being the absolute. Only the infinitely simple, or that unity-and-multiplicity, is one, is the absolute. If a ground for the antithesis is asked for, the request presupposes just that separation of the ground (whichever way this may be posited) and of the antithesis. It does, of course, bring both into a connection, but such a deficient one that each of them is still there on its own account—that is, since both are what they are only in connection with each other, both determinate, therefore neither the one nor the other is on its own account and the request for a ground sublates itself. For what is asked for is one that would be in and of itself and yet is to be at the same time something determinate, not in and of itself. [35]

It is evident that what is dialectical in the moments, in quality, quantity, and quantum, and in their moments too, has been nothing else than their being posited infinitely. Each showed itself necessarily as something infinite; but the infinite itself [did] not yet [show itself] with respect to them; that is, it was not itself posited. It [has] been brought to mind that the moments were therefore only infinite; they were not the infinite itself, because they did not express with respect to themselves the necessary connection with their opposites, or that the infinite was only the ground of their ideality. From quality the opposite is excluded; it is entirely on its own account, connected only with itself. Quantity is on its own account, but exclusive, and the opposite it excludes is not posited with respect to it either. With respect to quantum, however, the excluded is itself posited; it is itself the connection of unity and multiplicity, and what is now excluded is the unconnectedness of unity and multiplicity. To quantum pertain both terms of the antithesis itself; and what is to enter into antithesis within it is the connection of the terms themselves. Since each side now has the whole antithesis within itself, the one-and-many excluded from quantum now pertains to quantum itself; all that it still lacks is just the reflection that what is thus excluded is within it as something just as much not connected to one another; and so it becomes the infinite. In other words, the simple connection of the one-and-many has become something other than itself and has returned into itself; it has realized itself. In this way it is *the* infinite, because what is in each term is also in the other, or in each term itself its oneness with the other is posited; each has the same content. To keep the point in mind in a provisional way, this is the true cognition of the absolute: not the mere demonstration that the one-and-many is *one* [as if] this alone were absolute, but that with respect to the one-and-many itself the oneness of each one with the other is posited. The movement of that demonstration, the cognition of the oneness, or the proof that there is only *one* substance, proceeds as it were *outside* the one-and-many and their oneness unless this unity is conceived from the opposition itself—that is, unless it is unity as the infinite. But this movement of opposing itself (that is, of becoming other and of becoming the other of this other, or of the sublation of the antithesis itself) is within the infinite because the infinite is with respect to itself this oneness with its otherness. For that demonstration in which the substance is just one, not the infinite, [36] has on its own account, so to speak, the movement of the infinite, the becoming-other of the simple and the becoming-other of this other. In other words, the proof, not the *one* substance itself, is this absolute reflection.

3 / According to its concept, infinity is the simple sublating of the antithesis; it is not the sublatedness. The latter is the void to which the antithesis itself stands opposed. The absolute contradiction of the infinite wipes out within the simple what is opposed; but the simple is simple only insofar as it sublates this opposite, and it itself is as a

result of its becoming-other. But therefore the otherness or the antithesis is just as absolute; in that the simple is, the antithesis stands
against it, and the simple's being *per se*, which is indifferent to the
antithesis, would likewise be an indifferent being *per se* of the antithesis. However, the simple and the antithesis are just themselves the
antithesis again; for each is essentially not to be what the other is, or
is absolutely opposed only in the other and is self-sublating. Similarly
the annihilating unrest of the infinite only is through the being of
what it annihilates; the sublated is absolute just so far as it is sublated:
it arises in its perishing, for the perishing only occurs because there
is something that perishes. Thus what is in truth posited in the infinite
is that it be the void in which everything sublates itself; and just for
that reason this void is simultaneously an opposite, or one term of
what is sublated, the connection of the one-and-many, a connection
moreover that itself stands opposed to the disconnection of the one-
and-many, but that, from this standing-in-opposition in absolute in-
stability, is taken back into simplicity and is posited only as what is
thus taken back [and] reflected. In other words, infinity is:

II / Relationship

The hypothesis of simple connection—that what is is self-identical, or "Everything is what it is, and not another thing"—has sublated itself in the infinite
contradiction: what is is its own opposite, or "Each thing is in itself what it is
in relation to everything else."

We should notice that Hegel *uses* the Kantian categories of modality (possibility, actuality, necessity) as *stages* in the logical evolution of the triad of
relation. The modal categories are meta-categories, so to speak—and for this
reason the two *dynamic* triads in Kant's table must be deduced side by side.
The introduction of the modal categories at this stage is essential because
"necessity" is just what distinguishes relationship from simple connection.
"The rational as relationship" (Hegel said in his essay on "Scepticism") is
"*necessary* connection with another." But "the rational . . . has no contrary; it
embraces within itself both of the finite [terms] of which one is the contrary
of the other."[33] The terms to be *related* in the Logic (as a theory of cognition)
are the knowing self and the known world. Thus the fundamental relationship
is that between being and thought. But the equilibration of *that* contrast is

---

33. *Gesammelte Werke*, IV, 220; cf. di Giovanni and Harris, trans., *Between Kant and
Hegel*, p. 336f.

the task of "Proportion" (in which the Logic culminates). At the present stage Hegel develops the concept first of the *real world* and then of the *scientific truth* as a system of relationships. But his fundamental *speculative* concern is with the finite world of real *selves*, and the logical unity of the absolute self, which embraces the contraries.[34]

The world is both my world and not my world, because it is our world. Singular consciousnesses are accidents that come and go; but the continuum is indispensable, and it cannot exist without *some* singulars. Hence we must become conscious of the social foundation of our consciousness—and "we" means each one of us singly: "In all that is to follow, the relation stays together simply." It is the singular consciousness (as simple connection) from which the social concept of consciousness has been deduced. Thus far it is merely the (Kantian) formal concept of the self in its community that we have reached.

Infinity as the reality of simple connection is the totality of it. Simple connection has itself become as infinity the other of itself, [37] namely a manifold connection and the connection of a manifold. For α) that which gets connected in infinity is not the simple one-and-many; rather a connection of the one-and-many and the non-connection of the one-and-many, or the one-and-many posited as simple and the one-and-many posited as manifold. β) Similarly, the connection of these two terms is itself manifold: [first,] the pure self-equivalent connection or their non-being, the void wherein they are sublated; secondly, their *and*, or the same unity as their subsistence; for they are just as well not, within infinity, as they are. Simple connection, now that it has become infinity, is thus itself only *one* term; its opposite as well is the whole simple connection again, and its reflection or totality [is] the connection of its duplication and itself something duplicated within itself. On the one hand, [it is] the absolute ideality of both its shapes; on the other hand [it is] itself an ideality that is opposite to reality or only limit, the *and* of both its forms, which subsist outside it.

Infinity thus articulated is *relationship*, and this whole that it is must likewise become an other than itself and reflect itself into itself; although divided within itself and distinct, but also sublating its distinctions, infinity is something simple that must itself become infinite.

34. Anyone who doubts this claim should compare the logical discussion of the "one and the many" in Knox and Acton, trans., *Natural Law*, pp. 72–74 (*Gesammelte Werke*, IV, 432–33), with the opening paragraphs of the discussion of "Relationship" here.

In other words, against what is infinite the infinite itself must stand forth, and this, which it reflects into itself, must itself be the infinite.

In that the relation stands forth against itself, it remains simple. In other words, the differentiation, which it posits itself as, is not an analysis of itself; for that would be nothing but a going back through the preceding moments to simple quality. In all that is to follow, the relation stays together simply; its internal dividedness, which we have taken note of, is held together throughout; and the only thing to be done is to determine more closely this oneness of what is divided. In the concept of infinity it is initially nothing but this reciprocal sublating and positing, being and being-gone [*Verschwundenseyn*]. It is itself only the concept of infinity, not the infinite, posited with respect to it as infinite; for neither that which is an other is the infinite itself, nor is the infinite something that has come out of itself, but it has come out of something other than it is itself, that is, out of simple connection. Its arms are not themselves infinites but the connected one-and-many and the unconnected one-and-many. Thus the infinite [38] has not come forth out of itself and is not something that has turned back on *itself*; only its concept, not its reality, is posited.

With respect to the infinite, [each of] its unity and its separateness, its absolute self-equality and its absolute inequality, is distinguished. Each has been posited with respect to it or within its concept; each must be something that has come about through it, a returned unity and returned multiplicity, and since the infinite itself thus comes to be both of these, it is the other itself. It has fallen apart into a subsistence of itself as something duplicated; its nature, however, is the oneness of the opposites and the self-sublating of itself as thus duplicated or of itself as the other, so that it has come into being out of itself.

A / RELATION OF BEING

What Hegel calls the "relation of being" is both the logical ground of a dynamic theory of nature and a theory of the evolution of social consciousness. The "substance" that is its "immediate" form is what appears in the *Phenomenology* first as "the soul of the world" and later as "the ethical substance." The application to nature is easily visible, but the ethical application needs to be pointed out. In the ethical substance all of the singular consciousnesses recognize that it is the community alone that counts. But in its peaceful existence the community is just the system of common utilities. The common good seems to be directly identical with private prosperity. This means that it disappears—and with its disappearance the very possibility of private prosperity vanishes. The *differentiated* identity of self and community is the condition of the *possibility* of both.[35]

Hence the community must itself be a *negative* unity, an authority. As executive authority it is no longer merely possible, but actual. But as the actual unity of the community, this authority must be such as to preserve the prosperity of the members distributively. It must be not arbitrary, but lawful. (It is clear that Hegel's analysis applies to substances *generally* and not just to the ethical substance. But I suggest that if we apply it to that case we can see better why no reference to Spinoza is made until later, and why Hegel takes the moments in the order that he does.)

We take up relation immediately, as its concept has been determined. Its terms have significance throughout only in connection with each other; they are only as thus opposed to the other, and their unity is the duplicated, or positive, one that is what they have in common (or pure being) and hence just as much that in which they subsist as that in which they are sublated. Since they subsist in the unity, [the latter] is only their form; insofar as the unity is on its own account, it is the empty *and* of the terms outside which they both are. As this connecting *and* it is thereby immediately exclusive, negative unity, opposed to the terms of the antithesis, and itself a term whose other is the antithesis as such or with respect to itself.

As this its concept, relation is [39]

AA / *The Relation of Substantiality*

1 / The relation of substantiality expresses the concept of relation immediately; and the distinction both of the relation in general as a relation of being and that the concept of relation as substantiality relation is opposed to other forms of relation— [all this] is an anticipated reflection whose content produces itself only in what follows and justifies itself only further on; for the present it has merely the significance of a sign.

---

35. The discussion of "Ethical Life as Relationship" in the *System of Ethical Life* (Harris and Knox, trans., and *Gesammelte Werke*, v) illustrates the social application of Hegel's logic. But in the *System of Ethical Life* the logical distinction between simple connection and relationship is not clearly drawn because the concept of "consciousness" has not yet assumed its guiding role.

Since according to its essence the relation is infinite, its moments are themselves only the way they are within the infinite: in other words, they are posited only as sublated or simply and solely as such— the way they are with respect to the other.

a / Positive unity is initially, as it were, the space in which the moments of the antithesis subsist; or it is the being, the subsistence of the moments themselves. In this being the one is as good as the other;[36] they are both indifferent and external to each other. The space of the positive unity, or the commonality of being, is at the same time the *and* of the moments, which, however, is not over against them but as *and* is not present [at all] for them. Hence negative unity, which would be the *and* standing over against them, is not posited either; and substance has only the significance of being or subsistence; properly speaking, only diverse qualities have been posited, with the reflection that their being is what they have indifferently in common.

But in that the *one* determinacy is just as much as the other is, their essence is likewise only to be not indifferent to each other but simply and solely in connection with the other; and the being of each determinacy is the non-being of the other. It is[37] simply the case that not both are subsisting, but as self-sublating the one can subsist only insofar as the other does not. But equally the one does not just subsist; on the contrary, each in like manner has being insofar as the other is sublated. But just as absolutely each is not, insofar as the other is not; for each is only in connection with the other; or each is only insofar as the other is not; yet it is, only as essentially connected with the other. As a result, insofar as this other is not, the first itself is not, and insofar as the first is, the other immediately is, just as much as it also is not. [40]

The being or subsisting [*subsistiren*] that was posited previously is thus such that the determinacy is only insofar as the other is not; but insofar as the other is not, it itself is not. Thus its substance is only such that the determinacy is as a sublated one, and this substance is called *possibility*. The being of quality, having gone through infinity, has become what it is in itself; determinacy *is* only as a sublated, or

36. *Trans.*: Both "one" and "other" are neuter. To what do they refer? Should it be *das Glied* (understood), meaning member? Or, as we think, *das Bestehen*, "the subsisting"?

37. *Trans.*: We follow the ms. by using the singular verb. CE substitutes a plural one.

as a possible one. Being itself has become substance or possibility, a being of the determinacy, which being only [is] as a positedness of the determinacy, that is, as a sublatedness. On its own account this substance is the nothing, the void, or the pure unity. Determinacy has not disappeared within it, so that there would only be nothing—the nothing itself would be only a term of the antithesis against the determinacy, a form of the antithesis that has already been sublated— rather, the determinacy remains what it is; but its being is substance as its possibility. The content is the same; but the form that previously was being is what the being of the determinacy is in itself, namely, possibility. The content expresses nothing other than determinacy itself; whereas the form expresses the oneness of the determinacies that are kept apart from one another (that is, what they have in common), and this is the substance thus determined.

b / This substance, or being as a sublatedness, is thereby immediately something inwardly split; it is the nothing of the determinacies and their subsistence: as their nothing it is negative unity excluding them, the empty point; and at the same time the possibility of both or their being as sublated. The empty point, however, since it is at the same time positive unity, opposed to them and connected with them, is itself something determinate; it is no longer the nothing that is on its own account, but the sublatedness of determinacy, and hence [it is] itself a determinate sublatedness, or the being of determinacy as of something sublated. Determined as the sublatedness of both, the point is always something determinate, which has the other term of the antithesis outside itself. It is, as it were, the restricted substance, which is posited only as *one* determinacy, and as negative unity excludes the other from itself, determinacy in the form of the numerical *one*. And the substance, which is not pure numerical, but rather determinate, *one*—a determinate being with the exclusion of the other but in such a way that even the determinacy in being [41] itself is just something possible, something such that the other can just as well be in its place, or something that has, immediately, no more force of subsisting than the other—this substance is *actuality*. Quantity or connecting that excludes, having gone through infinity, is negative substance, or a determinacy that is only self-connected in such a way that it excludes the other as quantity does, but as an excluding determinacy it is itself only posited as a possible one. It is only something possible, which excludes the other possible; and the posited possible is substance. Within actuality substance splits what it is as possibility into two and steps to one side against itself or becomes an other than it is itself. It is actuality as its being posited in the mode of [*als*] negative unity, which now introduces an inequality into the positedness of both and has the one possible as something posited but the other as something not posited. What is thus not posited, the possibility that stands opposed to actuality, has become what is excluded and does not subsist. c / The dialectic of possibility, the being of the determinacies as a sublatedness of them, makes the substance into negative unity or actuality, but actuality as well has its dialectic in itself and cannot stay with itself.

Substance as actuality is a posited possible, the one accident which is in being; but this its positedness does not sublate its essence of being posited only as sublated. This accident is strictly connected with the other, and substance or being is in truth not the being of the one but the equal being of both, the *and* of both, posited in their sublation.[38] One is just as much something actual as the other and both are just as well possibles. Their substance is this: that each of them alike is actual as possible; that in its being or in its self-connection as actuality, it is essentially only as something sublated or as something possible. In other words, insofar as its inner essence as possibility is opposed to it as its becoming sublated, it must simply pass into this possibility, [42] that is, display its essence; and its possibility, as the opposite of itself, must rather be the actual. The genuine substance is this contradiction: that what is actual is a possible or that the possible is the actual. The differentiating *and* of the opposites, the immediate inversion into its opposite, or the substance, is *necessity*.

The concept of relation—that is, infinity—is posited in necessity as what it genuinely is. In possibility the moments of the antithesis only are as sublated—possibility itself is ideality, without being so in itself; possibility must posit itself as ideality, in which the moments are not as sublated but are sublated. But this numerical unity is itself a determinate one and is thus posited as actuality, in which relation as the ideality of the antithesis is rather the contrary of itself, that is, itself subsisting within it; or this numerical unity is determinate substance, which, as one with the opposed determinacy, is only infinite, or is necessity. Necessity expresses infinity as the self-equivalent unity of the opposites in the mode of absolute possibility, and at the same time expresses possibility as twofold within actuality, in one case being

38. *Trans.*: The ms has a semicolon after "both," only a comma after "sublation."

determined as in being, in the other as possible. But in necessity both are simply and equally as much actual as possible.

2 / Hence substance or necessity is nothing but the displaying of infinity as it is within itself: in its moments something which as possibility became other in actuality and is reflected out of actuality into possibility; but in such a way that these moments are not themselves what is infinite. What sublates itself within the other has not (as is required) been posited as something in being, yet it has to be like that; for the sublating, the ideality of infinity, is indeed only insofar as it sublates beings, in other words [only insofar as] those it sublates are in being. Within this relation of substantiality, however, only necessity or substance is in being; but since, with respect to its being as sublating, it still lacks its nourishment, so to speak, or the being of the moments, it is therefore not itself genuine. The moments themselves are truly in being; what is actual is with respect to itself, in its essence, something possible; likewise, within necessity the possibility excluded from the actual is just as well a posited or [actual]³⁹ possible. The infinite as substance or necessity is [43] in truth the contrary of itself, something not simple, but the connection of the sort of things that themselves are the unity of possibility and actuality, [that is,] necessary [things] or substances; and what is posited is:

BB / *Causality Relation*

If we take the ethical substance as our model, we can see why Hegel asserts that the genuine substance must be not the self-conscious God of Spinoza but a Leibnizian community of substances. That he *is* still primarily concerned with the evolution of rational consciousness is confirmed by the preamble to his analysis of the causality relation (see page 428 above).

According to Hegel's analysis the Spinozist definition of substance as "cause of itself" necessarily involves the mutuality of social recognition. The community is the "original Thing" (*Ursache*), which is manifest in its effective members. The law that expresses "necessity" *relates* its terms (this is true whether the law is natural or social, but the relationship is more obvious where the terms are "sovereign" and "subject"). The abstract law is merely a real possibility: it is *actual* only in the solar system or the *polis* (whose members are not mortal singulars but substantial families). These are the examples in

39. *Trans.*: The ms has "possible"; CE emends to "actual." We have not replaced but added.

which we can see clearly the identity of cause and effect, or of force and its manifestation.

Hegel deals with the conception of causal explanation in Hume and Kant in the first of the two following notes, and with the prevailing scientific conception of force in the second one. The relegation of these *external* conceptions of cause to the notes is further confirmation that his main argument is concerned with the concept of cognitive consciousness itself. The notes are relatively easy to follow; and they are especially interesting for the light that they throw upon the parallel discussions in the third chapter of the *Phenomenology* ("Force and Understanding").

In his two notes Hegel has shown the identity of cause and effect in the "external" applications of the category. Force in its relational sense is what *must* reveal itself. The cause is what is *completely* revealed in its effect. The two forces soliciting one another (or consciousness recognizing one another) are the two sides of one substantial reality. If we regard them as *distinct*, then their real nature is *hidden* and the *effect* revealed by their equilibrium is only a *limit*. But when we apply this insight to the *community* (whether it be the natural substance in the sky, or the ethical substance on earth), we find that the regression is not quite to the level of limit but rather to that of quantum (or whole and parts). Here the whole is a "true" infinite, not a "bad" one, but the distinction of the parts is not "real." Absolute possibility (that is, freedom) has vanished.

1 / It is the substance or necessity as a connection of opposites that are themselves necessary, or are substances. Substance as necessity is the disappearance of actuality. The actual opposed to the possible perishes in necessity; in other words, its essence has perished therein. We see that if it is to subsist, then it can subsist only in antithesis to an actual, and substance falls apart into opposed substances. The actual preserves itself in the face of necessity only by sublating it as unity and by dividing it into a duplicated necessity. The actual as something necessary in which there is no longer any necessity is self-connected, and within itself is infinite. In other words, its possibility is not outside the actual but rather inherent [*an ihm selbst*]; and it is thereby free. But it is connected with itself only in that it excludes out of itself this [fact]: that its possibility is outside it, and so what it excludes from itself is something actual. In that it excludes this, it is connected with it; it is thus only truly actual in that, in itself infinite,

it is connected with something actual by exclusion. Thus it is a *Thing* [*Sache*], and indeed a cause [*Ursache*].[40]

The cause has its possibility not outside but within itself; it is itself something actual and is connected with an actual. Since both are actuals, the necessity is just the equal actuality of both; that is, necessity is outside them, and so is actuality (or self-equivalence). This [fact], that the "both" is actual,[41] is a reflection that is not posited with respect to them themselves; with respect to them themselves there is only their being *per se*, not this connection nor their being equal to each other. Not only is an actual outside the self-subsistent [*für sich seyenden*] cause, but also [it is] actuality itself as the unity of both; hence the cause would not in truth be actual. [44]

Now the cause, as infinity, which itself only is in the form of possibility and has its actuality outside it, is called *force*; it is substance that has been held up in its positing of itself as actuality. Necessity did, of course, split into two actuals, but when this duplication of actuality is regarded as what it is in truth, then the actual that has its possibility within itself proves itself to be such that it excludes another actual from itself; and this exclusion is strictly essential to it. This connection is a differentiated connection; in other words, it is relation. What is excluded is of its essence just this: to be the contrary of what is posited. Since both are actuals, it seems, indeed, that infinity or necessity is sublated; each actual is posited on its own account. But these, which are posited thus solely as self-connecting, are in truth (or in their essence) not on their own account. What is posited as actual, the *cause*, is so only because it is the cause of itself, or has its possibility absolutely within itself [that is, because it is][42] the determinacy whereby the cause, as connected thereto within infinity, is sublated; and this its ideality is in the cause itself. The cause is the one[ness] of itself and of its contrary; but then its contrary, what it excludes from itself, is not actual, and we would be thrown back to the substantiality relation. But since this its contrary is actual, the cause itself is determined merely as something possible. Thus each of the

40. *Trans.*: In german the *Ur* is stressed.

41. *Trans.*: The ms has a singular verb; CE substitutes a plural. We have returned to the ms, taking the sense of "both" to be a singular conjunction, not a plurality of terms.

42. *Trans.*: The text has a semicolon here. The location of the verb in the next clause suggests that it is still governed by "because." We have therefore moved the semicolon to the next line, prior to a main clause.

two is connected with itself as infinite unity of actuality and possibility; and each is substance. But at the same time each is simply posited as excluding, as connecting negatively with the other. Each is in like manner an actual over against the other; the other is thus determined as a possible; and thereby in its actuality it is determined as a possibility at the same time. The cause is substance only insofar as it determines as its actuality precisely the possible excluded by it—in other words, because it acts [*wirkt*]. As this agent [*Wirkende*], or as determining what is excluded as its actuality [*Wirklichkeit*], [the cause] itself is strictly opposed to what is excluded from it; for it is only on its own account as excluding or negating. Since this excludedness is actual and is the contrary of itself, the cause is thereby determined as merely possible or as force, which in order to *be* or to be as cause must utter[43] itself or must sublate this antithesis.

In this heaping-up of contradictions, each moment only is to the extent that it is held fast before it passes into its contrary. But since it is thus secured only as [45] connected with its contrary, then its determining as something held fast is itself the display of its having already passed over into its contrary.

The cause is what is necessary in itself, which [is] thus necessary in itself only because it excludes an other from itself but is connected with the other in such a way that this other is only something effected [*bewirktes*] by it, that is, [in such a way] that in what is effected the cause posits itself explicitly [*als sich selbst*] as actuality. But in this way this other, the self-subsistent substance that is separated from the cause, is simply sublated. For this other substance is only that in which the first substance posits itself as actual; this other substance is nothing but the first actual substance. If the first substance were to be on its own account, and [if] the other in which the effect [*Wirkung*] happens [were likewise to be], then the former would not be cause—in fact, no effect would occur at all. There would be no relation, only a plurality of absolutely self-subsistent substances. But just for that reason these several self-subsistent substances would not be substances, not intrinsically [*in sich*] infinite, intrinsically necessary, for they would not be connected with another, as indeed they are. To the extent that they are indifferently on their own account they would merely be numerical *ones*, of which the dialectic has been displayed earlier. Thus the cause

43. *Trans.: Aussern* means both "externalize" and "utter." Baillie sometimes translates it as "expression."

is absolute only in the effect. Since it is only *qua* effective [*wirkend*], it is connected with another substance; yet at the same time as effective it is not so, for this other substance is in fact the cause itself as the actual substance. In that the latter is held fast as something other than the cause, this other than the cause is the cause as actual substance; and the cause is what it is itself as not this other, only as the possible actual substance; in other words, it is only as force.

We can see that, properly, force expresses the whole causality relation within itself, or the cause as one with the effect and in truth actual substance, but [that] also the causality relation is sublated. In other words, because cause is inseparable from effect and the distinction is null and void, their unity as force is the actual substance; for only because it posits itself as an actual outside itself [is] the cause outside itself only a possible. In force the antithesis remains as a quite ideal₂ one; it remains, for this actual substance is an actual simply and solely as being outside itself; it is an ideal one because the substance, being outside itself, is something that is on its own account merely possible—the whole—and the same as what it is *qua* being self-equivalent. Force as the merely possible actual substance has over against itself the form of actuality once more; in that the cause makes itself into actual substance, it [becomes] rather just a [46] possible one, just force. Its positing of itself outside itself in an other is rather a being-within-itself of the actual substance or its concept, since only thereby does it correspond to its concept. Through this coming to be outside itself it has become not its reality but its own ideality—that is, merely its possibility; and this possibility has its antithesis in its actuality. But this actuality of the cause is now no longer a substance proper, but merely form. [Inasmuch] as that possibility or force is the sublatedness of the duplicated substantiality,⁴⁴ force is what the cause is in truth; but against force itself there stands something purely ideal₂—that is, something that is only posited in sublation, the mere determinacy of actuality. Thus cause is not realized in force itself, but in order to be actual force must pass over into its opposed determinacy, actuality; it must utter itself.

In the utterance of force nothing else is left for the alteration or for the becoming other of force in its realization but the form of

---

44. *Trans.*: The "is" of the subordinate clause is in the wrong place for our reading. However, the "as" was inserted later, and Hegel may have overlooked rearranging the clause.

actuality. If force were essentially just a possibility, then in giving itself actuality it would cease to be. Force, which as possibility is connected simply with its actuality, would simply and solely be as actuality; but at the same time, in being actual it would cease to be what it is. The essence of force is thus its content, substance (or the oneness of actuality and possibility); and the antithesis—that this oneness itself [is] posited again as possibility—[is] a completely empty one over against the pure determinacy of actuality, an antithesis that has only pure determinacies as terms and dissolves itself in itself into nothingness. There is nothing in the utterance of force that is not in force itself; it is a completely empty distinction—the distinction between force and its utterance [Äusserung], or between inner and outer [ausserem] generally. Since force is opposed to actuality only [inasmuch] as actual substance [is] under the determination of possibility, therefore the positing of actual substance (or of the substantiality relation) as a possibility—that is, force—is something just as completely null and void. The dialectic that the causality relation has with respect to itself drives necessarily beyond this relation; but the reality that the actuality of the cause gained in force is a determination just as superfluous as it is null and void. [47]

N[ote] 1 / The causality relation, as the one in which relation generally [is] determinately fixed in the duplication of substances and seems to unite within itself both the being *per se* of a numerical plurality and also their connecting with each other, that is, [both] empirical intuition (or the being of nature) and the concept, offers itself just as much at first to the consciousness that relates itself to nature as its dialectical nature stimulates it to contradiction against itself.

The *superficial concept* that does not come to infinity takes THE ABSOLUTE BEING PER SE OF THE SUBSTANCES to be fundamental, and then connects them with each other. It posits them together as one, but just slightly so, so that their remaining on their own account does not suffer by it. But rather there cannot be any connection at all between such absolutely self-subsistent beings; for every connection, be it ever so slight, would be a sublation of *substantiality*. Because each is in this way on its own account, there also emerges in truth no *opposition*, no *difference*, for that would be a connection such that each of them would not be on its own account but only in its connection with the other; but the substances are to be strictly on their own account. In fact, *no relation at all* has been posited in general—and neither cause nor effect. The cause is to be something other than what it is as effect; yet both remain strictly the same. And what is separated is not something that is cause and something that is effected; on the contrary, just the *one* substance (which was to distinguish itself as cause and what is effected, yet remains the same) is posited at one time quite externally separate from another: two things that have nothing to do with each other and are quite accidental to each other and then are bound up with one another—just so externally, however, and in the bonding remain so much on their own account that they are connected with one another neither before the bonding nor when they are bonded; that is, they get bonded by something quite other than what they are themselves. Thus, for instance, the rain is posited as cause of the wetness of the soil, the wetness as effect; and the causality relation has the form A: a + B, where A signifies the rain, B the soil. The rain is at one time cause, but then also, as effect, is no longer rain but wetness, a property or condition [48] of the soil; and the dry soil has become something other than it was before through the agency [*Einwirkung*] of the rain. In this relation both rain and soil are and continue to be substances; but the rain is the actual that posits itself as actuality to the extent that it sublates the possibility that is outside it, that is, the dryness; and only thereby is it in truth rain as cause of dampness. But what has been posited here [is] not in truth a relation but merely its semblance; the rain does not therein become genuinely actual substance or infinity. Its opposition as rain and as dampness is radically null and void; [for] it is always one and the same thing that is to be separated into rain and dampness. There is in truth no separation here, and the causal action of the rain, [namely,] in producing wetness, is a completely empty tautology. Or if the opposition is conceived in such a way that on the one side rain, on the other dryness, are opposed absolutely, then the one is the possibility of the other. Yet in its acting [*Wirken*] the rain does not make itself so infinite that it posits its possibility, dryness, within itself, but only sublates the dryness with respect to this place, this determinate soil. This sublation would be a pure negating of dryness but never a positing of its possibility within the rain itself, not a genuine actualization [*Verwirklichung*]. However it is not even a sublation but purely a change of place of the dryness and the rain, or of the identical wetness; for the dryness has, so to speak, only gone to where the rain was previously. The rain itself has gone over to the other substance; but this is perfectly contingent for both: the wetness could have remained dampness of the air, even as it is now dampness of the soil, just as the wind that is cause of a motion of the leaf might as easily not have moved it—the soil could have stayed dry, the leaf at rest. Still less is necessity or the necessary connection to wetness or to wind posited in this determinate soil or in this determinate leaf—and soil and leaf are nothing if they are not "thises." Just as it is contingent for both to be bound, so they are contingent for each other within the bond itself; the damp substance and the inherently dry substance must simply continue as what they are, for they are both posited as beings on their own account. [49] In all the moments of this alteration nothing is posited of the essence of the relationship, [that is,] the being in connection with an other, or determinacy as it [is] in itself, namely infinite.

What is often called explaining is nothing else but the positing of a so-called causality relation of this kind. It is a requirement of explaining that the determinacy so posited be shown as an other, as its own contrary; but in truth, explaining by means of this causality relation does nothing but show the same determinacy in another quite contingent form, such as wetness as rain. Instead of infinity· or the transition into what is absolutely opposed, the absolute principle is rather that what is to be explained has already been present previously in all its determinateness, before it is there where it appears. The explaining is nothing but the production of a tautology—cold comes from the dissipating of heat; heat comes from incoming or outgoing calories, rain from water, oxygen only from oxygen, etc., motion from impulse (that is, from a motion that was there all the time before). The fruit of the tree comes from oily, watery, salty parts, etc. (or in more learned language, from carbon, oxygen, hydrogen, etc.), in brief only from what it [is] itself. Likewise, what is animal arises from nitrogen, carbon, etc.—it is indeed essentially nothing but these—and the causes that constitute it are the same things that it is itself, to which singular [things] an other is mingled only externally and yet an other is sundered. The whole process is a change of place of the parts, but the determinacies are what has being absolutely in and of itself, is indestructible, and remains strictly self-same. What appears in a body has always been preserved in it merely hidden and now comes forth from it, or was outside it and now comes to it; and the explanation is nothing other than the consequence of this identity or the displaying of the tautology. The differentiation or opposition, the essence of the determinacy, becomes a merely external one instead, something from elsewhere, something that is to have been together with another; and in truth no relation, no infinity is posited.

This absence of relationship in the causality relation is what justified

Hume in denying the necessity that after all ought to lie in it, and in explaining it as a mere illusion. In fact the necessity is just the substance as relation—that is, as the oneness of opposed determinacies, [50] which are not, like those materials, absolutely on their own account, absolute qualities or substances, but such as are in themselves this: that they are connected with another—in other words, essentially their own contrary. The identity that there is in the tautology of explanation that wetness is the cause of the wet, heat the cause of the hot, is oneness to be sure, but not the oneness of necessity, which passes from one determinate to the opposite determinate. In this causality relation an other appears as well—there are two substances, and the latter constitute the side of opposition; but it has nothing to do with the former identity. The substances are not in relation to each other; they endure [*bleiben*] on their own account, apart from each other and externally combined. The former identity remains simple tautology; the latter diversity a particular being *per se* of the substances; and the identity and diversity both fall asunder. The connection of the diverse substances is not a necessity, because they are not connected with respect to themselves. Kant has said the same as Hume; Hume's substances, which follow one after the other or are next to each other [and] are anyway indifferent (each on its own account) towards one another, remain so in Kant as well. It matters not at all that what Hume calls things are [for Kant] sensations, perceptions, sense representations, or whatever else he likes—[for in any case] they are diverse, self-subsistent; the infinity of the relation, the necessity, is something separate from them. That being *per se* of the diverse in its objective aspect Kant calls a contingent togetherness; and the necessity remains something subjective. That appearance is on its own account; and necessity as a concept of the understanding is likewise on its own account. Experience, of course, is the conjoining of concept and appearance—that is, the setting in motion of indifferent substances, sensations, or whatever you will, whereby they become determinate, existing only in the antithesis. But this relation itself is . . .—that is just what is hard to say; at least it is not what the things in themselves are! It is, to give it a name, something merely subjective. For with respect to them in themselves, what is connected is supposed to be outside the connection—the sensations are[45] self-subsistent singulars; and likewise the infinity of the connection, the

45. *Trans.*: We follow the ms. CE emends to "what is connected are supposed to be sensations, self-subsistent singulars, outside the connection."

concept of the understanding in and for itself, is to be outside what
is connected. And yet those self-subsistent beings are supposed to be
only appearances, not what they are in and of themselves; they are
supposed to be likewise the infinite connection, capable of a significance and a use in no other connection save with what are thus separated; [51] thus they are supposed separately to be empty *entia rationis*
without truth. In truth what are falling asunder—sensations, objects
of experience, or whatever one wants to call them—are mere appearances. And if the word "appearance" is not to be meaningless,
then it can only signify that those diverse [entities], thus posited as
self-subsistent, are not essentially in themselves but are rather in themselves strictly infinite, identical as their own contrary. In the same way,
what has been called "concept of the understanding" is the infinity of
the connection, as a connection that connects nothing, whose terms
would not be those absolutely relative [entities];[46] [it is] the pure unity,
a perfectly empty identity, or nothingness with respect to the concept
itself. And in themselves those [entities] (that is, sensations, objects)
as well as this concept (that is, the absolute relation) are both one and
the very same. The appearance alone of the sensations or objects is
what is objective, just as the *ens rationis* alone of the empty concept is
what is subjective. But precisely on that account what is objective in
the one case as what is subjective in the other is a nothingness; and
what is in itself is only the infinite relation. It would not hurt to call
this "experience" and thereby to [re]cognize experience as the in-itself
of the antithesis, if only experience itself did not in fact express the
relation again in the form of the subjective instead of in the form of
mere relationship and if only it did not usually rather signify the
contrary of mere relationship, to wit, precisely the causal linkage set
forth above, in which the diverse [entities] are not opposites, not terms
of a relationship, and [in which] the connection likewise is not the
infinite one, not the connection of relationship.
N[ote] 2 / Rising above the causal linkage that we have just explicated
is the concept of force. Force unites within itself both of the essential
sides of the relation, identity and separateness, and unites the former
precisely as identity of separateness or of infinity. The substance,
which gets posited as cause and effect, is this not in and of itself but
only in connection with something else; and this connection is strictly
contingent for it, something other than it [and] not in it. Water can

46. *Trans.*: We follow CE's emendation.

be rain, but it need not be; it is perfectly free, not under the necessity of wetting; the condition that it does wet lies entirely outside it, and hence this too [lies outside it]: that it be cause and effect. As force, on the other hand, substance is cause with respect to it; substance as cause is, of course, connected with an other, but it is not essential for it to be cause. But force is essentially the determinacy that makes substance into this [52] determinate substance; and at the same time it is posited as connecting with what is opposed, or as having its contrary with respect to it, so that [it is] cause not contingently but through itself. The moving force is not, for instance, a body that as mass is indifferent to motion and rest, but it is in itself the cause of the motion, being posited strictly as one with it. Force is the whole, the whole magnitude of the motion, the product of mass and velocity, whereas in causal linkage, on the other hand, mass is on its own account, and it makes no difference to it whether motion is conjoined with it, whether it connects with other substances through motion, and whether it is cause, or not. Just so attracting force is not a substance that is on its own account and to which the determinacy of attracting may or may not be added externally as a connection with others; rather, attracting force is in itself simultaneously the connecting with another. Since force thus expresses the idea of relationship itself and what falls asunder in causal linkage is sublated, the duality of substances falls away too. Force itself is just substance that (as relation) has necessity in itself, is inherently self-equal, and as this equality is the unity of opposites. Moving force is with respect to itself product of mass and velocity, a self-equal product, and at the same time a mass that, through itself as one with velocity, is the alteration of motion with respect to it. Just as the attracting force is self-equal and infinite within itself as the connection of one to an other with respect to it, and the connection itself embraces this one as well as the other—each is contained in its simplicity—so moving force not only grasps the opposites of location within itself, as motion does, but also comprehends within itself motion and mass together as one. In the same way, magnetic or electric force, etc., is not a substance that would have what is magnetic or electric outside itself, but it is posited with respect to it as one with it, so that this being is not contingently, but essentially, magnetic or electric. Whereas substance as such would only possibly have in itself what is electric or magnetic as well as motion, but would have the actuality of what is electric or magnetic outside it, substance as force has its actuality immediately within its possibility. On the contrary, the substance that is cause is to be cause with respect to it only possibly, and has actuality outside itself. [53]

In that force thus expresses relationship in truth, it is no wonder that the so-called discovery of attractive force or of general gravity, of the irritability of the organic, or of the force of chemical affinity has been accounted such an enrichment of knowledge in general, and that also what is relation has penetrated elsewhere (for instance, the relationship between mass and volume, density, what is dynamic as one energy, and the magnitude of what is thus simple, of force as an intensive magnitude). Just as attracting force is nothing but the implicitly posited connection of one with an other, so likewise irritability is this infinite that in itself connects with an other, since here the connection with an other as it were first appears as a posited effect of something else,[47] which is reflected, however, into itself or displays itself as a connecting not with an an other but with itself. In the same way the force of chemical affinity is just this: that it [is] the essence of this body not to be on its own account but to have its essence in its connection with an other. Just as dynamic density is the relation of space to mass, posited simply (so that this pair [*diese beyden*] is one and their difference is reflected into itself), so too irritability embraces both what the body is on its own account and what it is through something else, and establishes its own self-equality; likewise density saves the weight of the mass from its ideality as pure space, which destroys that reality; it establishes the weight, [and][48] maintains against its otherness as space its self-connection in the infinity of the simple oneness of mass and of space. The force of affinity is likewise the connection of the determinacy with its opposites, but in such a way that both these opposites [are] one in the relationship and the determinacy that exists only in connection with an other, or only as outside itself, maintains itself at the same time connected with itself in its being-outside-itself, as what it is.

Force thus ex[presses] relationship itself and the necessity to be within itself even in its being-outside-itself, or to be self-equal; in other words, it expresses infinity. But in order to express infinity truly, it must not, in the first place, be distinguished any longer from the substance or the thing, or whatever one wants to call the subsistence

47. *Trans.*: Lasson retains the original draft that Hegel later corrected: "effect of an other[ness]."

48. *Trans.*: CE adds a subordinate conjunction here.

of the one determinacy; for substance is in truth nothing more in particular but necessity—that is, force itself; and force is not a possibility to which actuality still stands opposed as substantial being. [54] Hence force, if it is to be infinite in truth and not express infinity (that is, relationship) merely in a formal$_2$ way, must express its inner opposition truly in itself; it must express its determinacy in these its ideal$_2$ moments and be just their connection. Force must not [run] together again into an identity and thus set itself against its actuality, its utterance; nor must it be again the differentiation that it has with respect to its [actuality] (as in ordinary causal linkage, a diversity of substances subsisting on their own account). But both alternatives are involved in force: it does oppose itself to its actuality, and in order to be it must first utter itself; it inheres as some such merely possible [being], or *ens rationis*, in a substance that is not force itself but is distinguished from it and that, as force without its utterance, it needs as its bearer. Because it is thus simply something possible and because as this identity it is a connection of opposites—though a simple one, just pure connection—what are connected fall outside it: set over against force and against each other, they are self-subsistent beings; they are not the idealities of the infinite, but substances.

Force must utter itself, for relationship as force is just something possible; it has actuality opposed to it. But what matters about this antithesis has been shown: to wit, it is the pure antithesis devoid of content, [or] force itself is in truth the whole relation. It is an entirely useless distinction to define relationship as force and oppose it to its utterance; there is in fact nothing but the relation itself; it does not distinguish itself from itself as ideal relationship, force, and as real, existing relationship. The utterance of force, the relation as an actuality (for instance, the actual attraction, the actual irritation, magnetism, electricity, etc.), is always and everywhere relationship itself, self-equivalent in its utterance. Relationship appears as a manifold of utterances; but this manifoldness is nothing but the multiplicity of the moments of the relation itself. For it is not something purely simple, an empty identity, but an infinity or unity of opposites; and the multiplicity that has been posited in utterance is the same in the force that is posited as not uttering itself. If the relationship is a restricted one, then its actuality depends, to be sure, upon conditions that are not within the relation itself; in other words, the force can be posited as one that does not utter itself—magnetism, electricity, motion, etc., appear actually in a single body (that is, they are not necessary), and utterance or actuality is separate from possibility. But this actuality has nothing to do with relationship, with the [55] infinite itself as such; the relationship is, purely and simply because the determinacies that are its moments are posited. For a relation that is itself just a moment in the system of relations, its condition is the relation opposed to it; but it is actual in the absolute system of relations. Its singularization, however (and the violence that can be done to it in this singularization), does not concern it as relationship. Thus, for instance, electricity is a relationship infinite within itself; at the same time it is a determinate relation, a moment within the system of relations or of absolute infinity. As this moment it has absolute actuality; it always is, and always utters itself. But the isolated display of it through the friction of a glass plate is no more its absolute actuality than the magnetism of magnetic ore or of iron. As to these single determinacies electricity may or may not utter itself; it is free from them. But its existence in these singularities is immediately something contingent. This lies in the concept of the matter at hand [*Sache*], since we are only talking about the singular positedness and that is something accidental, arbitrary, external. A singular positedness of this kind, however, is not the absolute actuality of relationship at all; it is actual even without this utterance in such single [cases]. Hence, relationship [as] distinct from such single utterances is not a force—that is, not the relation posited as merely possible; quite to the contrary, it is the absolutely actual and possible simultaneously—that is, what is simply necessary. And the singular activity, that being as a determinate phenomenon, is rather in itself an *ens rationis*, something that is not, in that it is. Singularized actuality of this kind will be dealt with in a moment; the relationship that would have its utterance and reality in the singularized actuality would have in itself to be opposed to it and would have to be determined as possibility in connection with it; and this may well be what should be said once relations have been defined as forces. But relationship as absolutely actual is removed from this actuality only in the sense that actuality is [re]cognized as ideality or as nothing with respect to it; and actuality is thus in fact also posited in the place of what is called force, since the entire infinity of relationship has been transposed into force. However, the determinacy of relationship as force, as possibility against actuality, is something quite empty.

Relationship, however, being thus *qua* force only as possibility, must simultaneously have its actuality with respect to it; for force only is as connection with actuality. And since it is strictly fixed as possibility and is not to cease to be possibility (or force) in its connection with actuality, [56] and is not to be one with actuality (wherein possibility would be destroyed)—[that is] it is not to be necessity—it follows that its connection with actuality is just a bad external bond, in which force still remains sundered from actuality and each of them (force as well as actuality) is on its own account. This is expressed by saying that force inheres in a substance. This being of force would again be nothing but the substantiality relation itself—in other words, the necessity in which one determinacy is connected with the other. But the force that inheres in a substance is not locked within itself or within the substance but has passed over to the causality relation, since this whole of the force as bound up with the substance is connected with an other that is necessary in itself; in other words, it is opposed to utterance.

That substance and force [are] now external to each other in this bond, that in truth each of them [is] on its own account, is expressed by saying that the nature of matter (which is precisely the substantial) is unknown, and that therefore we do not know whether force is of the essence of matter or whether it has been implanted in matter from outside. The bond of force with substance is also conceived more determinately as an imparting of force. In order to make this imparting clearer, force is better still posited as a substance or matter, specified again from universal substance or matter; and the bond is supposed to be a mingling of the specific substances, like the mingling of wine with water—so that, for instance, magnetic substance is poured into iron substance, or repelling substance is poured into light substance, or into the substance of the celestial bodies. In short, whether it be done by implanting, pouring, accumulating, piling up, or impulsion, force gets to be inside substance in a completely external way.

But as we have shown, this substance sundered from force is nothing but the actuality opposed to force (since force is relationship posited under the determinacy of possibility); but this empty actuality is a pure determinacy, entirely the same as pure possibility, pure simplicity in general. The infinite relationship, however, is itself this self-equivalent simple, and this [57] its self-equivalence is the genuine substance—though it is not at all the form as opposed to the self-nullifying determinacies but is precisely the one[ness] of their nothing[ness] instead; not something that is separated from the relation, but rather the essence of it. When the relation itself is something bounded, then it is, *qua* determinacy, itself a moment—just as, for instance, quality and quantity are things infinite within themselves, reflected, and at the same time moments; it is not the absolute unity itself but an expression of infinity that is only formal (that is, one posited in a determinacy), whereby, however, infinity as such is not affected. Instead, determinacy is, as it were, the colour of the unity of the relation which displays [itself] as infinite without stress or hindrance in this self-equivalence of the determinacy. Thus the relation, *qua* moment, is not connected with itself but with its determinacy, which is opposed to it. It is connected not according to its infinity but according to its determinacy, and as single moment it is distinguished from the whole of which it is a moment. But this whole is itself the infinite, the relationship; it is the substance—with which whole, however, the subordinate relationship, which is only a moment, is not bound up in a contingent way but is rather an essential moment of it. And *qua* moment it is not a fixed self-subsistent being (as force is defined to be) but is strictly just a determinacy; and this determinacy, as the whole relationship, only is in its connection with its own opposite relation, since its substantiality is just this unity with its opposed moment. Force is neither something separate from substance and over against it nor self-subsistent over against other forms of the relation embraced within the unity of the substance (any more than the substance as empty unity is). As force, the determinacy is even more fixed than quality in general, because determinacy as relation is infinite within itself. We shall soon have occasion to discuss this point when we consider what is dialectical in the causal relation itself, since the two substances in a causal relation are nothing but two things necessary or two relations which merge into One within it.

The relationship as it, defined *qua* possibility, is to inhere in a substance and is thus not to be absolute substantiality in itself, is on its own account separated from the substance that is its actuality, subsisting [*seyende*] with respect to it. But *qua* force the relationship is also connected with its actuality as something opposed to it, upon which it utters itself. The actuality bound up with [it] is its positiveness; *qua* essentially infinite it must be negatively connected with an actuality and hence must have it outside itself and sublate it, perhaps partially, in the connection. [58] Force thus becomes a connection between mutually opposed, self-subsistent substances, opposed to force as identity, [or] it becomes something purely formal. What are differentiated are outside it; they are not the moments of force itself as of something infinite; since it has these moments outside itself, force itself ceases to be infinite. Devoid of its moments it is something merely identical, a form in which any determinacy [is] posited; and it ceases thereby to be anything else but the same empty tautology as the causal linkage and serves only for the same nonsense as the tautological type of explanation. [The] attracting force of diverse substances, the force of affinity, etc., express a connection, but what is connected are[49] not absolute opposites, not moments of the infinite, but self-subsistent and indifferent [*indifferente*] beings; and the connection itself is thus not an infinite one but an identical or self-equivalent one, apart from which there is the opposition. Diverse mutually connected substances contain the contradiction: of being *per se* because they are substances, and of not being *per se* because they are connected. Since the substances are absolutely on their own account, the connection is what is absolutely alien to them. And the request for explanation that arises itself presupposes that the ground to be indicated for the connection is outside the substances, and it requires this indication. What gets indicated is the force of attraction or of affinity; or in other words, nothing else but the connection itself. It must be something other than the substances that it connects, for they are not connected with one another through themselves; on the contrary, they are only on their own account; they are connecting only with themselves. This other that connects them, what is it? It is nothing but the connection itself. Once that being *per se* of what are connected as substances is presupposed, there is no possible answer except this tautology. In order for it not to be a tautology, the connection would have to be an infinite one, so that what are related would be their own contrary. But the substances are only self-equivalent; and thus there remains for the connection nothing but their pure self-equivalence, or the tautology of their essence. "The substances are connected by connecting force" means nothing more than "they are connected just because they are connected." What is absolutely incomprehensible is the binding of self-subsistent substances with their connection, which posits them more [or] less as one and sublates them. And what is absolutely incomprehensible leaves one nothing more to say but "That is just how it is." Comprehension—in other words, positing the necessity—would be nothing else but the [59] substances' being connected with each other through themselves—that is, their absolutely not being *per se*, absolutely not substances, but being with respect to

49. *Trans.*: The singular and plural verbs are as in the ms.

one another each only in its opposite, outside itself, the contrary of itself. But upon the presupposition of absolute being *per se*, this necessity is not possible. So there is no necessity at all, but instead the connection is on its own account, separate from the substances, as they are from it and from each other; and the ground of their connection is the tautology that they are indeed connected. The pure being of "*That is how it is*" is empty identity, the absence of necessity; [it is] the space of absolute contingency, in which all things have their places, lying quietly and indifferently beside one another without mutual hurt, [or] particular substances that stay as they are on their own account; then, in addition, there is also a connecting—that is, a sublating—of the substances. But the staying as they are on their own account and the not staying so are external to each other; they do not touch each other; they lie quietly next to each other; all relationship has disappeared.

The tautology that explains the determinate connection has been driven to an antithesis by the need for explanation, which looks for necessity (that is, for the being of one in its opposite), and thus it hides its tautology from itself. The antithesis, which explanation then puts in the determinacy that has been made identical, is precisely the formal one of possibility and actuality, of force—of [its] inward[ness] and its utterance. This antithesis, however, is not posited in the relationship itself in such a way that the relationship would in truth divide itself thus with respect to it and be its infinite connection; instead, the relation has been made into the pure simplicity of a name and defined as possible. Force is exactly the same as it is *qua* appearance, or in uttering itself—distinctions that have nothing to do with force in itself (namely as relationship), [that are] not moments of force itself. Hence that explaining has indeed an opposition in its tautologies as well; but the opposition is just a semblance, since it has nothing to do with the essence either of the explanatory connection or of what are connected. To explain the rock's falling to the ground (that is, uniting with the ground) it is said that it unites with the ground not because it unites with the ground but because a force in the rock unites it, namely, the force uniting the rock with the ground. The explanation of the turning of the magnetic needle towards north or south, or the attraction of iron [60] filings to the poles of the magnet, or the repulsion between homonymous poles, does not just assert that the magnet turns to the north or the south because that is how it turns, that the magnet attracts iron filings because it attracts, that homonymous poles repel each other because they repel; but rather because in the substance in which all this is exhibited there is something other than the substance, namely a magnetic force, and this magnetic force is capable of turning the substance that way, of attracting such filings, of making homonymous poles repellent. Likewise electricity or irritability is explained as force in the way it appears. The content of the appearance and of the force is the same; the totality [*Ganze*] of utterances is gathered together within the force. Internally sundered as the relation may be, it still counts as one in name, a simple togetherness; and the separating that is posited with respect to the relation is one that is alien to it, a separating of force as something possible from force as something actual; so that the tautology of the explanation remains the same. From this it follows that for the cognition that is infinite in itself [and] is only concerned with the infinite and the necessary, there is no force; and that it does not consider moving or accelerating force but motion, acceleration, etc., not the magnetic, electrical force, etc., but magnetism, electricity, etc. Just as little does it consider the force of imagination, of memory, or the faculty of imagination, memory, understanding, reason, etc., but imagination, memory, understanding, reason themselves; and least of all does it consider attractive force or the force of affinity. For, although the electrical, magnetic, intellectual, etc., forces are nothing but pure identities and, despite the differentiation [produced] by explanation, are tautologies, these names do signify this determinacy of electrical, magnetic connection. But the forces of attraction and of affinity are completely empty; they express nothing at all except connection as such. It is indeed remarkable to find investigations of the question whether attractive force may not be an entirely universal force of nature, perhaps even of spiritual nature. This is in fact the case, for attractive force is connection as such, and there is, to be sure, no force more universal than the force of connection. The force of affinity is in fact much too empty, as is also the attractive force. To say "Alkali combines with acid because it has affinity for it" does not truly mean anything more than that they posit themselves both as one because they posit themselves as one; to say "Sulphuric acid combines with the lime of a lime carbonate [61] and drives the carbonic acid off, because sulphuric acid has a *greater* or *closer* affinity with the lime than the carbonic acid has" means in effect nothing else but that the lime prefers to combine with sulphuric acid rather than with carbonic acid. The metaphorical expression "affinity" can quite well be replaced by "drive to bond" or even "friendship," etc.; and in that case one might say "Alkali combines preferentially with acid, because it has a preferential drive to bind with it." We have remarked already that force expresses [the fact] that the connection of one substance with another is in the substance itself, or that it is in the relationship—[that is,] that it is of the nature of an acid to connect with alkali. Hence explanation in terms of the force of attraction or of affinity also expresses the fact that the connection is not a contingent but a necessary one. But the formula "Acid connects with alkali" signifies this necessity immediately, whereas "force" leaves it open whether acid or alkali could not be something sundered from their necessary connection (as if that connection were not their definition) and whether there could not be an acid without this force, just as there could be a magnet without magnetism, etc. Chemical affinity stands higher in the signifying of relationship, since whatever has this affinity is in fact nothing but something relative or (when posited with respect to itself) its own contrary. But just for that reason the utterance—for instance, the neutralization of alkali by acid—does not in actuality sunder itself from possibility or force. There is simply and solely one and the same necessity; and one can think of no diversity of actuality and possibility, or of a separateness of utterance and of force, even in connection with ordinary actuality, or the actuality of the singular. Iron is conceivable without magnetism, but not acid without alkali; that is, iron may be posited as self-equivalent or neutral without the differentiation of the magnetic poles, but acid and alkali are not neutral at all. In other words, when as salt they are neutrally bonded, then they are devoid of alkalinity and acidity, like iron without magnetic poles. But this again is just how their affinity is not to be taken; fixed by their nature as acid and alkali, each defined to be the contrary of the other and hence, as necessarily connected, the contrary of itself, this isolated determinacy is yet to remain substantial and be strictly self-subsistent. And while they fulfil their nature, or display themselves as what they essentially are (that is, to become as self-sublating [62] neutrals in the neutralization so that neither the one nor the other [actually] is), both are yet to remain what they are in their isolation. In other words, the affinity is posited in fact as alien to their essence, and they are posited as connected by something alien, still having these connections outside themselves even in the neutralization, and still abiding on their own account. Chemical affinity (which expressed the infinite or relationship immediately) thus itself comes to be once more a connection without differentiation or relationship; it comes to be quantum, the connection between a whole and its parts.

2 / Force, divested of its superfluous determinacy, is causal relationship in which substance, or what is necessary, doubles itself, and in this redoubling posits itself as actuality. Substance, as cause, connects through its effect with an other, and this its connection is its very actuality. This connection is the same infinity, the same relation, that each of its members is; and it is itself infinite. In that substance is cause—and it is in virtue of its essence that it connects with another through itself as determinacy—this other itself is substance (for the infinity of substance is cause) [and] only is infinite, the sublating of the otherness, in that the other is. However, the connection of cause with the other substance is nothing else but cause positing its determinacy in the opposite substance as effect, yet just in that way sublating its own determinacy as well as that of the other and positing both as *one* only as sublated. The substantiality of the two necessary [terms] disappears as a being *per se*, for each is essentially infinite determinacy reflected within itself; the positing-in-one of both is the sublatedness of both determinacies and the becoming-one of doubled being. The actuality of what is necessary, as a positedness of its determinacy, is the oneness of the doubled necessity. Substance realizes itself only as going out of itself, and only as going out of itself to itself, [or] as absolutely self-opposed. The other substance is nothing but this opposed determinacy substantialized; and the effect is not the severing of the determinacy from the cause, but the going over of its essence (which is determinacy) to its opposite, not to some indeterminate other being. What is wholly annihilated is the empty duplication of sundered being. The determinacy itself is not annihilated as one with its opposite. It is only sublated as self-subsistent; at one with [63] the other, however, [it] is their mutual, complete permeation, so that they are posited—for each was infinite, reflected into itself; they were not pure determinacies—but they are posited as sublated. Actuality is the product—this oneness with respect to which only the possibility occurs of sundered, self-subsistent determinacies, in which, however, they have ceased to exist as determinacies of this kind.[50]

---

50. *On an inserted page*: That is green, moved; this derives from a green-making cause, thrust; it is effect. About the cause, force, we know effects; that is, we know nothing but the green, the moved. Therefore, not even that it is effect.

Rightly have the limits of reason been laid down just here: that we do not penetrate

The character of the substances conceived in the causal relation is thus determined. Both are posited as infinite or necessary, yet they are at the same time mutually opposed. The one [is posited] as passive, self-connecting, expressing the concept of necessity with respect to it. The other, however, [is posited] as possible, [as] the cause that has its actuality outside itself; as force, therefore, but in such a way that its actuality consists in its connecting with its opposed determinacy, in itself, yet as with another substance; as having its actuality, then, only in this connection, that is, in the sublation of the self-subsistent actuality posited outside it. This other substance is infinity connecting with some other infinite, the unity that is infinite only in that it is not a determinacy but sublates an infinite determinacy. It is on its own account, connects with itself, but only through the sublatedness of something infinite. The actuality that comes to be in this way is not the actuality posited in the concept of infinity—which infinity is formally a positedness that in itself is only possible or in its positedness excludes the other, though in truth [it] does not exclude but is connected with it. Here the positedness has excluded the other in truth, in that the latter is another substance; and at the same time it truly connects with it as with something [64] that [is] within it, and thus its very excluding has become sublated. The infinite thus ceases to be a being; with respect to itself it is this movement, over against another substance that is passive but self-connecting. The essence of each is the opposed determinacy; and actuality, the causal relationship itself, is the unity of these determinacies, which only are as sublated.

The actuality that has thus come to itself from infinite determinacies or from the sublating of substances is simply and solely *one* substance, *one* necessity. How [it] distinguishes itself from the concept of necessity is demonstrated, since for this concept what sublates itself was only simple, not infinite, connections: the connectedness of one and many and the non-connectedness of one and many—in other words, possibility only as simple motionless unity (an indifferent being of opposites), [and] actuality, the negative determinate being of one together with the exclusion of an other.

In this actuality of the causal relationship, however, the being *per*

---

to the inner of the matter of force, of matter; for reason starts from here; it is totally unreasonable to make of green [or] of what is moved something distinguished from itself as cause and effect, for both are always just one and the same green [or] moved.

se of the infinite collapses. The product (and it is only product) is their unity; their separateness is sublated. Relation is quite simply as this sublatedness, or as the product, since the self-subsistent substances are essentially determinacies—necessary, infinite determinacies, but only reflected into themselves; and in truth they have therein no subsistence. What the causal relationship is in itself is this product: the having-disappeared of the self-subsistent determinacies; a third in which they are united in such a way that they no longer distinguish themselves and their self-distinguishing lies outside it. Quantum has emerged again, but in this way: [a] the product, the connection, is something completely simple, not distinguished into whole and parts; and [b] what is excluded is the being-distinguished of what are not distinguished in the product (what are distinguished outside the product do not thereby continue at the same time within it); rather [c] the continuity is broken altogether; the distinction is not this external one of the limit of quantum, but an absolute one; [d] what are distinguished are sublated in the product as they are outside it—within it their unity is as actuality. [It is] a unity that is a positedness, something purely self-equivalent and not something empty; [it is] rather one that has emerged out of infinity, or is determined with respect to itself as a sublatedness of opposites. The opposites, as separated outside the product, are only sublated, purely possible, absolutely unequal to themselves. [65] Thus absolute being stands opposed to and unconnected with absolute possibility. The product is perfectly self-contained; and in causal relationship it is rather its contrary—not diverse substances, not a cause and its effect in some other substance, not an opposition and infinite, self-generating connection; rather, something simple as substance.

cc / *Reciprocity*

The reciprocal dependence and independence of the substance and its substantial member-elements must emerge. In "Reciprocity" Hegel shows us the problem from the side of the atoms or monadic selves. At this stage the bad infinite triumphs. The whole—whether physical or ethical—is infinitely divisible.

The world as an infinite community of independent substances within one substance is logically projected in the *Monadology* of Leibniz. This is the topic of Hegel's two notes. First he shows that only God is real in this system, and that he is a "paralysed infinity." Then he shows that this infinite cognition is inconsistent with the reality of life. Living nature is not a perfect "chain of being." The life that is *free* cognition must "rend" this harmony.

The transition from the relation of *being* to the relation of *thought* is necessary because of the freedom of cognition. The consciousness that the single member brings to the ethical substance is the concrete fulfilment of the substance. Being and thought are its necessary attributes. Thus the true *reciprocity* of being is the interaction and dependence of human culture, through which the consciousness of the social substance is maintained. The transient mortality (which appears first as the bad-infinite divisibility of being) is the means by which the true infinity of thinking is maintained.

Instead of realizing itself in the relation of causality, the infinite has rather fallen apart in it. The infinite is in itself the connection of the unconnected; it is the simple that becomes an other to itself, which in turn is the other of its self and thereby the first simple. In the relation of causality, the becoming-other is sublated; the simple is only the sublated otherness; and the opposition, which likewise is in the infinite, is nullified. It is, however, the essence of the simple in the relation of causality to be a sublatedness of the determinacies; its simplicity is only an abstraction from their being *per se*, yet their being is for that very reason essential to it. The simple substance, posited only as their sublatedness, is itself a determinacy, to which stands opposed the other, from which it abstracts; it is not connected with them; they are separated by the void. But its essence is thereby no less connected with the opposition; and as this abstraction it does not display in itself what it is according to its essence. Its substantiality, its being *per se* as what it is posited, contradicts this conditionedness through the opposition that, instead of being in what is simple, is rather completely outside it.

Through this isolatedness, the other outside the simple first comes to be for it a genuine being *per se*, an absolute substance. In the relation of causality, substance is realized only as one; here the multiplicity is posited simply through its not being connected. What is excluded from the simple product is the separating of what are opposed; it is itself, however, a being *per se* and as such, self-equivalent as the product is, or in truth it is something just as simple. It is the [66] pure possibility of the former [that is, the product]; inversely, the latter [that is, the separating] is just as much on its own account, and the former is its pure possibility. In this way they are equal to each other, properly undifferentiated and undifferentiatable; for in the second [possibility] as the separateness of the determinacies this [separate-ness] likewise falls away, and the determinacies [fall] together. For they are connected not with the first substance but with themselves; and they are connected in that they are on their own account. "Being on one's own account" means being connected with oneself, or a sublatedness of the opposition; that is, outside of the first, a simple substance is also posited, and again outside of that there is also the separateness, which collapses into simple substance. This self-positing, the positing outside itself (or otherness) and the sublating of this otherness is infinity, albeit bad infinity, since the other[ness] of what-ever is posited is outside it—so that whatever is posited subsists. In truth nothing but the bad-infinite multiplicity of numerical *ones* would be posited. As the simplicity of opposed determinacies, however, sub-stance is determined in itself to be simplicity, and the separate, op-posed to simplicity, is determined with respect to itself as separated. In other words, in the equal simplicity of both, they are opposed; the antithesis does not fall outside of them as bad infinity. For it is in general the basis of quantity that is posited, [that is,] unity susceptible of multiplicity (which in bad infinity is posited as falling outside of the many), and thereby in truth opposition as well. Through this being, which is something communal—that is, separating them—op-position is posited with respect to them and itself stands over against the simple product initially as something separate within itself. They are, but as pure possibilities for each other; they are both unconnected substances. What is simple as self-determined thereby expresses de-terminacy with respect to itself; in other words, in the simplicity of what are thus opposed, it is, as compared with something else, exter-nally just as much the separation, having determinacy in it as its essence. The other is just as simple; both [are] simple in the same way and in their simplicity determinate, mutually opposed. In that the determinacy vis-à-vis each other, thus taken up into the simplicity, substantiates each on its own account, it is indeed posited under the form of externality, of quantum; and infinity (as negative unity) is external to them. Bad infinity occurs with respect to them—the sub-sistence of determinacy which just for that reason is indeterminate vis-à-vis an other, [that is,] as quantum. The absolute determinacies are as something simple in the substances that have this same content. [67] The simplicity is this same content—is at once an externally, quantitatively determined one; and the pure neutrality of what is simple is a continuity to the point of their separation. In other words, as determinacy it is an indeterminate continuity of transition into its absolute opposite. What are absolutely opposed are the same connections of determinacies; within the medium of the commonality of this content they are indifferent to each other. Their connection is a continuity, and their opposition is the external one of quantum, according to which that continuity is divisible *in infinitum*. For as continuity and determined by means of quantum it has simply no immanent limit, does not have negation, absolute opposition in itself, but has limit as an external, indeterminate one, only as limit in general; as external it is only something called for.

In this way, where a quantum is posited, actuality is something infinitely[51] divisible within it and likewise something infinitely extendible outside it. It goes through infinite mediations over to what is opposed; and the latter itself is not [absolutely opposed]. For as absolutely opposed it would have its limit—determinacy—in itself, not as something external.

In this way self-realizing infinity has once again fallen back into quantum; paralysed in the product of the causal relation, it ceases to be the annihilating of what arises as separate. And it is their sublatedness whereby it [is] an external, purely possible, empty, negative connection; the unity [is] a subsisting continuity of infinitely divided differences—not empty unity but the simplicity of opposites, a simplicity that itself expresses the difference as something external. This fulfilled continuity is the unity of what is infinite; the being of its opposites is the subsisting of what is thus distinguished. And their sublatedness as determined vis-à-vis each other is that each singular determinacy has its opposite purely outside of itself; the sublatedness of each is only the equal being of this other. In the relation of causality the one substance as connecting with itself is something to be sublated vis-à-vis the other that is connected with what is thus passive; it is determined as the opposite of the latter, and the cause is likewise determined thereby through that on which it acts. However, it is only posited as determining or as the connecting of opposed [68] determinacies. Here each one in the same way is connecting with itself and is not[52] posited as being negated through the other, each as determined through the other. However, this determinateness, as the reciprocity of the substances, sublates just thereby what is negative in

51. *Trans.*: Following ms rather than CE.
52. *Trans.*: This "not" could govern only the first clause; or it could apply to both.

the connection, in that each is hereby posited equal to the other, and their distinction is indeed posited with respect to them but as an indifferent one, connecting only with itself, neither of them positing itself in the other nor on its own account connecting with the other. Instead of bringing genuine movement forth—the reciprocal being of each in the other—reciprocity posits them rather in the calm of equilibrium in that it sublates the distinction with respect to them. Each [in] its essence is equal to the other; each is the same simplicity of what are opposed; and the distinction, which just thereby must be posited, is only something external.

N[ote] 1 / The activity in the relation of causality shows itself to be rather a non-activity too immediately for [it] not to have had to go over into reciprocity. For if the activity is the positing of the determinacy of the one substance in the other and therewith the sublating of the determinacy of the latter substance, so it is just as immediately the sublating of the first. And insofar as the first is active, it is precisely not active. The activity as the sublating of both determinacies is their simpleness; in truth it is what we have called product. When substance is posited as active, its determinacy is sublated too; and with that the other is in truth also active. In place of an effect of the first on the second, rather the reciprocity is posited—the equal activity of both absolutely opposed determinacies, a duplicated active state. The doubled activity, however, is nothing but the expression of the fact that each of the two determinacies is sublated in the same manner. It cannot be that the one meets the other, so to speak, at any other point than where this other is active, so that each would be divided into an active and a passive side. For the activity is simply and solely the connection of determinacy to the opposed determinacy; and only this opposedness, or the negation, the ideality of the antithesis in itself, is the activity. Thus neither is active towards another that is not opposed to it, or that would not be the very activity of the other. That is, there is only *one* activity or, what comes to the same thing, only a product; [there is] no reciprocity. Both determinacies reduce [69] to a simple unity. And only in that this [unity] itself is a determinate one does it indeed have external determinacy,[53] antithesis against another. This its reciprocity, which is a determinateness of both as connected with one another, is their indifferent being *per se*, a rest without relation, a positive, not a negative, positing of determinacies, or the multiplicity

---

53. *Trans.*: Lasson reads "does it have determinacy, however external."

of diverse substances. The relation, the absolute activity, is simply not in the being of the same whole or the same simple as would be doubled and should have the external form of opposition in it; it just reaches this paralysed infinity.

N[ote] 2 / This reciprocity is no more a living entity than it is what it displays itself to be in truth: namely, rational cognition as an infinite mediation of transition. Cognition is thus only cognition as infinite, in absolute opposition. As the otherness of spirit, nature has in itself infinity only in this external way of mediations; in that it is the same simple unity of opposites, it [dis]plays this opposition itself, not as being infinite in itself, but simply, and only externally as separation, as a determinacy that is in the more or less of the emergence and preponderance of one or other opposite. Cognition must first rend this unity absolutely, display the extremes purely and simply, and thus sublate them as qualitatively opposed. The transition, mediated *in infinitum*, has already given the moments of the antithesis; in what is simplest, where such cognition begins, there are at least the traces of the antithesis that subsequently emerges and articulates itself further. What is essential to the idea—[that is,] the relation of determinacies— does not come into consideration as relation, as infinite; but [it does so] as an appearance of determinacies, which are here the same as in all forms of mediated transitions and are distinguished solely through the more or less, the one and the other. And just as what is essential here, namely, the relation, does not come into consideration, so too it does not come into consideration in connection with its diverse determinacies, which are themselves once more the relation among themselves; rather, the qualitative is reduced to a quantitative. The metamorphosis, which forms a system of its conditions, is only a range [characterized by][54] a diverse, quantitative mixture and [by] stronger and weaker emergence. [70] The identity of determinacies (which thus in the relation ought to be a diversity of aggregates over against one another and which alone is what is rational) and equally [the identity] of the determinacies as inner (that is, as moments of the relation itself, as its own in the way the relation appears in them as a whole) becomes rather a self-equivalence of the separated matters which only increase and decrease; but in addition each is on its own account already and originally presupposed as present. The interruption of the uniform streaming forth of the waxing and waning

54. *Trans.*: The German has the genitive case.

aggregate (through what is qualitative in the pure moments of relation, over which the quantitative or formal in nature cannot become
master) creates gaps in the ranges and scales, which no longer pertain
to this historical view of what is simply present.

2 / Relation is realized in reciprocity since its moments preserve a
subsistence; they are themselves necessary infinite relations. But this
reality is at the same time the sublating of relation, its absence. Since
relation as paralysed infinity or reciprocity is the reality of relation,
it must be set forth in respect to each of its moments as just this bad
infinity—that is, in its two forms, the relation of substantiality and the
relation of causality—not with respect to their immediate determinacy
of relation. For this is not yet the totality of relation; but insofar as
they [are] relations at all, [they are] this totality under the determinacy
that they only are just as relations, that reality is expressed with respect
to them—which at the same time can be, not this indifference of
reciprocity, but reciprocity only under the determinacy of the form
of the relation. In other words, the substances in the reciprocal relation itself, as determinacies according to their essence, are themselves only under the form of incomplete, ideal$_2$ relation; and the
relation that has gone back into itself as reciprocity displays in itself
the moments of its going back into itself; that is, it displays itself as
formal reciprocity. Since it reverts in this way to its ideal$_2$ moments, it
thereby preserves, as it were, the moment of ideality that it lacks,
although it affects it with the subsistence of the substances.

a / The relation of substantiality, as the concept of necessity, is the
positedness of substance as of one determinacy with exclusion of the
opposite one; [71] and since necessity [is] absolute possibility at the
same time,[55] it [is] indifferent to it which of the opposed determinacies
substance may be under. Through the causal relation this indifference
is sublated. The substance as actual is opposed to the other as possible;
but in reciprocity each has equal actuality again. This equal actuality
contradicts the relation of substantiality; in this actual the essence, the
simplicity of the opposites, is this very [actuality]. In the relation of
substantiality this simplicity is indeed only empty unity, connected
with both, only their possibility. The separated accidents are the fulfilment of possibility. But in this way the unity is fulfilled—the possibility, the pure substance itself, what is simple in the opposites.
Possibility over against this posited simplicity [is] the same simplicity

55. *Trans.*: Lasson has a comma before "at the same time."

in a determinacy (or stage of transition) other than the posited one. The connection is that the one substance only is, in that the other is not; and at the same time [it is] the equal necessity of both. The positedness of each determinacy in the relation of substantiality is only something hypothetical, something possible; if the substance is in one accident, then it is not in the other. Here, as the simplicity of both, it is in itself necessary—as determinate substance. Not in the equal possibility, not in the empty unity of the two opposites but in itself, the accident is at once the contrary of itself; thus it is the totality of the relation of substantiality, not merely *one* side within its unity. This actuality of the determinate substance is at the same time only a possibility of the actual substance that is determined in the opposite way; and vice versa, this [that is, the actual substance that is determined in the opposite way] is just as necessary. And they cease to stand indifferently beside each other, in that the fulfilled unity of both is the same. In this way again there is only one possibility on its own account. It is the reflection on this unity of their essence or of their fulfilment that puts the relation of substantiality back into reciprocity, whereby the substances as such [become]: the one becomes actual over against the other as possible. Since each is equally necessary, the being of the one is the non-being of the other; and the being of each is as necessary as its non-being; that is, the one must *pass away* and the other *arise*. The opposition of both is infinitely mediated; and the passing away, just as much as the arising, is this infinitely mediated transition [*Übergehen*] itself, not as an already completed transition [*Übergegangenseyn*] (as [72] in the concept of reciprocity itself) but [as] negatively posited. In this way transition, the mediation itself, is the unity that, in the form of substantial unity, separates into the opposed accidents of arising and passing away, and is thus realized. Reciprocity is the concept of transition or mediation, a unity in which there is posited in an indeterminate, external way an otherness that progresses in accordance with an absolutely arbitrary unity by continuous addition—that is, precisely by external increments. TRANSITION is in truth substantiality, the determinacy of subsistence itself. In the pure relation of substantiality there is subsistence, the pure self-equivalent being. As transition it is this inherently self-determined and differentiated being; but differentiated only as something indifferent, as something diverse, multiple, as expressing only a tendency towards [*gegen*] opposition,[56] that is, as expressing every-

56. *Trans.*: The German could equally well read "direction against opposition."

where just the demand for the same [opposition]. The negative positing of this demand, the actuality that excludes, is itself thus merely
a demand for actuality. It is connected with its not-having-been only
as one that comes to be (that is, timelessly, a being of the determinate
substance, in that its other ceases to be); and [is] passing away (a not-
being of what is posited, in that its other'is). The transition or mediation divides, sets itself against itself; it is the actuality of the determinate substance connected with its possibility. This connection is
just as much possibility *qua* the first, which posits itself as actuality—
arising—as [it is] the contrary, the actuality that posits itself as possibility—passing away. [This is] a separation that occurs only in reciprocity, since in it is the necessary *qua one*—that is, itself under the
opposedness of the determinations; and so it is something necessary
both as possible and as actual. The necessary that is possible, however,
must connect with actuality—arising; [and] the necessary that is actual
[must connect] with possibility—passing away. In the relation of substantiality itself this connection is one only external to both; the necessity [is] not in itself the antithesis of the possible and the actual,
but each [is] just as much possible as actual: *either* the one actually and
then the other possibly *or* the reverse. Here each [is] itself the two
[together] and at the same time, the two separately.

The opposition is, however, a formal one, simply required, in that
the arising [73] and the passing away is something absolutely mediated, something external to the substances. What is arising has posited the other of itself absolutely, as a being outside it, as another
determinacy not reflected with respect to it. The simplicity, in which
the substance is turned back into itself, is its undifferentiated basis,
which has outside itself the being of the determinacy as an opposite,
and only one as actual. The negation is being excluded, a not-being-
actual, merely a having-been, or a possibility of arising; and the indeterminacy of the antithesis makes the arising and the passing away
into something absolutely mediated.

b / The arising and passing away, however, is essentially only through
the in-itself the necessary connectedness of the determinacies with
one another, [that is to say,] through their ideality with respect to
them, or through their absolute though only formal opposition—that
is, the relation of causality. And through the latter it is the mediated
arising and passing away. Determinate substance arises or comes into
actuality as the possibility of an other that ceases to be. But "It comes
into actuality" means nothing other than that it does not exclude the
other but is active [*thätig*]; it sublates the opposed determinacy as its

possibility, its ideality; and only so, as acting [*wirkend*], is it actual [*wirklich*]. Its arising is through itself, through its activity, the self-equivalence, which is infinite—that is, which takes its possibility, its other, back into itself, that is to say, acts [*wirkt*]. But in that substance arises through itself, just so is this immediately its perishing; for this is what it is: this determinate [substance]. In that [it] equates itself to the opposed, [in that it] acts, becomes actual, it [sub]lates itself in itself; it perishes through itself. Just as before only the concept of arising and perishing was posited, so it is here with respect to substance itself. This transition is, however, infinitely mediated; it is at the same time posited as something external with respect to the substances. "With respect to themselves and external to them" means that they are divided; through the essence of reciprocity they are separated,[57] each for itself, and in their actuality at the same time connected—they are so only in part, [and] separate themselves determinately into an unalterable and an alterable part. This is not the pure accident; for in the opposed substances, determinacy *qua* reflected within itself is the essence itself, not the void of unity; yet at the same time [it is] substance subsisting too, thus something simply parted within itself into several substantialities.

In its becoming actual the substance passes away; or rather its becoming actual is the arising of another substance, though one part is[58] passing away with respect to the active and passive substance. But by the same token this substance that has arisen is actual only [74] within activity; it is a determinacy, opposed immediately to what is separated, whose simplicity it is: a determinacy reflected within itself, but as a being-reflected, not through this substance itself, [not] through its activity. The substance that has arisen must likewise have on its own account, negatively, the one opposed to it, must sublate the latter, actualize itself, and in its actualization thus pass away, become another substance than it is. If the perishable seems thus to be diminished in that only one part passes away, enters into the new substance, and one part is always thrown down, precipitated, as separate, self-subsistent, imperishable, this is nevertheless only one determinacy, and now actual just as the other is. The line of arising and passing away proceeds forwards and backwards *ad infinitum*, and in the same way

57. *Trans.*: Following Lasson, we omit the comma before "separated." The ms requires "They are through the essence of reciprocity, separated each for itself."

58. *Trans.*: We read *als* as *ist*.

there are infinitely many lines and infinitely many parting and starting points. This infinite criss-crossing and entanglement of arising and passing away makes actuality into an arising-and-therein-perishing being of substances. The essence of its movement is the self-equivalent simplicity of opposites; yet this simplicity is what is latent, not posited, in this entanglement. Because such—fulfilled—unity lies outside it, it falls wholly into bad infinity; and there appears in general this simple unity of opposites *qua* substance, the fulfilled and self-equivalent being, and alongside it a multiplicity of arising and perishing substances. But what is arising and passing away is in fact nothing but the determinacies. The reflection of determinacy into itself—singular substance—is infinite only in this way: that precisely in the simplicity it is as determinate, and as determinate sublated or the contrary of itself. But this contrary of itself is only in the simplicity something sublated (the singular substance itself being something sublated); yet something posited as the other is not. This inequality equalizes itself through its becoming sublated, in which the substance itself becomes the sublated one as well, yet in which it is a posited one, as the other is. But, to be sure, if both are here posited and sublated in the same manner, their sublatedness (the simplicity of opposites) falls outside their alternation [*Wechseln*]; as the substantializing of determinacies it is itself multiplied. And if the simplicity is the same for all, it is, of the separated determinacies, numerical *one*, not infinite unity or their sublation. Since what is simple is posited thus in the form of numerical *one*, it falls outside the unity of sublating; it is rather its multiplicity. But in fact it is rather the equivalence of all these determinacies posited as substances, is fulfilled being; and in this there is [75] no distinction at all. The determinacies as such are distinguished only vis-à-vis one another. Their distinguishing is not a subsisting of the one and the non-being of the other, but rather they are for their part immediately sublated, posited as sublated and ideal$_2$. [It is] not a non-posited, a vanishing into simplicity, but [it is] rather what the determinacies are inherently, something posited in the same manner, though as sublated, in their *one* self-equivalent simple unity, a unity that is their non-positedness.

Reciprocity, thus returned to itself, is the sublatedness of the separated substances. It is simply and solely a substance, but absolutely fulfilled substance, the rendering indifferent of all determinacies that are posited in it as sublated. Relationship has fulfilled its concept; it has not stepped outside itself. And the fulfilling of its concept is that it posits itself as what [it] is in itself, a fulfilled oneness of opposed determinacies, and *in* this sublatedness at the same time their being-posited as sublated. But relationship has thereby become the contrary of itself. For in its concept the opposites were in being, [while] their oneness [was] itself something differentiated, connected negatively with them. Yet here those are merely posited as sublated; this latter is self-equivalent, connected purely with itself, the connectedness of what are ideal$_2$, or the ideality in them. It has gone over into the relationship of thought, into *universal* and *particular*.

B / RELATION OF THINKING

The proper model for the paralysis of the infinite, which we arrived at in the "Relation of Being," is not the One Substance of Spinoza[59] but the divine Monad of monads in Leibniz. The "paralysed infinite" is the Great Chain of Being. The thinking consciousness of the cognitive subject breaks the paralysis that the completed cycle of the categories of being has produced. On the objective side it produces a *Platonic* theory of science, in which life is viewed as the universal that specifies and individuates itself *necessarily* (yet freely, and subject to contingency). This universal is identical with its own logical process of *division* (or judgment); and in cognition it comes to self-possession as the mortally singular rational animal. (Formally speaking, this identity of the concept with its process of determination is an impossible operation—like the imaginary number $\sqrt{-1}$) But now that we have passed over to the territory of "subjective logic" (though only relationally, just as Hegel proceeded from the categories to the forms of finite cognition in "concepts, judgments, and syllogisms" in 1801),[60] it is quite *evident* that the appli-

---

59. As the Italian commentators (especially Chiereghin, *Logica e metafisica*, p. 342) believe. Chiereghin's interpretation of the transition in *Faith and Knowledge* (*Logica e metafisica*, pp. 350–51; *Gesammelte Werke*, IV, p. 354, ll. 27–34, and p. 359, ll. 1–3; Cerf and Harris, trans., pp. 107, 113) deserves study because Hegel does have Spinoza's substance in mind in the preface to the *Phenomenology*. But his own account of the relation of substantiality here points forward to his mature rejection of Spinoza's theory as acosmic. The Leibnizian conception of the Great Chain of Being gives the finite term of the relationship of being its *necessary* place. Evidence of the importance of Leibniz in the evolution of Hegel's logic and metaphysics is supplied by his "Scepticism" essay (*Gesammelte Werke*, IV, 229f; di Giovanni and Harris, trans., *Between Kant and Hegel*, pp. 346f).

60. See Rosenkranz, *Hegels Leben*, p. 191 (Cerf and Harris, trans., *Faith and Knowledge*, p. 10); compare the Introduction, pp. xvif above. If the parallel between 1801 and 1804 is valid and can be extended, then "Proportion" corresponds to the transitional

cation of Hegel's argument to the mortally singular rational animal is what matters most. In this context it is the "ethical substance" perfectly stabilized by its constitutional customs that is the paralysed infinite—and the single consciousness is the moving particular, a mortal "identity of non-being and being," which subsists stably as a reproduction process (as the family, which is the unit of the polity).

In the ethical substance, universal and particular are immediately "in one another." This is the "determinate concept." The universl here is (negatively) the customary law that makes all citizens members; and positively it is the common territory that they share. Socrates the Athenian knows that his whole existence is at the disposal of "the laws"; but the injustice of the verdict upon him is the "contradiction of the determinate concept within itself."

As realized reciprocity, the infinite has become paralysed. It is the fulfilled oneness—that is, a oneness of [opposites] that are not *qua* opposites—and equally a oneness of the same, so that they are *qua* opposites, but as sublated; and their connection, their simple unity, is just that oneness. This it is that has arisen; contradiction (or the infinity that [consists] in a oneness of opposites, wherein as such they are not at all posited and wherein as ideal$_2$ they are at the same time distinguished) is what is dialectical in this relation, which [76] in its very realization has to posit itself as our reflection. Right here nothing concerns us but what has thus necessarily arisen; and just as infinity is brought to rest in it, so we too must bring our reflection to rest, as it were, and only take what is there. Our reflection will become the reflection of this relation itself.

The *universal*, as has been shown,[61] is not pure but fulfilled unity, the self-equivalent oneness of the opposites. The *particular* is not a substance; but what is distinguished is something posited as sublated, what is as what is not: a determinacy, yet not determinacy in general but in itself, infinite, or posited as such. The determinacy is in itself in this way because it is reflected into itself out of being *per se* and is itself posited as the identity of non-being and being. It *is* not—that

---

discovery of the speculative meaning of the syllogism in 1801. The connection of the syllogism with mathematical "proportion" is made through the Platonic doctrine of the "truly beautiful bond" (*Timaeus*, 31c–32a; compare *Difference*, in *Gesammelte Werke*, IV, p. 65, ll. 31–37; Harris and Cerf, trans., p. 158n).

61. *Trans.*: The ms includes "not" with "shown," separating it from "pure" with a comma.

is, it is not connected purely with itself; as what is not it is not sublated, not at all.[62] Rather, it is the unity of both: it is connected with itself, sublated; and, in this state of having become the contrary of itself, connected with itself, equal to itself. This self-equivalency in its sublatedness, its form, is substantiality as something universal. Yet this universal is not merely this form, but it is what is fulfilled, what is simple in the determinacies thus posited as distinguished in their ideality$_2$ [*ideellseyn*]. The universal as this connection of what is distinguished [*des Unterschiedenen*] is its ideality and negative unity; but as the sublatedness of this opposite [it is] hence the indifferent connection of just these that are[63] not set against one another negatively, in that they are so with respect to themselves. Likewise the universal is not opposed to the particular, but it is immediately the form of the particular; determinacy is, as sublated, reflected into itself, and the universal is this its reflection.

A / Determinate Concept

The connection of the universal and the particular just now determined, their simple being-in-one-another without antithesis, is the determinate concept. Determinacy is no longer substance, not something posited as positive numerical *one*, but as something universal, something reflected into itself; and determinate being has received a completely different [77] meaning. For it is in truth nothing other than the determinate concept, realized being, just as the relation of being is properly the realizing of it; that which is usually understood as determinate being is rather the determinate concept. The accident of substance that is something actual has its connection, its otherness, outside itself and therefore *is* not; it is only something possible, not something that is in itself. Only the reflected accident, the determinate concept, is within itself; it is something determinate, and thereby itself only something possible, one only in connection with another. But as this possible, it is posited; it is, not for the reason that it is something possible—on the contrary, this [its being possible] is its coming-to-be-sublated; but it is for the first time, through this its being posited as

---

62. *Trans.*: Lasson omits a comma, to read "It is not what is not, sublated, not at all."

63. *Trans.*: There is a shift from singular to plural here, because the universal is a species of itself.

something possible. What is determinate inherently disintegrates within infinity; it is a nothing. That it is something that is not is for it an alien reflection; it is *in* itself only this [thing] that is not; and [when][64] posited as something sublated—that is, as determinate concept—it is posited as it is in itself; or for the first time, it is. This being is simple infinity, infinity brought to rest; it is the existing of what is determinate; its being is synonymous with universality. It is something determinate, but as something particular; [it is] as something determinate that, just because it is outside of itself, is, with respect to itself, connection with another; for in the relation of being, determinacy is with respect to itself not at the same time reflected into itself; rather, it goes only outwards.

. In the determinate concept *determinacy (and reflection)* is *strictly one, simple*. Determinacy without reflection is not *the particular*, else it would be nothing; likewise reflection is of itself the void; for it is only as what has come back out of opposition—that is, out of determinacy. But the determinate concept is in truth not this simple [thing], of which the concept has been established. It may be considered from the side of its having come back out of opposition, out of the relation— then it dissolves itself into the relation again. But [when] this relation [is considered] as simple, in the way it has come to be, then this simplicity must carry this determinacy of being conditioned upon itself as a trace in another way. It has the form of freedom; but that it does not in fact have it absolutely, as we realize (even though the bridge has been broken off through its simplicity), this it must therefore display in itself.

The determinate concept is subjected to the same dialectic of which it [relation] is the quality; which quality is determinacy in the form of pure being, into whose place reflected being, being-in-itself, has here stepped. There is in fact a contradiction [78] present between determinacy and being reflected: the former is only *one* side of the opposition; the latter is the unity of both. The relation of causality was the negative, the moment of reflecting itself into itself, wherein determinacy was to sublate itself; but it was only a formal sublating. Similarly, what is reflected did not of course remain the initial [determinacy] (for that became one with its opposite); yet this one[ness] is itself something just as determinate and therewith has being-in-itself only as form in itself, to which in truth it is not equal. It can

---

64. *Trans.*: Replacing *es*, or "it."

just as well be posited again as one with its opposite, but it still remains something determinate; for as something reflected thus it is on its own account and simple, yet just thereby opposed to those whose unity it is. It exists indeed in a two-fold mode: in one way as being something determinate and thereby as connecting with negative unity, which is its infinity; however as unity reflected into itself it is itself negative unity, though of a kind wherein the negated *is* [as] sublated. It is negative unity posited in the form of positive unity, as simple positive unity; in other words, as universality. Through this it is itself preserved in that connection, whose infinity is thereby formal, opposed, a negative *one* instead of negative unity. In this mode of subsisting determinacies that are reflected into themselves, it is this substance as negative *one*. The substance is their separated being *per se*, yet is like the determinacies. However, their[65] dead *one*, as this *one*, is in connection with the being *per se* of determinacy, or their universality; [it is] what is determinate and indeed what is absolutely determinate, what is negative, the particular, which is contingent to the universal. Universality as reflection is the non-being of particularity; and the singularity of the substance is what is accidental or merely possible. The singular or the substance is a particular, not a mere singular, in the positive connection with the univesal—a particular that is in the universal as in its universal space wherein it is connected as excluding. Conversely, substance is equally the universal as (negative) *unity*, in which apart from the determinacy, which is the universal, something other is also posited, or in which this universal in just the same way is connected negatively as determinate, excludes the other from itself, though the other is its like, such as is equally in the form of being *per se*, [79] of positive universality—just as in it the negative *one* [excludes] other *ones*. The univcrsal is *one* PROPERTY of substance along with others; substance is something particular, something posited in the universal along with other particulars. Each is subsumed under the others, but these two subsumptions go in opposite ways: the particular is negative *one* and the properties according to their determinacy and in opposition *are*; the universal is the positive unity of numerical *ones*.

This our reflection about what is essential in the determinate concept, developed with respect to it, is its realization or the reflection of the same into itself. The determinate concept is determinacy comprehending itself, or determinacy reflected into itself. Reflection as

---

65. *Trans.: Ihr, ihre* could be singular and refer to "substance," rather than plural.

the simple, or the universal, is in the form of determinacy; and the latter is the self-subsistent being and the sublatedness of the determinacies, the negative unity, the merely possible, posited precisely as possible; substance is absorbed in it. Insofar as substance is posited, the universal is what is essential and this substance is posited as something sublated; in other words, the negative *one* is subsumed under the universal. Conversely, substance is the particular, what is subsumed, connected with the universal, posited in it as sublated, indeed positive unity as well, something universal; and the determinate concept is through its determinacy something only posited as sublated and therewith posited rather as what is subsumed. For, since it is something reflected into itself, substance cannot disconnect itself from that; just as, opposed to this reflection, [it is] connected with its opposite and thereby with negative unity, in its being *per se* having in itself only to be as the connection with negative unity. Thus, the contradiction of the determinate concept within itself is that it [is] this doubly opposed subsumption in itself; the determinacy is contradictory to the reflection within itself, and the positing of the determinate concept is this $\pm \sqrt{-1}$. Its positing is its square; its reality, its concept is this opposed possibility.

The determinate concept, expressing what it is in itself—[expressing] not the determinacy reflected into itself but that the determinacy equally sublates [itself] therein and that the concept is a *one* that posits the determinacy at the same time as sublated, but simultaneously [is] a universal that posits this its being sublated as sublated—is *judgment*. [80]

B / *Judgment*

Here "bad reality" follows the "bad ideality" of the determinate concept (contrast the order in "Simple Connection," CE 31 above). In the first moment we reflected. Now Socrates himself is the subject whose judgment "subsumes" the whole community of the Athenians (including himself); and through him the laws speak—so the subsumption goes both ways.

Hegel's treatment of the forms of judgment is itself formal. But if we take him to be concerned about how the community is present to the citizens as the laws, we can see why he orders the forms of judgment as he does. "The law-abiding Athenians are Athens" is convertible; "All Athenians are Greeks" is inadequate; "Socrates is an Athenian" is accidental; only "If Socrates heeds the laws, then Athens is," is necessary. (Note that Hegel gives the hypothetical judgment this odd form.) This is "the reflection of Socrates the Athenian into himself."

The reverse subsumption goes: "Socrates is not just the human animal that he was born" (because of his education—but this is accidental); "Socrates is not a lion, but an Athenian" (which is a necessary truth but a superfluous statement, even though a circus lion might be called "Socrates"); "Socrates is an Athenian, or he has not heeded the laws but has fled to Boeotia" (which is a *choice* that he does have). The *disjunctive* is the absolute judgment because it expresses the freedom of choice implicit in Socrates' being a "human animal" to begin with. What is *realized* in judgment is contingency or freedom; and that is not yet named. Hence the advance to syllogism is necessary.

1 / Judgment is the moment of otherness of the determinate concept, or its (bad) reality, wherein what is posited as one in it goes asunder and is distinguished on its own account. In the determinate concept there is reflected determinacy as taken back into itself out of the otherness; yet it is not so in truth, but rather still determinacy, and still in otherness. And the reflection into itself is the negative *one*, or the posited side of the sublatedness of the determinacy.

Judgment is the expression of what the concept [is] in truth; therefore it includes within itself a negative *one*: a substance that, however, [is] no longer posited as such on its own account (as in the relationship of substantiality) but rather [is] what is reflected into itself, itself connected with the reflection into itself, with the universality, [and is] subsumed under what is reflected into itself [and] posited as merely a sublated one. In other words, substance is something particular, or *subject*. But just as [substance] is posited through the universal as sublated, so in its turn as a negative unity it posits this universal (which at the same time is a determinacy) as something sublated. This universal is not posited as being in itself but rather only with respect to an other as subject; and it is a property of it, something other than it itself is. This otherness, or the being in an other, is necessary; [it is] the expression of substance as of a determinacy, [it is] what is opposed to opposed determinacies whose negative unity is the subject. The substance has [them] next to itself as other properties in general, not as [things] that are connected with each other through themselves ([that is,] are only as [each] the negative of the other) but [has them] rather as reflected, self-subsistent, and indifferent to one another, [things] that do not relate to each other as their possibilities but rather each of which is on its own account as opposed to the other ([that is,] is only an other like the others). [They are] qualities whose being *per se*, as subject, is however just as much opposed to them as it also is in them; they are in the form of the subject.

To this subsumption of the universal under the particular, under the subject, is tied the opposite [subsumption]. These properties are universal, positive [81] unities; [they are] a self-equivalent being *per se* in which the negative unity is sublated or (insofar as it is posited) is designated with this determination: to be posited only as sublated—that is, not as substance but rather as subject. Just as the predicate, regarded from the perspective of the subject, was also posited only as something sublated and this expressed itself in the fact that it had others beside itself, so too this positedness of the subject as something sublated through the predicate is expressed in the subject [*an ihm*]. And regarded from the perspective of the predicate, the subject similarly has others beside it, against which it [stands] even as it is indifferent to them. Its connection with them is outside of it. Just as the connection of the properties is outside of them, namely in the subject, or rather the subject is this connection itself, so is the connection of these subjects something other than they—namely, the predicate. It is their equivalence; [it is] what in this its otherness, the diverse subjects, remains self-equivalent as reflected into itself, and thereby posits this its otherness only as ideal$_2$, as sublated.

These two opposed subsumptions are unified in the judgment; in the concept they are in simple unity; what the judgment expresses is a reflection alien to the concept itself. The subject and the predicate are what is essential in the opposed subsumptions; in whichever, when one is the essential, the other is posited as the ideal$_2$ or sublated. The simplicity of the concept has vanished; its reflectedness of determinacy has divided (or doubled) itself under opposed determinations. And the simplicity of the connection of their connection[66] doubled is not the concept, but rather the copula *is*, empty being, non-reflected connecting. And the judgment does not so much accomplish the realization of the concept, but rather in it the concept has come outside of itself. That it may be maintained in the judgment, the subject and predicate must make themselves equal even in their antithesis, must both express in themselves the determinate concept, a simple oneness

66. *Trans.*: Here we follow ms; CE omits the second "connection."

of universal and particular. The question is how the judgment is able
to do this in itself, how this necessity is displayed in it and, in the
inability of having the concept in itself, drives it out of itself. [82]
2 / The subject and predicate coupled in the judgment, the former
the particular and the latter the universal, contradict themselves through
their antithesis to themselves and through the opposite subsumption
that they exercise over one another. Each is on its own account, and
each is connected in its being *per se* with the other and reciprocally
posits the other as something sublated. One just as much as the other
must display itself as positing this ideality in the other; in the manner
in which they are connected with one another in the concept of judgment, the contradictory being *per se* of each is posited. Each is, however, only on its own account in that the other is not on its own account;
in the manner in which they are in judgment, each is on its own
account. Thus the being *per se* of the one must make the other into
something other than what it is posited as immediately in the judgment. This self-preservation through the coercion of the other under
it is therefore immediately the becoming-other of this other; but at
the same time the nature of the judgment must equally validate itself
in this alteration and simultaneously sublate the otherness; it is thus
the path [of] reflection of this other into itself. The realization of the
terms of the judgment is in this way a doubled one; and both together
complete the realization of judgment, which, however, in this its totality has itself become something other. For the determinacy of the
members essential to judgment has sublated itself through its reflection into itself, and it is rather the empty connection that fulfils itself.

a / Being *per se* of the Predicate, and Reflexion
of the Subject into Itself

The fact that in judgment the predicate on its own is not subsumed
under the negative unity of the subject makes it cease to be a property—makes the predicate into what is self-subsistent and the subject
into what is posited as sublated.
α / The subject is itself a universal when posited immediately as sublated in its determinacy of particularity. It is not a numerical *one*, but
itself something positive, a determinate concept. It must at first be so
posited, for it should be on [83] its own account and not as substance,
as actuality. Rather, it should have in itself the being *per se* such as it
has now become—that is, universality. In order that the judgment,

however, not cease to be a judgment, the subject must still retain vis-à-vis the predicate the relation of a particular to its universal; besides the subject there must be contained in the universal other determinate concepts. "A is A" or "Matter is heavy" is no judgment, for "What is heavy is matter" or "A is A" is just as correct; that is to say, the possibility of converting the relation proves that what was previously posited as particular is likewise a universal and that the universal still loses nothing of its universality in being posited [as] particular; [it proves] that for these terms the distinction of subject and predicate is something quite external, not expressed in their essence.

As this determinate concept that retains vis-à-vis the predicate the relation of particularity, the subject still remains thereby a negative *one*. But a *one*, taken up in universality, expresses itself as *allness*; and the judgment "All A are B" (or, when the negative unity is brought out even more determinately, *"Every A is B"*) determines the subject equally well as negative *one* and also as something universal.

This restoration of particularity in universality itself, however, is not a positing of what the subject as such is. The subject should be on its own account, and precisely as subject. Yet as allness it is in fact not subject but has the universality of a predicate and is something particular simply and solely in this connection with it. And the predicate does not preserve itself in its universality; rather, the subject is likewise something that subsumes, something universal, just as the predicate is. The latter only remains the universal in that the subject becomes a negative *one* and is posited as such above all. The subsuming of the predicate is sublated by the universality of the subject; for the subsuming to occur, the universality must be restricted and must express in itself this becoming subsumed.

β / The judgment in which the universality of the subject has been restricted in this way is the *particular* one[67] "Some A are B." Here the subject is no longer something universal, particular only in connection with the predicate; rather, it expresses negativity with respect to the predicate itself.

But the particular judgment ceases in fact to be a judgment. It is through and through only a problematic judgment, for the subject "some A" is something wholly indeterminate. [84] A distinction is drawn [in] the sphere, [that is to say, in] the universal A, but only a

---

67. *Trans.*: In the following, *particuläre* and *besondere* are used as indifferent synonyms and translated indiscriminately as "particular."

quite general distinction, one that is without any determinacy; and the opposite judgment "Some A are not B" is equally correct. Precisely because the connection of B with A is possible in the completely opposite manner, it is an indeterminate connection just as well positive as negative: B is connected and also not connected. Suppose, however, that the negation is connected with the predicate and this is determined as not-B; the predicate would then cease altogether to be a determinate concept; it would be, rather, something fully indeterminate, something sublated, instead of being what it ought to be: something that preserves itself. In that the connection of the subject in a particular judgment generally is considered without reference to the possibility of [its] opposite or negative, the predicate is connected in truth not with some A but with A generally (partly positive, partly negative, from which we here abstract)—that is to say, we would have again the previous universal judgment altered only by the requirement of a restriction. The particular judgment only claims "B *should* not subsume A as universal"; for the subsumed is immediately a particular just because it is something subsumed. It is also nothing but the mere "should," however, that is asserted; the requirement that the subject be posited as a negative *one* is not in fact fulfilled.

γ / The mere "should" of the particular judgment is sublated; and in that the subject is a numerical *one*, something singular, what is problematic in it is determined in the *singular*[68] judgment "*this* is B." A "this" is *per se* a particular, a negative *one*; it is opposed to the universal and freed from it. But just because of this, it is rather only a singular, not a particular, for the singular *qua* particular is at the same time posited as connected with the universal. And in that the subject thus posits itself on its own account—what it is vis-à-vis the universal of the predicate: to be only subsumed under it—its connection with the predicate is in fact sublated in it too. In the way it must express in itself the connection, the subject is no longer a particular. Just as the subject as universal has destroyed individuality within itself—it is not posited as particular—just as little is it posited as singular in that it has now destroyed universality. The middle between the two, particularity, is the negative unity of both, something merely *required* in the positing of universality and singularity as one. [85]

δ / The true union of both consists in singularity being posited, but as a sublated, as a merely possible one. The subject expresses its nature

---

68. *Trans.*: "Singular" translates both *singuläre* and *einzelne*.

in this way since its content is a substance, a numerical oneness, and this oneness (as at the same time only possible) is both distinguished from its possibility and connected with it; [it] is thus itself expressed as a proposition. When the subject is posited in judgment in this form, the latter is the *hypothetical* judgment "*If this is*, so is в." The "this" of the singular judgment is the subject of the judgment, but in such a way that this "this," this actuality of the numerical *one*, is posited at the same time as only a possible, as a sublated one. The predicate в governs the whole judgment. It is the universal that this subject subsumes under itself, so that the subject is not something positive but only something possible; or so that it expresses at the same time its determinateness by means of the universality (since it is a "this") and displays fully developed in itself the nature of particularity.

In the hypothetical judgment the preservation of the predicate has been established. In the universal judgment the predicate is equal to the subject, and the relation is lost. In like manner, since the subject expresses only its connection with the predicate—[that is,] its being in the universal—it is for its part not as particular; it is this, rather, only relative to the predicate. As merely for this relation it is thus subject: [that is,] what it is in itself in the relation;[69] and its becoming-other is its coming to be on its own account. In the particular judgment the predicate is indeed the universal, but it dispenses with the subject. It both connects with "these" subjects and also not with "these"; that is to say, it connects with some of them and not with others. And that with which it connects in general throughout its duplication, or in respect to which it does not have this indifference, is in fact the а, or the subject as universal. The subject in this particularity is something other than the way it is merely in relation, connected with the universal. But it [is] an otherness only externally, formally posited with respect to the relation, something that *should be*, something non-universal, not a "this." In the singular judgment the predicate is indeed the universal that subsumes the subject but is itself still a property of the subject, something determinate; and its subsumption of the subject under itself is not expressed with respect to the subject. This is accomplished only in the hypothetical judgment. But thereby the judgment is in general a problematic one, for the "this" is posited as

---

69. *Trans.*: The German reads: "es ist so Subject bloss für diss Verhältniss, was es im Verhältisse an sich ist." An alternate English reading: "It is thus as subject what it is in itself in the relation, that is, merely for this relation."

sublated; and the predicate has not emerged from its [86] subsumption under the subject by means of the developed particularity. The subject is indeed posited on its own account as what it is in the relation; but because of this, were the subject posited ideally₂ by means of the predicate, the universal for which the subject is posited as sublated would itself come to be negative unity. But the subject of the hypothetical judgment is thus posited on its own account as something only possible. From the side of its "this" it is connected with the predicate, but not as something sublated; or "this" is not its substance whose accident it would be, its necessity. The condition is a possible cause; but it would cease to be cause and necessary precisely in virtue of this non-identity. Both are connected, to be sure, but in such a way that, since the subject is only as possible cause (as ideal₂ cause, that is), it is in truth as something separate. The connection of the universal and particular is a simple being of the particular in the universal. In judgment the two separate; the connection must become again the differentiating one [that we saw] previously in relation. The realization of the judgment comes to this point in that what has come apart connects. But it becomes necessarily a realization that is not that of the cause but that of the condition: the condition, namely, that the subject not become an other in the predicate; or [that] its otherness only consist in its remaining identical, its own self; and in its being bound only with another. In this being bound with another, its simple being *per se* as cause would stand out against this bonding of itself with another as with the effect. Rather, the cause remains as subject on its own account; and its connection with another is not a bonding of itself to another in which the connection would be a real₂ crossing over. On the contrary, what is here identical, which is [also] in the other, falls away. The cause is posited ideally₂; necessity is a connection that does not express itself as identical. The relation of causality is A: a + B; that of condition, A: B.

The hypothetical judgment is thereby a requirement of necessity, which as such (that is, as the identity of opposites that are at the same time self-subsisting) had disappeared until now in this relation and [which] first comes in again with the hypothetical judgment; for here the opposites are posited again as self-subsisting. But necessity emerges simply and solely as something required, as something negative; for in the being *per se* of the subject that has realized itself, and in the being *per se* of the predicate (for the preservation of which this happened) in their very selves, something positive in identity is not expressed: that the A might be in B, or B in A, the one or the other a uniting of both. Rather, what is identical is [87] just the negative: the fact that just as the predicte is a universal that is posited as sublated, so too is the subject (which as unity of actuality and possibility is the resolved universality) the realization of the previous relation as itself something connected, or as *one* term of the connection. This relation of the relation of actuality and possibility to the universal, to the predicate, is a necessity that should be. The terms are posited as ideal$_2$; they are what is fluctuating, unstable; and what is required is the middle term that would be their expressed necessity, their *posited* identity. This demand is what is last in the realization of the subject; it can be satisfied only by the realizing of the predicate, of the universal.

β / Being *per se* of the Subject and Realization of the Predicate

αα / The subject preserves itself as a posited particular in that it realizes the subsumption of the predicate under itself or displays it as subsumed under the subject according to its determinacy, just as previously it preserved [itself] in the contrary way, namely, as reflected into itself, as universal, as that which already on its own account would be the sublatedness of opposed determinacies. Displaying the predicate as something determinate in itself (as it is in itself *qua* one property of the subject) can be nothing else than its self-sublating and its being posited as one with the opposed determinacy, whereby a new unity, a higher universal, originates.

The immediate display of the judgment "B is A"—that A, the predicate, is something determinate and subsumed under the subject B, in other words, something sublated through its negative unity—is the positing of A as not-A. It is the expression of the *negative* judgment, in which the predicate is posited according to that moment in which, as determinate, it is in fact something that is not in itself but rather something going under within its opposite through its negative unity.

Negative judgment, however, is just for that reason problematic, like the particular judgment; for the subject is not connected with something universal. There is posited only the universal form of the judgment, not a judgment itself; in other words, it is problematic whether there be a judgment. The predicate is not-A. This universal just as it is is something absolutely empty, a determinacy not reflected into itself. However, this not-A, as reflected into itself or as positive, can also be the determinacy opposed to A. The negative is something with a double sense: the "not" in general, pure nothing or being; or the "not" of this determinate A whereby it is itself a determinate "not," which is [88] opposed to A as positive. If the former is intended, the judgment is something completely indeterminate in its predicate; it is no judgment. If the latter, it is something determinate; what it is, however, is totally problematic and such that one just as much as the other, and the one as little as the other alone, must be intended.

Were not-A itself something positive, then the judgment "B is not-A" would in fact be a positive one, "B is C." And since C is expressed not as C but as not-A, then the subject would connect with C as with something opposed to A and thereby with the unity common to A and C—the higher universal that incorporates A and C in the same manner and is their negative unity or their universality.

Since B is connected nonetheless by means of A with a higher sphere not yet posited, what is required—the sublatedness of the predicate as a determinacy—has not been achieved through the negative judgment. As we have shown, it can only [be] realized (or the predicate be completely displayed as something annihilated) [in] that this equivocation of not-A cease, and it be posited as nothing. And this can only happen [in] that the connection of B with the higher sphere D, common to A and C, completely fall away.

ββ / In negative judgment lies an unexpressed but indirect connection of B not with A but through A itself with the not-A opposed to the A as C, and the higher sphere of A-and-C. "B is not green; it does not have this colour." By that is meant: α) it has some other determinate colour, and β) it has colour in general. For the predicate to be posited as sublated, the other colour, as colour in general, must fall away, and with colour in general also every other determinate colour falls away. The negative judgment has become an *infinite* one: "Feeling does not have a red colour"; "The spirit is not six feet long"; and any nonsense of the same kind. That is to say, it has simply to do with the fact that the connection of the subject with the sublated predicate is at the same time a sublating of the sphere, which as unity has the negated predicate for a negated term opposed to it. The predicate as such is negated: in the negative [89] judgment the subject does not have this predicate; in the infinite it has no predicate. The negative expression of the infinite judgment must therefore be so constituted that not through this determinacy does the connection with its universal still [subsist], but rather that this universal just as well, hence the predicate, is sublated in general.

An infinite judgment of this sort therefore presents itself immediately as an absurdity because, since the predicate is completely negated, no judgment at all occurs, but only an empty semblance of one (a subject and a connection with a predicate having been posited), which dissolves into nothing. As the negative judgment to the particular, so the infinite judgment corresponds to the singular judgment; the latter's subject is posited completely on its own, but just thereby it steps out from under subsumption and in fact, in its not being subsumed, [its] not being reflected under the universal, is not on its own and is also no judgment.[70] So in the infinite judgment the predicate is completely negated by the subject; at the same time, it has thereby stepped outside the subsumption under a subject and is completely on its own, just as the subject is. But just thereby the judgment falls apart and is no more.

However, the negation, the nothing, is not at all something empty; it is the nothing of this determinacy and [is] a unity that is the negative of opposed determinacies. It must thus be posited with respect to the predicate as it has been determined by us under the negative judgment.

γγ / The negated predicate, or (as it is for the subject in relationship) the property that is posited as determinacy only in a sublated way, is such that, being determined as A, it is connected strictly with its opposed determinacy and is a not-c, just as c is a not-A. And in that both of them are as reflected into themselves, the connection, [or] their negative unity, is equally something reflected into itself, a universal, what is common to the two, which are particulars for it; yet [they are] not as negative *one* but [them]selves as universal. For each on its own account is not the *one* of opposed determinacies but a formal *one* of this kind, reflected into itself, determinacy, [so that][71] outside of their own reflection [there is] equally a reflection into itself. Their sphere is indeed *one* of this kind but it is also at the same time [90] opposed to the subject. It is the positive unity, the subsisting of the opposites; it is just their common reflection—that is, a universal.

---

70. *In the margin*: subject in the particular moves towards the being of actuality, in the infinite the predicate towards nothing.

71. *Trans.*: The ms reads "determinacy, which one, outside of their proper reflection [is] just as much a reflection into itself." We have followed CE's emendation.

With respect to the subject as such the opposed determinacies do not
in fact subsist. The subject is their negative unity; its properties are
completely indifferent to each other. As the being of its properties it
is a formal universal, not negative unity but unity. The properties are
only other for each other, not differentiated as against one another.
The subject is the empty *one*, paralysed substantially, or determinate
substance, which, as not particular, not posited in the universal itself,
connects its determinacy infinitely with the other and sublates its actuality. On the contrary, the subject as *one* reflected into itself is particular substance; or the essence of this *one*, posited in the form of
negative *one*, is universality and is thus its determinacy reflected into
itself, not sublating itself as actuality. In connection with their determinacies, the higher universal is their negative unity; but opposed to
the subject [it is] what is self-equivalent in these particularities. Opposed to the subject, the negative unity is a universal and does not
appear as negative unity; but rather the determinacies just on that
account [appear] in it not as self-sublating but as sublated and thereby
external, independent of it. The negative unity is only their common
space; the determinacies are not its accidents but its specifics [*Beson-
dern*]. The negative unity is in this their otherness the self-equivalent,
but the determinacies as this its otherness are equally such as are self-
subsistent in their determinacy.

The predicate, posited in the judgment in this way ([that is to say,]
that the subject is connected with the predicate and its opposite and
thereby with what is universal in both of these), is something that
excludes its opposite, and the opposite does the same; thus both subsist
in the same way. The subject that is connected with the one cannot
be connected with the [other]; yet it must be connected in this way
with both. It is connected with both at once in such a way that the
connection with the one excludes the connection with the other, hence
also not with both at once and positively only with their universal.
This judgment is called the *disjunctive*. It is the counterpart to the
hypothetical; as in the latter the subject, so in the former the predicate
attains its totality (which is here developed as determinacy reflected
into itself). It is determinacy, and thereby at the same time is with its
opposite and hence is also their universal.[72] The judgment in which
the predicate is thus developed is disjunctive—the [91] subject con-

72. *Trans.*: We follow CE. The ms could read " . . . and hence also their universal
is."

nected *either* with A *or* C. That is, the predicate excludes its opposite from the determinacy; yet it is equally excluded by it; and one no more and no less than the other. The subject is connected with each in such a way that in this connection it excludes the other, yet in the connection is thus also connected at the same time with this other.

Through this totality of the predicate, the subject has genuinely preserved itself, or has made the predicate into what it is in truth in this relation, namely, a determinacy, something posited as sublated in the negative unity of the subject. This now pertains to [*ist an*] the predicate in that it is not the predicate that is the exclusive determinacy of the subject; rather, its opposite is connected with the subject in the same way. They are both at the same time not nothing, as in the infinite judgment (which is no judgment at all), but both pertain to the subject just as much as neither the one nor the other does; and right through them the subject is connected determinately only with their sphere, which is present as undeveloped.

The judgment is thus completed through the two opposed subsumptions: of subject under predicate [and] of predicate under subject.
a / In the first, the predicate preserved itself as universal; and the subject was posited with respect to it as what it is, not outside this relation but rather [as] what it is in it. In other words, it travelled the path of reflection into itself and set itself forth as determinateness of negative unity through universality. Thus, in the [second] subsumption the subject remained a particular, undeveloped, and the predicate developed itself as what is determined by the negative unity of the subject. The determining [term] (in the first case the predicate, in the other the subject) was posited as the one that remained whatever it is, as the self-subsisting; but in fact it is rather the other, which displays its reflection into itself, the self-subsistent or real$_2$. For it displays in itself the totality of relation, while the other preserves itself only as the fixed term of the relation. And the bad and true reality stand in converse relation: in the first subsumption wherein the subject is determined through the predicate, the subject is rather reflected within itself, real$_2$, just as the predicate [92] is in [the] second. In this their genuine reality, both cease to be something positive. In the hypothetical judgment the subject is posited as something sublated, and similarly in the disjunctive judgment, the predicate; and so they are both posited as what they are in themselves in truth. The subject is in itself not a particular, a self-subsistent being, but rather a singular

that is only posited as something possible; the predicate is not a universal as determinacy (in other words, not the determinacy as reflected into itself, as self-subsistent); but rather it is in itself only as the either-or, the equal being or the contingency of opposed determinacies.

Thus it has come about here for the first time that what we have hitherto opposed ([that is,] the bad and the true reality) and what in each fell outside one another in the exposition (namely, the one as the determinacy of the concept, the other as its totality) are here opposed in one and the same relation. But at the same time the doubled subsumption falls apart, and the true realization of subject and predicate is itself a bad realization of judgment; for judgment has not returned into itself out of its duplication. In the duplication judgment has only come outside itself, for this doubled judgment is a problematic one; [it is] the hypothetical [judgment] as necessity merely called for, with respect to which the identity of necessity is not posited. The disjunctive judgment is equally problematic, for the subject is in fact not bound to the posited predicate and its antithesis. Rather, that with which it is necessarily connected, namely, the sphere of both, is what is not posited; thus there is necessity in it in like manner.[73] In the hypothetical judgment the predicate is what is necessary, while the subject is contingent to this necessity and the other [that is, the subject] is lacking. And conversely, in disjunctive judgment the subject is posited as one term of the necessity, but the other, the predicate, is lacking to it. In both, what is posited as essential is not even connected with that with which it stands in connection (rather, this is posited as ideal$_2$, as sublated); but *through* this [it is connected] with an other that is not yet posited. The subject of hypothetical judgment is ideal$_2$, like the predicate, and at the same time a "this," but the "this" is not posited. In disjunctive judgment the predicate is ideal$_2$, but the determinacy is similarly not posited. In virtue of the fact that previously the subject was one-sidedly identical with the predicate and now the predicate is one-sidedly identical [93] with the subject, the principle of necessity is present. And in the hypothetical judgment the predicate, through its identity with the subject (which at the same time is also something determinate, a singular), can be bonded with the singular that is posited, which is just thereby identical with this subject. So too the subject in disjunctive judgment is identical with the predicate, which is posited on the side of its determinacy;

73. *Trans.*: That is, the necessity called for (explicitly added by CE).

this predicate is at the same time a universal, and the subject can thus be bonded with something of the sort through the realized predicate. For the subject and predicate there is present the form of the necessity of a connection with something not yet posited. But it must be posited. The hypothetical and the disjunctive judgment are problematic, but there must be a judgment; and it can only happen now because in hypothetical judgment the particular, outside of this subject in which it is as sublated, is posited [as] self-subsistent in the way it was in the disjunctive judgment—because the subject of the hypothetical judgment connects with the subject that is self-subsistent and with it constitutes indeed a judgment, which it can do since it is itself a universal. Likewise, [it can only happen now] in that the predicate of disjunctive judgment connects with its sphere, or rather only posits this connection; and with it constitutes indeed a judgment, which it can do since it is itself something determinate, thus takes up the self-subsistent universal in the hypothetical judgment. In this [way] both these judgments, the disjunctive and the hypothetical, are united; the self-subsistent subject of the disjunctive and the self-subsistent predicate of the hypothetical are posited; and the realized predicate of the former and the realized subject of the latter are both one and the same; [they are] the middle between the extremes, between the self-subsistent subject and predicate. There is hereby posited one judgment split within itself, its middle being a fulfilled, developed universality, the unity of particular and universal; and subject and predicate cease to be bonded through the empty "is" of judgment. They are *interlocked* [*zusammengeschlossen*] through the fulfilled middle, which is their identity, and thereby through necessity; and the judgment has come to be the syllogism [*Schlusse*].[74] [94]

c / The Syllogism[75]

Judgment establishes freedom in its problematic aspects: contingency and choice. Syllogism realizes freedom as reason. The concept of the ethical substance (formulated in the "Relation of Being") is now "reflected into" Socrates

74. *Trans.*: *Schluss* means both "syllogism" and "conclusion"; the English does not catch this.

75. *In the margin: Concept of the syllogism*

Trans.: The marginalia and the frequent underlinings in this section suggest that the ms was used later either for lectures or for preparing another ms. The text is not as carefully edited.

the thinking subject. As the incarnation of the laws he is not just the singular subject but the middle term through which the concept of the ethical substance becomes the syllogism of self-definition. He "subsumes" both his own singularity and the universality of the law in his own activity of self-realization (and as family member and citizen he is also subsumed).

As freedom of choice the subject is "the actual itself as universal." As family member he is resolved, and the contingency of his decision is wiped out. Through birth and education Socrates is one of "the Athenians," and this is his identity (as it is the identity of the family also). The hypothesis of the judgment is positively asserted. Socrates is an Athenian because he is the "son of Sophronisus," born of an Athenian, and now head of the family. The ethical Thing contains many such particular universals, and they have both different private interests, and different social functions. But the absolute determination of all of them is that they are Athenians. Because they are free agents, however, this determinacy is not *necessary*. Socrates can abandon Athens just as Athens can condemn Socrates. The disjunctive syllogism is voluntary. The subject realizes itself by defining itself.

The community has its own logical process of realization. It must sublate the privacy of the family. Hence it divides into the government and the governed. It does not depend simply on voluntary consent (which is a contingent judgment). The citizen as middle between city and family must obey or perish. (The form of rationality here is inductive: what a good citizen does is what all must do.) The sovereignty of law is "the calm simplicity of the connection."

The infinite in the "Relation of Thinking" is stable but not "paralysed." At this stage the new transcendental logic has sublated the older tradition of rational ontology. Up to this point the "critical" Logic of 1804 should be read and interpreted as a reconstruction of the Kantian position. "Practical faith" is not necessary because the logical structure of scientific language is the real supersensible world. The theory of the finite categories (including the forms of subjective cognition–concept, judgment, and syllogism—which serve an architectonic function in the critical philosophy) is the *formal identity* that understanding produces by *copying* reason. In "Proportion" the finite reflection of the understanding sublates itself and becomes *"absolute* reflection." Absolute reflection—cognition as self-conscious self-position—forms the transition to authentic speculation (metaphysics).[76]

76. Thus Hegel can say that "Logic ceases at the point where relationship ceases" (CE 126, l. 2); but this is ambiguous. As the *system* of reflection, logic includes the bringing of the two great "relationships" into the "proportion" that makes them one.

1 / The subject and the predicate preserve themselves in the realization of the judgment as what they are in determinacy vis-à-vis each other; and at the same time—in that each realizes itself in itself, each constitutes itself with respect to itself to be the totality of relation—they both coincide. Each in itself [ex]presses the development of universality in itself, the particular as much as the universal, since each is equally a determinacy reflected into itself. The subject that remains in its determinacy connects, not determinately with a predicate thus developed, but through the predicate with the sphere of the predicate as something determinate. And conversely, the predicate that remains determinate [connects] not with the subject thus developed but through it with something determinate. Both judgments are *one* syllogism, since the developed subject and predicate are the same development. In this manner the subject and predicate, thus interlocked, are not immediately as in the judgment; but [are] through this development, which has taken the place of the empty "is" of the judgment and through which the judgment has become something necessary. For the middle term is the posited middle of the extremes; it is universal and particular at once: α) it is a determinacy, hence equal to the subject, [and] a universal, hence equal to the predicate; and β) the connection of its relation is the converse of this equivalence, for this allows no relation. It is the universal over against the subject and subsumes it; it is the particular over against the predicate and is subsumed under it. Both these subsumptions, expressed as judgments, are common, simple judgments, and precisely the interlocking of subject and predicate. But the interlocking no longer has as judgment any meaning at all; rather, what is essential to it is not their connection in general but their connection through a middle, or the necessity of connection. The judgment is not as such on its own account, but is returned into the concept and subsumed under it. The [95] determinate concept obtains its reality in the syllogism. As middle it is the simple oneness of universal and particular, since the development

---

For the struggle of the understanding to *copy* reason, see the outline of 1801 (Rosenkranz, *Hegels Leben*, p. 191; Cerf and Harris, trans., *Faith and Knowledge*, p. 10) and the *Difference* essay (*Gesammelte Werke*, IV, 16–19; Harris and Cerf, trans., pp. 94–98). The philosophers who pushed this effort to the limit were Plato and Aristotle, who thus "perfected natural consciousness" and made logic (as *systema reflexionis*) possible. The *systema rationis* is a distinctively modern achievement, for which the long journey from the Stoics to 1789 was essential.

preserves itself in the unity. Its moments are simultaneously set apart
from one another as the extremes and determined vis-à-vis each other.
As relation of the extremes to the middle, the judgment is realized as something
duplicated; but it is at the same time posited as sublated, for what is subject
in one of these two subsumptions is predicate in the other one, and so the
determinacy of the judgment is destroyed through the opposite.[77] Yet
ideality is not merely posited through[78] this duplication of opposites
but—in that the interlocking of subject and predicate as extremes
does not have the meaning of a determinate judgment but rather of
not being a judgment at all—is immediately to be the identity of the
mediating concept, the emanations of which are the extremes and
only as such are taken up in it. The simple circle of the concept has
narrowed itself *and cast* itself *apart* into *the line, whose middle* is *the* narrowed circle itself, gathered together into a point, and whose extremes
are the universal and the particular.

2 / In the syllogism the concept has returned through the judgment,[79]
in that it is this casting apart through the judgment of its antithesis
yet is the essential middle term of the antithesis. But the syllogism
has immediately also the higher standpoint of being *relation returned*
into itself generally, the identity of the relation of being and thought.
Relation in its first realization has become something other than itself,
though the realized other relation is the other[ness] of this other[ness]
and the return to it. In the self-realizing judgment, in the hypothetical
one, the entire universality, distinct from the particular, steps aside;
but the universality becomes precisely for this reason purely negative
unity, numerical *one*. The subject of the syllogism is in fact particular
only in connection with its [96] subsumption under the middle—that
is, as enclosed in the circle of universality; but it is just as much
opposed to this middle, and on its own [is] pure singularity of substance. Yet substance is no longer mere substance itself; rather, as
what has gone right through the concept and emerged out of it, the
alternation of accidents is *brought to rest; [and these] accidents* are *not self-*
sublating and opposed but are other only for one another, and therefore other in accordance with bad infinity. In other words, this sub-

77. *In the margin: falling apart of the realization of subject and predicate* in hypothetical
and disjunctive syllogism. Ideality of both.
78. *Trans.*: We follow ms and not CE by placing "posited" before "but immediately"
and by not inserting a *sondern* before "is to be the identity . . ." later on.
79. *In the margin*: subject of the syllogism is the substance returned into itself.

stance is an INFINITELY DETERMINED one. *Substance has returned into itself*, for as the negative unity of absolutely altering accidents it is this *one*—that is, their self-equivalence. It is opposed as much to the particular as to the universal. The universal is the predicate, the particular the middle of the syllogism; for it itself is, as particular, the unity of singularity and universality; and its singularity is therewith particularity—universal over against the subject, and unity of singularity and universality, or particularity, over against the universal.

⁸⁰In the syllogism the subject, as a "this" to which the relation of universal and particular has returned, is connected with the universal through the particular, not through itself; it stands only in immediate combination with the former and in subsumption under it. Three levels of ASCENDING or DESCENDING are herewith posited: a pure "this," absolutely singular; a *particular*, at once this and universal (that is, as taken up into the positive unity, the negative, infinitely determinate *one*); and a pure universal. Just as the two extremes of the pure "this" and the pure universal α) *are contained within the middle*, β) so are they *also opposed* to it—they *are on their own account*. The *determinate concept* of the middle is as such the *simple unity* of the universal and singular, and as such *its doubled connection* is for the concept something external. It is our reflection that has developed it into these extremes. The concept is the universal unity of the two; but over against it as well stands the pure universal, which, just as the "this" is no longer the particular, is equally no longer determinate concept, but purely universal. Since this has appeared outside the middle, just for that reason the middle is not at the same time the genuine middle, subsuming both. The unity of both extremes in the middle and [97] their separation in it are not themselves united again: *in the separation the middle is merely the means that is not on its own account but [is] the point of transition in the ascending of singular to universal or in the descending of universal to singular.* In the concept of the syllogism, that which is opposed to itself is thus this *being-subsumed of both extremes* under the middle, as well as *the being per se of both* and their *relation to each other*, by which the one as purely universal subsumes both positively, just as conversely the subject subsumes both negatively. The middle is what is common, on the one hand in that it is subsumed under both in the opposed, positive and negative, manner, and on the other in that it subsumes them

---

80. *In the margin*: Contradiction in the syllogism α) the being subsumed of extremes under the middle β) the not being subsumed.

both. In the middle the extremes are related by way of opposition, equally as subsuming each other and being subsumed. The syllogism must realize its concept, in that it displays this contradiction in itself. The middle displaying itself as subsuming both would be the universal itself, and the realization of the middle would coincide with that of this universal; over against that realization stands the realization of the singular, which displays itself as sublating the particular and universal in negative unity. The two paths are opposites. But in this current, flowing opposite ways, both will be penetrated; and the equilibrium of both will be the realization equally of each singular.[81]

α / The Realization of the Subject as Singular

The subject as "this" infinitely determined [singular] (which is also called the individual) emerges here not merely into actuality; rather, the actual itself [emerges] as [something] universal. The actual as "this" is the negative unity, which is connected through determinacy simply and solely with the opposite. In the particular this connection, which turns its actuality into possibillity, is wiped out, and the determinacy is posited in the form of universality reflected into itself, although only in the form of being *per se*. For this form is opposed as the universal to the particular, and the latter has not freed itself from this connection. [98] As subject in the syllogism[82] it emerges from the ideality in which [it] is still posited in the hypothetical judgment; and as negative [one] it is in and of itself *determined absolutely*, or *absolutely in its determinacy*,[83] the *unity of many, indeed of infinitely* many *determinacies*. For as negative unity the subject is the unity of opposed determinacies; but having UNIVERSALITY in itself, AS SUBSUMED, these determinacies are other only relative to each other, and each is freed from that for which it is only a possible [determinacy]. The subject has subsumed under itself not only particularity, the middle, but universality, the other extreme. It is something universal, but in such a way that its negative unity [is] what is essential (the universality with respect to it, posited only with respect to it as something sublated) in this way: that it has infinitely many properties. Universality is just this: their being with respect to the subject, indeed their being only as the

81. *In the margin: Opposite realization of the subject and of the universal.*
82. *In the margin: Subject in the syllogism.*
83. *In the margin: singular or subject is unity of absolutely many determinacies as universal.*

being of others and according to bad infinity. For their being *per se*, their unity, is not just their sublatedness; but it is outside of them, as one[ness]. It [is] moreover infinitely many; its multiplicity is not determined through the unity. This so-called individuality should have reality: "it *is*" is what is said of it, since the merely possible being in the hypothetical judgment is expressed as actual.[84] Thereby the *hypothetical syllogism* is posited, since the subject of the hypothetical judgment turns itself into a positive proposition. The "is" of this subject is, however, nothing else but wholly empty being, which is perfectly equivalent to nothing. "This c is,"or "c is a *this*," means the same thing. The "this" is the "is" added to the subject as predicate. The reality of the subject remains an empty *thisness*. It should have reality only insofar as it is a "this," not insofar as it is the unity of these determinacies. For this reality would be quite another necessity, an inner necessity: unity of positive and negative unity in which the numerical *one* is completely lost in the positive unity.

It is the simplicity of the "this" that as absolute being and as absolute certainty [99] validates itself[85] in ordinary cognition *as absolute truth*. It is the concept of infinite determinacy: the pure "this" dissolves itself immediately into nothing; the "this" is not thus empty but rather *reflection into itself*, determinacy as totality, whose form is just the "this," the numerical *one*. As totality, however, it has a content: it is the unity preserving itself in the opposite; and the opposite is, as shown, the determinacy as multiplicity, though as *completed multiplicity*, as absolute determinacy. Yet *the multiplicity is not completed*,[86] for these many are properties reflected into themselves. They are on their own account as many; they have unity outside themselves; and so they are simply not [the] *all*.[87] What is completely determinate, or the "this," is a mere *ens rationis*. Of course it seems as though the mere "ought," an unfulfilled demand, is only this: to display these properties, these absolutely many determinacies to thought, and to exhaust them; [it seems] as though the subject in and of itself, without connection with this enumeration, is yet something completely determinate precisely insofar as, in that independence, it would be a "this." Now, the subject in the syllogism should be on its own account, not as subsumed under

---

84. *In the margin*: the hypothetical syllogism expresses the "is" of this subject.
85. *In the margin: In the ordinary cognition the simple this is absolute truth.*
86. *In the margin: The properties are not fulfilled.*
87. *In the margin: The properties are neutral vis-à-vis one another.*

the universal, not posited as sublated, but rather as subsuming the universal in general under itself. However, just this being in and of itself *of the absolutely determinate is* this: that it have infinitely many, separated *determinacies, neutral [indifferente]* to one another, *outside of which their one* is precisely *indifferent* to them; and this [is] an *ens rationis*, for it is null, *this indifference* of the determinacies whose essence is only to be in connection with another; and this their connection or their differentiation over against one another is their immediate negative unity, their essence, which is not simply outside of them, not indifferent to them.

So the subject is essentially *not* a "this," something *absolutely determinate* and subsuming the *universal* under it, but rather equally something subsumed; and subsumed, indeed, not merely through the determinate universal or the particular—[not] through this, since it is itself something subsumed through the pure universal. But this is in [100] fact not the pure universal, for it is immediately the universal of this particular that constitutes the middle. The subject is not a pure "this" but essentially *something subsumed in a necessary way through one determinacy under a higher one*, just as it subsumes it.[88] In this way the universal itself [is] just as much not a pure universal, for the reason that it is subsumed under the negative unity by the particularity and through this by the subject, [and that it] is hence opposed to another and is itself something determinate. So the subject's being *per se* consists in this: *that* in the twofold manner of subsumption it is interlocked, *not immediately with one determinacy*, but *through this with a higher, relatively universal one*, so that the connection of the subject with a predicate is a necessity; and in essence this necessity alone is what is real$_2$.

But *the question* is *whether this necessity is posited through this interlocking*. To begin with, the subject must be connected with the middle term; as numerical *one* and at the same time [as] something particular it must be determined as universal. But as subject it *is absolute determinacy and therefore equally as opposed to the infinite multiplicity of the determinacies*; it *is indifferent to the determinacy of the middle term*. The determinacy is a "this," just as the subject came to be considered as a this and as such is equally null. The subject *thus* determined would be this singular determinacy; but just as little as it is *a singular*, a numerical *one*, so little is it a singular determinacy.[89] In the *disjunctive judgment* it is connected in the same way with A = − c and with c = − A. To sublate

88. *In the margin*: the subject is subsumed *through* ONE *determinacy*.
89. *In the margin*: But it is indifferent vis-à-vis this its determinacy.

this *either / or* and to posit the one with respect to the subject while excluding the other in the DISJUNCTIVE SYLLOGISM means nothing else but to posit here as *this* predicate what is in the hypothetical syllogism as a "this" subject. It is of course the pure unmediated positing, the *minor* of the disjunctive syllogism, about which we are talking. But as numerical *one* the subject is posited essentially as substance and simply indifferent to the opposed predicates, which as accidents in their actuality (in which they are to be posited as singular determinacies [101]) are affected by possibility—in other words, by not being posited. Insofar as the determinacy would be neutral beside the infinitely many others, however, it has as "this" no priority at all to be posited before another; in other words, infinitely many others are just as good as it. And in respect to the subject as non-substance yet as infinitely determined, it is contradictory to posit only a single determinacy. However, it is not this determinacy of the subject, either, but rather its necessity as reciprocity that is to be posited. For the *connection of the subject* is not with this determinacy but rather THROUGH IT only with another, and indeed, in such a way that it is reciprocally subsumed under the universal as well. Since as "this" it is DETERMINED, just for that [reason] it *is* also SUBLATED. This sublating of the subject through the universal is, however, itself always a determining sublating, a determinate being-bound to a predicate. But this, too, cannot so come about that it would not be bound up with it immediately, but only through another, through the *syllogism* in general or the *simple syllogism*. But the syllogism in general binds the subject to the predicate not with necessity. The latter, although universal, is itself something determinate; and the subject as this determinate substance is through its determinacy precisely the contrary of this determinacy, and through this is interlocked with the contrary of the predicate.

[90]If the predicate with which the subject is to be interlocked has only the appearance of subsuming the particular, the middle, but is in fact equal to it and the judgment is only a *tautological proposition*, then in general all that is present is a judgment in which in place of the predicate only another expression is substituted. *If the middle and the other extreme are* in fact *related* as particular and universal, then *the interlocking of the* subject with this last is rather a sublating of its determinacy,[91] which is its connection with the middle as a determining

90. *In the margin: Identical judgment* in the syllogism.
91. *In the margin:* as relation of universal and particular the interlocking is a sublating of its determinacy.

of the subject. Insofar as this universal is itself a determinacy, it is [an] absolutely contingent [matter] to interlock the subject with it. For the latter as absolutely determined can be *interlocked with infinitely [many] others*—which just thereby must also *contradict* themselves. [102] For the subject through its nature as negative unity is the unity of opposites, equally connected with the opposed determinacy and interlocked through the latter with the determinacy opposed to the previous universal. Thus, instead of the necessity of the bonding, its *contingency* and the *contradiction of what is combined* is posited. And what comes to be through the syllogism is something quite other than this bonding. As absolutely determined through the determinacy with the determinate universal and through its infinite determinacies with the pure universal, the subject is in fact in and of itself something universal in its determinacy. It is the neutrality of infinitely many determinacies, their reflectedness into themselves. It is negative unity, though posited as a universal, not as substance; rather [it is posited so] that in and of itself the possibility is not connected with the determinacies or only with respect to them, but is in itself. And the subject is *not interlocked with the universal through the determinacies but immediately in and of itself*.[92] *The subject* completely *sublates* the separation that is in that line of the syllogism in which the subject and the universal are combined through a middle dividing them; the subject is a universal. Its absolute determinacy, reflected in this way into itself, is itself something simple, not the pure empty negative unity but determinate, just as its universality is the determinate one. But this determinacy, excluding the opposite, is posited as being in itself, as the essence of reflection into itself. The subject is a particular; this determinacy is what remains the universal self-equivalent in its pathway of becoming-other. Particularity is *a particular*;[93] through its determinacy it is connected with other negative *ones* and opposed to them. It has its completion outside itself; but its completion is just as universally reflected into itself, in and of itself. The subject is the middle that has come to be itself,[94] the middle that, turned against another, is opposed only in diverse connections. This subject is realized particularity, which in itself, turned inward and

92. *In the margin*: subject is not contingent, that is, interlocked through *one* determinacy with the universal; rather with all[ness] it is inherently universal turned back into itself.

93. *In the margin*: it is *a particular*.

94. *In the margin*: the middle that comes to be itself.

outward on its own account, is on its own account; [it is] itself reflected into itself only by being determinate, [103] for through this it is other to itself. But in this its otherness it itself is; that is, it is determinacy as such, which reflects itself into itself. Determinacy as a universal or as a particular is only formally reflected into itself as unity of opposites. But the third or synthesis—what proceeds forth posited as simple— became something other; and this other again an other, the first once more; but this first, insofar as it has become the third, distinguished itself from the first simple through this very having-become. It is the realized particular, however, which in its proceeding forth is already itself: [the] "this" that has become, and thus maintains itself on its pathway of reflection. That is to say, the subject is its *definition*.

b / Realization of the Universal

The universal in the syllogism—how the subject realizes itself as particular in that it posits the universal with respect to itself—must realize itself in that it posits the middle and the subject with respect to itself. *Its essence is to posit determinacy within itself as sublated*; it is opposed to negative unity as to the particular in that it, as universal, does not exclude the opposite of the determinacy but is equal to it, or is the positive of the disjunction. The subject is negative unity, positing the opposites as sublated, and thus itself universal; but as universal it is something determinate. The universal (negative unity, but as such only the universal [on condition] that it itself is again something determinate) is the side of the subject in which the universal comes into consideration in connection with the subject as subsumed under the same. But as a universal, as it is on its own account, it is not connecting with a subject through the determinacy but as the *reflection into itself*, dividing itself into *the opposed determinacies*, and *positing* them *as sublated*[95]— *self-enclosed reflection into itself*.

What is more determinate in this totality of the universal is that it connects with the "this" that is posited as sublated in the *hypothetical judgment*; but it connects not only with that: it has likewise other conditions. Its reality is not only the interlocking with this determinate and with a "this"; [104] it subsumes the same[96] and posits it as sublated,

95. *In the margin*: the universal as self-subsisting divides itself into opposed determinacies.

96. *In the margin*: it is the subsumed "this."

in that it posits others equal to it. Through this equivalence the "this" ceases to be a negative *one*, for as such it would exclude all equivalence, all connection; there is one particular and beside it several more particulars. But this their indifference is sublated through their determinacy; they connect with one another in that they exclude each other in the *disjunctive judgment*. But just as little as the hypothetical syllogism posits the universal in its reality, so little does the disjunctive; rather, the universal is the contrary of both. The universal is not through the being of the "this" in the hypothetical, nor through the excludedness of some other determinate in the disjunctive and through the being of this determinacy alone, but in like [manner] the universal is linked to the other; and it is not purely on its own account but only in connection with these particulars; it is their negative unity. This is the realization of the universal: that like the subject it is negative and positive unity at the same time, not in such a way that according to its determinacy the universal would have the opposite outside itself, but rather *it embraces both and posits them as sublated*. And *it is not* interlocked *with negative unity through a middle* but is immediately the unity itself. The reflection of the universal into itself is this: that as A it becomes the antithesis of the B = −c, and c = −B, and in this it is equal to itself, recapitulates itself out of it, for it sublates [it] in its self-equivalence. The reflection of the subject is that it [is][97] as equal to itself, as B, in that it becomes something other than +B against c = −B, and again sublates this "plus" of its determinacy.

The positing at the same time of the universal as a particular (in other words, its realization, but as self-subsistent being that would at the same time not be negative unity) would be the demonstration of the major premise of the syllogism or of the subsumption of the middle under the predicate. That with which it is interlocked cannot be something singular, for in the connection, in its determinateness through the universal, it is a particular. *The syllogism, which displays the universal as subsuming*, interlocks it through singularity with the particular, and is *induction*. The fact that the subject is this universal does not exhaust it in its [105] universality; it is absolutely many, this universal. For the universal to be posited as it is, the whole aggregate of this many must be posited under it; and in that this aggregate together, as subject, as one, confronts the universal, it is itself a universal against

97. *Trans.*: Lasson and CE insert "determines itself" as the verb here.

the singularity of the aggregate and a particular against the universality of the predicate; what previously was the nature of the middle is posited as an extreme in that the subject has become the particular from being the singular. But this interlocking is no more valid; for the singularities, whose togetherness the subject should express, are as singularities absolutely many and have as such no reality. The connection of the universal sublates the negative unity and is thereby immediately bound up with the particular, separating itself precisely as negative unity into the particular.

The syllogism is the connection of the singular with the universal through the particular. The pathway of reflection is that the singular at first becomes the particular and displays its subsuming of the middle and of the other extreme under itself. In this the universal is not satisfied; its subsuming must display this as well. And an immediate oneness comes to be out of the mediating connecting. In the relation of being, the simple infinity of the connection passes over into the infinite mediation, into synthesis. In the relation of thinking it passes back into the calm simplicity of the connection; and in this it is itself complete. The connection is that of equivalence, and each side of what is connected is itself a relation, under opposed forms that are posited as ideal$_2$. Each is a universal and a negative unity, and the unity of both; and the determinate form under which they are opposed is each of these two that are sublated with respect to them, namely, each with respect to the other.

III / **Proportion**

"Proportion" completes the Logic by providing a synthesis of self-conscious relation and the simple connection of consciousness. (Thus it is analogous with "Reason" in the *Phenomenology*.) It is probably called "Proportion" in homage to Plato's doctrine of the "truly beautiful bond."[98]

98. See *Timaeus*, 31c–32a. Hegel quotes (and translates) this passage in the *Difference* essay. His version (in a literal translation) goes as follows: "The truly beautiful bond is that which makes itself and what it binds one [. . .]. For whenever, of any three numbers, or masses, or forces, the middle is such that what the first is for it, it is for the last, and conversely, what the last is for the middle, the middle is just that for the first, then since the middle has become the first and last, and the last and first conversely have both become the middle, in this way they will all necessarily be the same; but things which are the same as against each other are all one" (Harris and Cerf, trans.,

The first section is the theory of self-definition. This is no longer regarded formally. It is now applied. The concept of self-definition explains why (in natural science) living species are defined in terms of their self-preservative capacity. But the actual self-definition of reason makes the singular consciousness into a concrete universal. This is not a static concept—it involves the motion of division and is achieved in cognition.

In the animal process division is sexual. ("The universal sunders itself into two mutually connected definitions"; quite apart from the influence of Plato, the natural model of sexual division explains Hegel's insistence on a dichotomous theory of logical specification.) The species emerges here as the true subject, and the definition applies to all species members. The wholeness of the breeding community involves the syllogistic structure of cognition.

The Italian commentary points out, very aptly, that there is an important correspondence between "Definition" and "Division" and the two sections of "The Syllogism": "(α) The Realization of the Subject as Singular"; and "(b) Realization of the Universal"—see especially CE 97, lines 20–21; 103, lines 10, 29–30; 107, line 33.[99] This is just what we should expect, since "Proportion" in 1804 has entered into the place of "the *speculative* meaning of the syllogism" in the outline of 1801 (compare page xvii, note 16 above).

The equivalence of both relations is the connection turned back into itself. It is so simply as this connection; and the opposed are themselves the two relations posited ideally$_2$. The concept is realized in that it has preserved itself and both its [106] sides have been posited with respect to it just as it has been. The syllogism as the bad reality of the concept has gone back into its circle. Out of the absolute inequality of its extremes it has become the contrary.

a / DEFINITION

The oneness of the positive and negative unity,[100] *the subject as a determinacy both posited and reflected into itself,*[101] is something real that is immediately interlocked with the universality in its determinacy, an absolute being

---

p. 158). That this passage expresses what Hegel called in 1801 the "speculative meaning of the syllogism" is confirmed by his discussion of it in the *Lectures on the History of Philosophy, Theorie Werkausgabe*, XIX, 89–91; trans. Haldane and Simpson, II, 75–77.

99. Franco Biasutti, in Chiereghin et al., *Logica e metafisica*, p. 397.

100. *In the margin*: oneness of the positive and negative unity.

101. *In the margin: determinacy reflected into itself.*

per se that in its determinacy is on its own account. The excluding is here for the first time real; the positive connection with what is excluded ceases; and it is the going back into itself. What thus far *sublated the determinacy* was that it only was in connection with the opposite; now, however, it has its reality. The subject is something determinate only according to this determinacy. It ceases to be something infinitely determined in manifold ways; and only this determinacy is the subject's essential determinacy. For the essence is the being *per se* or the having been returned into itself.

The subject that is equal to its definition and nothing but this is thereby not something singular. Its essential *determinacy* is the one in which the subject [is] *turned against other particulars* and in this *being-turned-against-them preserves itself.*[102] In the *definition* of living things, therefore, *the determination of the weapons for attack or for defence* has necessarily been taken as [the determination] of that whereby they preserve themselves vis-à-vis other particulars. [One] must determine the weaker *plant kingdom [Pflanzengeschlecht]* according to that whereby it likewise preserves itself, yet only as universal; as singular, however, it *goes aground*, namely through *relation of* [107] *generation [Geschlechtsverhältnis]*. The inorganic, weaker still, does not ever preserve itself as *genus in its going under* but *therein ceases altogether to be* what it is, and its *essential determinacy is that* IN WHICH IT GOES UNDER. What is essential to the subject that preserves itself thereby as an individual, as a singular, is that it be self-equivalent in this its being-turned-against-others, [that it] be connected only with itself. It remains self-equivalent since in its becoming-other it does not cease to be what it is but rather sublates what is thus other than itself. *Self-preservation or definition* has as immediately *one* what was hitherto separated, or was only our reflection: that the *one* as universal in its otherness is immediately equal to its concept, to the universal; it is, only because it has separated off this otherness or its determinacy from itself as something other. According to its determinacy it is completely on its own account in virtue of the fact that it annihilates what is opposed to its determinacy. Its being *per se* is not an abstraction from the opposite; but it is connected with it. And the oneness of both is not the sublating of both; but the *one* is itself the universal in its determinacy, or the sublating of the other.

102. *In the margin: The subject preserves itself* through its *determinacy* or it is through the determinacy turned back absolutely into itself.

This genuine reality of the "this"—that its particularity is, subsists, and, having been taken up as such into the universality, is on its own account—expresses the concept of proportion in general; in it the relation goes completely to one side; the particular is immediately incorporated within the universal, and the "this," connected immediately with both, has only their unity for its essence. It itself is that side of the relation according to which [the] "this" is negative unity, the *one*. And the two relations that are posited equal to each other are that of the negative *one* (the essence of the relation of being) and that of the positive *one* (the essence of the relation of thinking), so that the merely self-sublating determinacies of the first at the same time subsist in the universal element of the second—are in and of themselves—and the indifference of those that fall outside of each other in the second disappears through the negative unity of the first.

[103]Yet this reality, or the definition, is in fact a reality of singularity, or of what is determinate in general. The universal has not achieved its due; and the determinate that is posited as self-preserving can not in fact preserve itself. The determinacy is posited as being in itself and as [108] determinacy equal to the universal; and it is so posited that the universal [has] separated off its otherness as an other from itself and is so connected with it in a nullifying way that it is as universal in its sublating and preserves itself as this determinacy. Yet in truth only the side of its universality is what is thus self-preserving—what is equal as the unity of the opposites; and the sublating of the determinacy is not the sublating of one and the subsisting of the other but absolutely the sublating of both. In definition, therefore, the proportion is not completely expressed; the one side is only that of the negative one (not its expression as relation) or the "*this*" that should be simple; the other is its expression as of a relation but not of it as of a negative unity. For embodied in the universal, the determinacy subsists; that whose negative unity is the one side is the universal and particular. The former, however, *is not a genuine universal, for* it is only posited as subsuming one of the opposed determinacies. These terms are not posited as what they are in truth; the determinacy [is] not something ideal₂; at the same time the universal is not a real, non-negative unity.

Definition therefore expresses only the demand for the absolute reality to have returned back into itself. Directed outwards it is a

---

103. *In the margin: Dialectic of definition*; it posits in fact a singular.

negative *one* that excludes others from itself and preserves itself, is on its own account. Its positive connection is not at the same time a sublating of its own determinacy but its persisting. And the moment of universality in it is not true universality but rather is the whole under the determinacy of particularity. The particular is a unity of universality and determinacy, but conversely the universal [is] not also as unity of determinacies [that are] opposed as a universal and a particular; that is, the universal is only posited as determinate. And the same [the determinate], as reflection of the determinacy into itself, is therefore only formal₂, not real₂, as expressing what it is with respect to it [the universal].¹⁰⁴ Reflection into itself must not have the other as an other separated off from it, indifferent to it, vis-à-vis which it posits itself in a differentiated way and sublates itself in the connection; on the contrary, this other is in it according to its essence; it is the unity of both, and the sublating is the sublating of both determinacies. It is the ideality just as much of itself as of the other; in other words, the subject is essentially a universal. As reflecting itself into itself and sublating the determinacy, it sublates its own [determinacy] and is as a universal. That is to say, definition passes over into *division*. [109]

b / DIVISION

a / Since in its immediate oneness with determinacy *the universal* is itself something determinate, *this unity of both* is *a determinate unity, and something* particular; *this particular, as it thus reflects itself into itself, becomes rather a universal*, one that sublates its determinacy.¹⁰⁵ This universal is the equivalence of both opposites—that to which they return—and one is what the other is. Thus the self-preservation of the particular is rather its ideality, and a production of the universal. Since its self-preservation, its reflection into itself, its being *per se*, is this universal, it does not properly [re]turn to universality. Universality is not the product or the result; it is rather the being *per se* of the particular—that from which [the particular] originates just as much—the first, but in general the essence of the particular.

---

104. *Trans.*: We have introduced "the determinate" and "the universal" as our interpretation of an ambiguous text.

105. *In the margin*: The particular sublates rather its determinacy, and becomes a universal.

This universal is as such the empty undifferentiated space, the subsisting of the determinacies. It is yet more: it is the reflection into itself, the absolute being *per se*, which in its otherness is self-equivalent. *The determinacies* thus posited in it are themselves this other, this opposedness *or the duplication of the universal*, so that this [is] the essence of both; and they are in virtue of this alone. As something determined, in the necessity of the universal alone, they are *themselves to be an other*. But this their reality is essentially the equivalence or the sublatedness of both, and as strictly simple or self-equivalent the universal is the sublatedness of its otherness, or of its duplication, the negative unity of its parts.

The division that the universal makes with respect to itself *renders the definition* ideal₂, *for the universal sunders itself into two mutually connected definitions*,[106] which, as indifferent to one another, subsist both in the same manner. [It is] not [the case that] the other of one is sublated through the other as in the one-sided definition. But this their equivalence is their substance, and because of this it posits them both ideally₂. The determinacy that is reflected into itself is at the same time [110] sublated, and sublates itself. It is simply and solely in connection with what is opposed to it, and just in this connection it is itself ideal₂.

The terms of the division in which the universal realizes itself—posits itself as opposed to itself, and as finding *itself*—are determined immediately through the nature of the universal itself;[107] for the latter is only such insofar as it becomes an other, and becomes itself out of this other. The two moments whose unity the universal is (it as something simple, and it as an other to itself)[108] are the moments of its concept, and just these are the terms of the division. As moments of the concept they are only opposite, purely ideal₂. When posited in the *one*, however, each is as it is in itself or really₂, having in itself the determinacy of the other, so that it is posited as the essential. In the universal as such they are completely equal to each other, so that neither is what is essential with respect to the other; both are rather equally ideal₂; the universal is the ideality of both. However, the reality of the concept is this: that each is alternatively what is essential, and

106. *In the margin*: In the division the universal sunders itself into opposed definitions.

107. *In the margin*: The terms of the division are *determined through the nature of the universal itself*.

108. *In the margin*: it as something simple, and it is other.

the other is what is posited ideally$_2$ in it. For the concept of the universal, insofar as it is the equal ideality of both, is itself the determinacy of the universal vis-à-vis the particularity, and the concept is itself again the *one* term of the division; as opposed to the particularity it is itself something particular. This determinacy of the terms of the division is as such ideal$_2$; but it is as reflected into itself, as posited equal to the universal, and the duplication of the definition. In this reality both are indifferent to each other; each is in and of itself, for each has in itself the essence of the whole. They are not *per se* turned against one another, as in the case of the singular definition with respect to the opposite determinacy; for each preserves itself in the same way as the other, and neither can do so at the expense of the other, for both have equal rights.

Because of this the determinacy obtains just this indifferent [expression]. (Its differentiation vis-à-vis the other is, as it were, outside it). On its own account [it] is a pure quality that abstracts from its contrary; and the most indifferent expression of this determinacy is number. The universal, the genus, becomes through this embodiment something purely universal, something communal; and the *division is a multiplication of* definitions whose unity is outside them [and] is indifferent even for them. For as negative unity the universal is, only in that it posits the [111] determinacies (whose negative unity it is, in virtue of sublating them),[109] to be their other. This otherness, while it remains itself, is the dividing up of the universal, so that the universal is as the continuous unity, outside of those in which it is.

b[110] / Division makes the subject of definition into something universal; and the relation of the definition itself is converted into an aggregate of subjects. Division brings out the universality that was suppressed in definition, which had not received its due in that it was not posited as preserving itself in otherness, in multiplicity. In the division itself, however, universality preserves itself only as falling outside the many. Connected with the terms of *the* definition, it is the same in A, B, C; but [it is] not [thus] on its own account. A, B, C, are indifferent with respect to one another; instead of the universal being on its own account, it is rather each singular that is on its own account. There just must be, not this [universal] divided into particulars, but rather

---

109. *Trans.*: We follow CE in inserting a comma here. The ms would read "since it posits the determinacies . . . to be sublating them as their other."

110. *In the margin*: Dialectic of division. The divided are indifferent to each other.

simple negative unity, which just because of its simplicity is what sublates their multiplicity in connection with them.[111] The species must
stand in connection with one another simply and solely as moments
of the one whole of the genus. And because of this, the genus itself
is a negative unity,[112] which posits the moments in itself as ideal$_2$ [and
posits] itself as undivided. As a result [it is] a substance that sublates
within itself the differentiation and is on its own account. But it sublates the differentiation only insofar as the differentiation was [pre-
viously] present. It is the universal posited as singular, as pure point
of unity, as a positive (a manifold in itself) that disintegrates into parts
and equally sublates this disintegrating once more.

c / COGNITION IS POSITED

Here we have reached the self-definition of rational consciousness. Thus the
reflective character of logic is overcome. Cognition is the *form* of the "true
infinite" (which will be *realized* in metaphysics) reflecting upon itself and constructing itself. The discussion is a recapitulation of the earlier reflective
argument in this light. Logic concludes by discussing its own method.

It seems that Hegel's object in comparing logical proof with geometric proof
(the heading "Proportion" comes from Euclid) is to show us how cognition
continues to be *reflective*. Self-cognition is *reconstruction* and involves supple-
mentary constructions, but the argument dictates these step by step. The
"circle" of cognition goes from the "fact" to the "reasoned fact"; and this is
the whole pattern made (deductively) by the Logic. We should notice that
although the explicit criticism of geometrical construction is the same one
that is made in the preface to the *Phenomenology*, the attitude towards the
mathematical model of reasoning is different. The Italian commentary points
out that this phase of Hegel's argument seems to be guided by Plato's discussion of the "third hypothesis" in the *Parmenides*.[113]

---

111. *Trans.*: We follow ms, not CE.

112. *In the margin: The genus itself is negative unity.*

113. Franco Biasutti in Chiereghin et al., *Logica e metafisica*, 408–9. This insight
comes from earlier works by F. Chiereghin that are there referred to. The influence
of Plato's "truly beautiful bond" can still be seen in the theory of the "speculative
proposition" given in the preface to the *Phenomenology* (or so I would argue). But the
mathematical terminology (like the Spinozist parallelism implicit in the concept of a
"proportion" between being and thought) is there abandoned. Dialectical development
is regarded as a kind of organic *growth* rather than as a kind of *construction*. But it was
the fact that logical thought is a *self-directing* process of *accumulation*—that is, it was the

The way up from singular to universal, and the way down again, met in the singular consciousness as family member. "What passes through the circle of reflection is not itself this absolute circle." Cognition belongs to the historic link in the chain of generation. Thus the empirical self that is the sublated content is perpetually novel, but the content of absolute cognition is the circle of self-determination. This Fichtean contradiction is what makes the transition from formal logical idealism to real metaphysics necessary. The absolute knowledge (pure cognition) that has *emerged* from experience must make a circle of circles that returns finally to the moment of simple self-identity from which its emergent evolution began. (Half of sheet 39 is missing, so we do not know exactly how Hegel developed the dialectic of absolute cognition and finite experience. But the general review character of the whole discussion suggests that the "three determinacies of cognition" are the moments of "Proportion": definition, division, and totality.)

a / *Until now* the *transition* of the concept into its becoming-other, or into its reality, and the taking back of this becoming-other under the concept *was our reflection, a dialectical manipulation* that developed the antitheses that were present undeveloped in what was posited. The latter, however, or the [112] content, was not of the kind that would thus move on its own to its becoming-other and back from it; rather, it was something dead whose movement was outside it: pure being is sufficient unto itself [*für sich befriedigt*]. The *infinity* into which pure being or nothingness went over was this being and not-being of the antitheses, their vanishing and coming forth. But this movement [was] only an external one—that is, one in which only the being of deter-minacy came forth—and then its not-being as the being of some other. That from which what came forth proceeded and [into which] what vanished lost itself, the inner, the zero of the passage [*Durchgang*], [was] that empty being, or the nothing itself. The absolute concept is itself what is without concept, uncomprehended; the equivalence is only the nothing.

In the *relations* each was posited thus: as connecting with the other—

---

preservative aspect of sublation—that caused Hegel to accept Schelling's extension of the Kantian doctrine of "construction" from mathematics to philosophy in the first place. This is quite unaffected by the change of terminology.

The criticism of geometry from the *Phenomenology* is to be found at paragraph 42 of Miller's translation, p. 24.

in its being *per se*, only being in the equivalence with the other, or as self-sublating. There was expressed only the requirement of being *per se*, which could not be realized; what was posited as self-subsistent being vanished instead in its realization. Only in the relation of thinking did being *per se* define itself as what would be because it is equal to its contrary, and would maintain itself as itself in its contrary—[that is,] as reflection into its very self. As definition, the latter posited a determinate, negative unity as this reflection into itself, to which universality or positive unity was restored in division; and both [unities], *qua* posited in *one*, are cognition: the positing of the numerical *one* as of something universal and divided, and of the taking back of this divided *one* into the negative unity. *Here reflection describes itself.* Cognition a) has a definition, the display of the *one*[114] of self-subsistent being in such a way that it has taken up its determinacy into universality—an immediate oneness that has already *come back* from the movement of separating and of sublating the separation and in which, in the immediate unity of the determinacy and the universal, the movement and the being-apart is nullified. Definition is not merely the *definitum*, nor merely the definition, but precisely the unity of the two: the *definitum* [is] the *one*, the singular, immediately the "this"— the definition, the same [one] released from its immediacy and simple unity and divided in itself, in such a way, however, that [113] what is divided is not *per se* but rather posited ideally$_2$, as sublated; and its unity is precisely the *one*, the immediacy of "this." b)[115] But it was exhibited as what is dialectical in definition that the *definitum* was not in fact posited as something universal (but rather, as *one* it excluded what was opposed to it and abstracted from it), and that it is to be posited as definition, as reflected into itself, as universal. What is opposed would not thereby fall outside what it abstracts from but would rather be what is equal to itself in its being-other, something divided. The presentation of the subject as thus divided with respect to itself, as an indifferent being that remains itself in multiplicity, is its *construction. It is the division*: not however of a universal, or of a determinate concept—that is, of the [kind of universal that] would be something merely communal, whose parts [are] on their own account while as self-equivalent unity it would fall outside them—but rather, it remains the ground, the sphere embracing the parts, while they

114. *In the margin:* Cognition has (a) *a one, a definition.*
115. *In the margin:* (b) is what is universal, and division; *construction.*

[are] simply and solely parts—that is, connected with one another. It is *precisely* the exposition of their connection that *sublates*[116] this semblance of the being *per se of what is divided,* and BRINGS FORTH the *universal* as *connection,* as the definition. The exposition of the connection is the negative unity that subjects the parts to itself and thereby has exhibited the ONE of the definition as unity—not as one in which differentiation *is* sublated and which abstracts from it, but which is rather *unity*—that is to say, which has division but *within* itself—that is, which is with respect to itself the sublating of the parts. This bringing back of the division of construction to the unity of definition is *proof.*

This movement of cognition has until now always been the exposition of a concept as reality or totality. The first potency was the concept or the definition itself; the second, its construction or its exposition as bad reality, its coming-outside-itself or its becoming-other; and the third, the true reality, or the totality, the moment of sublating this becoming-other through its subsumption under the first unity. With respect to the first unity it was demonstrated that it has in fact a separation in itself; in the face of this separation [it was demonstrated] that the connection rather is essential to it. The negative [114] turning of the separating against the unity, of the unity against the separating, becomes a positive result in reality, which interlocks both [of them] in that it is a universal, self-reflexive definition in which the first and [second] potency are not nothing but are posited as sublated or as ideal$_2$. The spinning forward of the concept through its moments is in this [way] a movement turning back into itself, and its circle is reflection; self-subsistent being is only as this whole of the circle or of reflection.

Through cognition there is first realized the definition,[117] which from the side of the subject is displayed as determinate *one*; and because the *one* is not *qua* unity of the definition but *is the one of the definitum,* the *determinacy* is not *something* sublated as determinacy through the negative unity but subsists as *quality* of the *one,* this being an infinite aggregate of qualities.[118] *On the other side definition is* the same, but *bounded,* as *relation, one* particularity reflected into itself. [The terms

116. *In the margin:* (c) *sublating of construction* [;] *proof.*
117. *In the margin:* Cognition realizes the definition that is α) multiplicity of determinacies, empirical intuition.
118. *In the margin:* β) relation.

of] that aggregate, however, are[119] indifferent vis-à-vis each other; each quality excludes its opposite; and together they make up the whole of so-called empirical intuition, that is, of the being *per se* of the subject as a "this." The determinacy reflected into itself is that of self-preservation, which, being in itself directed outwards against others, turned back into itself, and connected with itself, has sublated inequality in itself. Thus the definition of a right-angled triangle is that a right-angled triangle has the square of the side opposite to the right angle equal to the sum of the squares of the other two sides (its catheti). The former determination[120] [is] that of determinate quality; the latter is that of reflection; for out of the antithesis of one side to the other there is expressed the return or the equality. In its own way the antithesis is that of *one* side against two.

The *definitum* is the *one[ness] of the three sides, figure*; and the *construction* has to demonstrate this one[ness] of the *movement* of the proof. The triangle must be divided so that the indifference of its subsistence may cease and it may become differentiated [115] and thereby come to negative unity. The proof sublates the division in such a way that, out of that first division of the definitum as of something that is, and out of the unity of the parts as a whole, it exhibits the second division and its unity. The first one is the indifferent relation of the whole and the parts. For the second division to originate from it, the first must in fact already be contrary to the whole of "this," must deform it as such, must dismember it (as in the cited example, the figure of the right-angled triangle in fact is lost), and in general must be engendered through helping lines and figures—figures that criss-cross and duplicate the whole piecemeal. It is not this first relation that results from the proof, but a differentiated one in which one part of the whole is equated to another, or to other parts, so that the parts are not equal to the whole but determinate parts are equal to others, [so that] therefore an equality is posited in the inequality or opposition; that is, the whole as unity is a unity returning out of the inequality. What are compared here are not parts of the whole but its moments; the angles and lines of a triangle are not what constitute the figure as a whole, but moments that presuppose the numerical *one*, the principle of the figure, and are its determinacy. The result

119. *Trans.*: This verb is singular in the German text.
120. *Trans.*: "The former determination" = "right-angled triangle"; "the latter" = "its definition."

of the proof is that the indifferent relation of the whole and the parts is at the same time a differentiated relation of the moments. The proof fastens both relations together for the first time; it contains the ground—that is, it discovers that in which the former is indifferently the parts and the latter is a differentiated *one*. In the proof of the Pythagorean theorem it is shown that half the square on one side is equal to half a rectangle produced in the construction by dividing the square on the hypotenuse, since both are equal to a third triangle.[121] All these triangles belong to the construction, the dividing of the figure posited with the square of its sides. From them there is eliminated what belongs to the triangle as figure, and there remains only an equivalence of opposed moments.

This transition from the indifferent to the differentiated relation, and thereby from the positive to the negative [unity] and from parts into moments, is what constitutes the nature of cognition and of real definition. In the [116] concept of proportion or in the definition it is first a question of the determinacy reflected into itself as an essential characteristic that is embodied in the genus, maintains it on its own and makes it into something singular. Through the division the subject becomes for the first time something divided into moments; and cognition displays the unity of both relations.

b / In this way cognition displays what has previously taken place, namely, the transformation of the undifferentiated relation into the differentiated one, and the equivalence of both. Just as the former is itself an equivalence of the whole and the parts, so the latter too is an equivalence of what is posited as simple and what is posited as separated; and cognition is the equivalence of these two equivalences. The antithesis of the second equivalence can be nothing else than that of the two relations. The relation of being is the transition of the infinite or of relation in general into the equal that is equal to itself, into the equal reflected into itself, the universal; the relation of thinking is the transition from the universal into the separation of [the terms] interlocked by the middle, by the unreflective equal, the relation. In the preceding example the relation of being is the right angle, the relation, something equal that is not displayed as equal; and what is equal to it in the triangle (with the side angle beside it) goes over into the hypotenuse as a non-relation, non-equality, but something simple and self-reflexively [*in sich reflectiertes*] simple that

121. *Trans.*: See Euclid, ii, 14.

has posited itself equal to itself, the square on the hypotenuse. Opposed to it stands the breaking up of that line into the opposition of the sides that have a relation to each other [and] together constitute an angle, so that, being [first] self-equivalent as squares in their duality [and] then conjoined as a sum out of their separation, they are equal to the other simple square. It appears not to be the case that here only moments or lines are being compared, rather than figures or parts of the plane triangle or even plane figures; for as squares they are posited equal. However, a square is precisely not a quantum, not a part, not something externally limited.

In cognition, therefore, the preceding is recapitulated; it is the totality of the totality of simple connection, of quantum, and of both relations; and in itself [117] [it is] this circular movement whose content (that passes through this movement) is the definition of this circle. Cognition equates the whole divided into parts to the *one* distinguished into moments—the former undifferentiated equivalence to the latter differentiated equivalence. The whole alone, through its determinacy, is capable of division. It itself is determinacy reflected into itself; and in its indifference it preserves itself through abstraction from the opposites. The other division into moments is the inner determinacy, which, opposed to itself, does not abstract but posits both in itself; only thereby is it the whole equivalent to itself and connected with itself. The relation, or the second division, is as such a/b; but as unity it is the c, = a/b, the quotient and indeed a determinacy, the simple determinacy of the whole, which has the opposite outside itself. What is self-equivalent in the relation is something coming back out of its inequality, something sublating the inequality, and just thereby an opposite, which has, however, annihilated in itself the form of inequality. Thus it has in itself only the form of universality, but in fact is determinately abstract.

Cognition, therefore, posits both relations equal, for within itself it splits the determinacy of the indifferent whole; yet this split, like its reflection, is in fact always something determinate. Thereby the movement of cognition is indeed the universal. But what moves in this way is a particular; for it is a "this," a singular. In other words, it is formal and not equal to its content, which is not absolutely universal.

As the division of the indifferent whole into parts at first indifferent, construction is just for that reason completely indifferent in itself; it turns into a dividing [*Theilung*] into moments, or passes over into division [*Eintheilung*], differentiated relation. Yet as indifferent division it has this principle of differentiation outside itself, and its dividing insofar as it is determined and ruled by the second division, is indifferent vis-à-vis the whole—that is, is not determined through it. In mathematical cognition it indeed turns out at the end that this construction is necessary for the proof; but it has proven itself to be necessary not through itself but only through the proof. That is, it is indeed cognized that the indifferent passes over into the differentiated relation; but this transition is not itself cognized; it is not grasped. The wonder of mathematical proofs is this remaining lack of satisfaction, which indeed passes over from what appears to be contingent in the construction to the necessity of the proof, but which does not grasp that construction [118] through itself because it is not a concept, not something differentiated, and therefore also not the transition.

But the fact that cognition—this reflection of the indifferent whole out of its bifurcation and otherness into its self-equivalence—is still formal, follows from definition being self-preservation—that is, the reflection into itself of the determinacy as such, something determinate posited simply, something that is. It passes over into division; that is, as something universal it becomes differentiated, negative unity. What is dialectical in the definition brings it to this point; and cognition itself is at first nothing but this transition of definition into division. The transition between them is what is empty, the [mere] requirement that definition come to be division, the equivalence of both in general, their interlocking; but *the equal*, their middle, has not yet come forth. Since definition passes in this way into division, it does presuppose for its [middle] the only authentic one among the absolutely indeterminate partitions; that is, definition would just as well have properly to proceed backwards, from division to construction. But so far only *one* path has been pointed out, that of movement, and not this, [namely,] that definition and division precipitate out of the totality itself.

Just for that reason totality or cognition is indeed reflection, which from definition returns by way of division back to it and posits the two as equal—that is, sublates the inequality that issues from the second moment. But since cognition is essentially division as well, the definition does not preserve itself as what it was; self-preservation succumbs to the differentiated unity; and in its reconstruction out of division, definition becomes something other than it was.

The internally reflected determinacy of the definition, or the singular dividing itself, passes over into internal difference, into a duplication of the definition; and the reconstituted unity is the equivalence of both definitions, but an equivalence where the very determinacy of the first sublates itself. This is what makes determinate division possible, a division that collapses once more into what is simple; but what is one in the parts is itself that determinacy of definition. The definition is the self-partitioning universal, and itself one of the parts. In the Pythagorean theorem the determinacy of the right angle α) changes from an external equivalence (or, in other words, from [119] one that has its equivalent alongside itself) into an internal equivalence of [terms], both of which—the hypotenuse and the sides—are posited in the figure; the right angle remains what is equal, universal. β) The right angle becomes something else, a part opposed to it. From being a relation it becomes a line, quotient, determinate magnitude, the hypotenuse opposite to which are the sides. It is thus the equivalence of the square of the hypotenuse and the sum of the squares of the sides, and is present as a moment, as one aspect [*Seite*] of this relation. The definition is produced thus: its determinacy comes to be the universal, the exponent of the relation, which as aspect of that relation at the same time is sublated; but in that aspect the exponent, being determinacy against the other aspect, was universally reflected into itself, and this is what gets lost. Thus, with respect to definition as such, what in cognition preserves itself is not that definition is the determinacy reflected into itself; but rather what preserves itself is reflection, and the sublating of this determinacy with another's having come to be, since the sublated determinacy along with its opposite becomes something simple, which again has the opposites outside it. In other words, cognition is *deduction*. The realization of the concept, which the first moment expresses and which is the universal of the whole sphere, is posited as such a universal—a simple, not reflected, not opposed; in its reflection the universal becomes all this and simultaneously becomes sublated according to this its determinacy. What remains equal with itself and preserves itself is so *qua* unity, *qua* connection (though what is connected becomes another, and thus the whole). The remaining-equal is merely formal; the realizing by means of construction and proof is a transition of definition into division and, from these two, which themselves are the parts of the construction, into the gathering together of both. There is something other than the definition, just as previously in the realization of the concept something other than the concept itself has always arisen for us. What remains equal to itself in its totality is the pure unity, which, however,

comes to be a negative unity, sublating its own as well as the opposite
determinacy. The result is that the universal of the sphere is something deduced, something for which the antitheses, being ideal$_2$ and
extinguished therein, are as simple moments (which were the real
moments for the other that was its concept). It is the universal that
realizes itself just as much, that [in] remaining equal to itself duplicates
itself and thus constructs itself. These real moments (of which the
universal in its determinacy is itself one, ideal$_2$,[122] posited as sublated,
in a negative unity) form its totality, which is reality and something
other than its concept. It is the antithetic path of the climbing of the
singular to universality [120] and of the universal to singularity immediately united. The deduced sphere is a singular, negative *one*, as
unity of the preceding moments. As realizing itself once more, itself
as something determinate, and as in the contrary of its determinacy
remaining equal to itself, it is at the same time as singular immediately
a universal or a particular. In the totality, however, annihilating these
determinacies one through another, it is universal. Conversely, the
sphere as unrealized is a universal, which in duplicating itself comes
to particularity and [which] as negative unity of its duplication [comes]
to singularity.

These two paths of climbing up and down cross each other and
meet in the middle term, which is particularity or bad reality, not in
the absolute middle. Only in connection with an other is the sphere
its·deduction, a singular, not in the connection in which the other is
a universal—in other words, not within its own sphere itself. For in
the latter the other is universal; and as totality it becomes singularity
again, though an other singularity than what it was before.

Therefore, as absolute reflection on its own account and [as] equality
of the simple connection and of both relations, cognition has in itself
this inequality, which appears distinct from the indicated aspects as
well. What passes through this circle of reflection, the content, is not
itself this absolute circle; content and cognition fall asunder. In its
reflection into itself the content becomes something else instead, while
the cognition is deduction, itself a circle that in its return is transition
into another circle. In its repetition in the diverse spheres into which
it passes, cognition is the same. But the content is a diverse one, and
becomes unlike itself; its return into itself is rather a spinning forward
into another; inasmuch as its negative unity alters the moments whose

---

122. *Trans.*: CE has made this an adverb rather than an adjective.

negative unity it is. *Qua* negative unity enclosing itself within itself, it falls outside cognition and is what is passive vis-à-vis the othering of cognition; *qua* content, or negative unity that moves within cognition, it differentiates itself within itself, becoming instead unlike itself. Content either preserves itself, thus falling outside cognition and having cognition outside itself; [or] it is the movement of cognition, thus arriving outside itself and becoming an other than it is itself.

The inequality develops to the point where, opposed to a cognition that remains the same [in] all spheres, a cognition as the transition [*Übergehen*] from singular to universality, or conversely, as diversity of content, opposed to what is going over [*dem Übergehenden*], there stands cognition itself, inasmuch as in its reflection (that is, the finding of itself) it is an other. The in-itself, [121] what is self-equivalent, is not what is posited as reflected into itself, but cognition; though this—as the movement of this transition, of what alters itself in reflecting—is the universal, the particularity of which comprises the moments of this cycle but which presupposes a content, a negative *one*, whose rest is set in motion through [that universal]. But in fact this form of what is at rest, of result or product, is itself a moment of cognition, the welding together of the moments as self-sublating. And cognition is in and of itself a pure self-equivalent cycle. Since cognition is deduction, what it starts from—the negative *one*—is itself again its final term. For the universality of cognition there is only unity of opposite moments; and their determinacy falls away along with the fact that what is deduced is an other than what it started from. Yet deduction coincides wholly with cognition—that is, is itself reflection. Over against this self-equivalent [cycle] there nevertheless stands a self-altering content. With respect to it cognition is essentially deduction; for content exists as simple unity, determinacy reflected into itself, which in its realization does not turn back into itself but is a moment of another simple unity. Because of its determinacy, content as a universal must enter on the one side; in its moments cognition is indeed itself something determinate; yet in itself [it is] a universal, inasmuch as it is the unity of its moments, the entire cycle. With respect to content, determinacy is posited as reflected into itself, as something indifferent; with respect to cognition it is posited only as something sublated. The moment of content with respect to cognition is thereby not negative *one*, indifferent determinacy, but negative unity, infinity, absolute (that is, self-sublating) determinacy, which [has determined] itself to be what it is. What cognition separates itself from is the indifferent *one*, undifferentiated determinacy reflected into itself. Inasuch as it fixes itself as negative unity, it sublates itself as this deductive process, which runs off without rest or respite backwards and forwards into bad infinity—a grounding whose very ground, according to its essence, it is necessary to ground once more. For as negative unity it incorporates the antithesis of what is grounded, while as determinate, it is itself once again only a moment, which as negative *one* must be deduced but which can itself exist merely as moment in a proof for which the *one* is to constitute the ground. Being this determinate content, the ground must be deduced, [122] and so on in an infinite regress. As the universal of the sphere—that is, as ground—it is not that which interlocks; but it was so as a result of deduction. As ground of the sphere it is the basis, the universal, of the construction; but in the proof it has become just *one* moment and sublated, since it is negative *one*, and cognition proceeds from it to the totality in which it has become an other. But insofar as ground is the universal or the basis of the construction, the totality is its realization. In it the ground becomes negative *one*; its particularization is not comprised within [the ground], but to the extent that it, as determinate, places itself on one side as a moment, only to that extent it sublates itself. Insofar as it is considered only as universal, however, the universal remaining the whole process of realization, to that extent its reality stands opposed to it. It is indifferent, posited as being in and of itself; and the movement of cognition proceeding from it to reality is for it something alien. For the necessity of thus proceeding would lie only in its determinacy, which, however, because ground is supposed to be being *per se*, is out of the question; proceeding in this way the determinacy would sublate the ground.

Cognition is the universal as totality, since in it the whole content of the universal is displayed in a developed way; it is the whole reflection, which in its alteration remains simply self-equivalent; it is free from the content, which, as something indifferent, abstracts from its determinacy and which has separated it from itself outside itself. Through cognition, which is directed towards its determinacy, however, the content comes to be posited in the way it is with respect to itself, namely, as an other. The universality of cognition is itself this form of indifference, in which the content enters, or the cognition is only content, what is posited in this indifferent form. The determinacy itself becomes only a content, by way of the form of cognition. Cognition itself, however, expresses itself with respect to the content, so that its positing itself in this way is a deductive process—in other words, so that the content alters itself. The nature of the content is thus the same as that of cognition; the content as determinacy reflected into itself goes over *qua* determinacy into another. The content realizes its reflectedness, and sublates itself as this determinate indifferent [thing], and becomes another indifferent [thing]. Cognition is itself just this transition; the content falls asunder; it is a series of indifferent [things] that enter as isolated, each on its own account. The unity is the differentiated unity of cognition. The indifferent [things] form a line; the unity is a circle and is only deduction, itself a series of circles as to content or as seen from the side of content. *The content* is again itself this repetition of reflection into itself, for each of its singulars is what is reflected into itself. Its [123] determinacy, or what the content is for the differentiation of cognition, consists in its having other content next to itself. This [latter] content is not for it. In other words, it is not its differentiated unity; but rather this unity is cognition, its inner or outer, which is the same; only it is not what the content is posited to be. The self-equivalent circle of cognition is in this way itself something indifferent [*gleichgültiges*] to the content, wholly fulfilled in itself, the absolute reflection into itself, but only as a universal.

Cognition, as a universal itself from the side of negative unity, sublates the content as indifferent [*indifferent*]. The indifferent content is itself derived from it; and cognition goes over into the content. From definition, cognition comes to be cognition through division; for cognition is itself a definition, and it has not sublated itself as definition. It is itself still formal. It is the transition out of definition through division into another definition; and as definition it again stands opposed to the first definition as an other one. The former one would be sublated, of course; but cognition itself is determined as a definition stemming from it; and thereby the former is for it just as well, or [is] another one. For as this moving or sublating, cognition is opposed to the former rest or being; and *qua* not at rest, *qua* not in being, *qua* a moment of cognition, definition is something other than the cognition whose moment it is. It is on its own account determinacy reflected into itself; but cognition as self-subsistent is the sublatedness of the determinacy, and into this rest it indeed passes over as a universal and becomes through it a content next to another content. For it to be its concept absolutely and not formally, it would itself have to be its own content, its moment; and the moment would thus be indistinguishable from the whole—in other words, from the universal.

Cognition is therefore the self-equivalent reflection into itself, which, though not itself a moment, not yet posited as a singular, has as a universal another content than itself, whose movement, however, it is. The self-equivalence of cognition preserves itself in virtue of its sublating the content, which is other than it, making [it] into an other than itself. It thus asserts against this alien [content] that it is not alien to it but is rather posited *qua* alien as sublated. What is thus sublated as alien is itself, however, once again a content; for it is to itself posited as not sublated, coinciding with cognition, an other, and so something determined again. The former, however, still alien to cognition, something not determined through it, is outside [124] cognition, or just on that account also its inner. Both together, cognition is still. . . .[123]

. . . the content, determining it, as the movement, or rather as the differentiated unity, as positive in the preceding moment. The former, distinguished as totality in itself, determines in both of the latter the antithesis of cognition as totality over against its moments, or determines the determinacy of the content in opposite ways.

Cognition itself is the universal, or the basis of these three ways of considering—in other words, of these three determinacies of cognition itself, posited indifferently vis-à-vis each other. It is that which subsists in itself, the absolute, since it is what is closed within itself, absolute reflection, and since as this reflection it is the universality of the antithesis posited in this universality. Reflection, as opposed to the content, is reflected into itself in such a way that it expresses this antithesis in the totality of its moments, and is intuition—that is, their self-equivalent indifference.

Such being in and of itself, or cognition, is the last to halt immediately: for in the circle it turns back into itself and, although the content always alters, it remains self-equivalent in it—does not itself spin forward any more, but as content (that is, as something determined by standing over against the determined content) is rather not content, and simply falls outside of the movement of cognition; it is not [as] moment, but in and of itself. Cognition is what is thereby taken from the relation; for the content is on the contrary what is

123. *Trans.*: The inner half of the double sheet 39 is missing.

differentiated. Cognition only solicits in order rather to perish in the content, and in its cycle to be determined and altered rather than to alter and determine. In this way cognition is the realized infinity, which is thrown apart in the doubled relation and returned to itself. Their moments were abstractions; the moments of cognition are themselves infinite, are relations. The whole pathway has been nothing but an enrichment of these moments. Cognition, as this in-itself that has withdrawn from all connection with another and whose moments [125] are themselves totalities reflected into themselves, is no longer [the] object of logic (which has constructed the form up to its absolute concretion) but rather of metaphysics (in which this totality must be realized in the same way as the totalities have been set forth up to now, they being only moments of the absolute totality). What meaning the realization [will]¹²⁴ receive here—whether this idea itself [will] go over into something else, whether it still has in itself a determinacy— will become clear in this science itself. [126]

124. *Trans.*: CE inserts "must" here. We have chosen the milder alternative.

Metaphysics

The discussion of cognition at the end of the Logic is like the section on infinity at the end of "Simple Connection." Only a formal review of cognition can be given in the Logic because cognition is the proper topic of Metaphysics. In the Logic it is a climax that poses a problem. The logical self comes to the recognition of itself as the free agency that the ethical substance sustains, and upon which the fate of substance itself hangs. Now the problem is: how is the identity of this absolute cognition with the historic moment of consciousness in which it has emerged to be realized? The first step is for cognition to comprehend its own objective structure. Metaphysics shows us the process of logical consciousness from the side of the substance itself. It is the absolute self-consciousness of the substance. (Thus Metaphysics corresponds to chapters 6 to 8 of the *Phenomenology*; and cognition is only the formal "certainty and truth of reason.")[1]

Hence every moment is *eternal*. The absolute transience of simple connection is now seen as the absolute permanence of the principles of rational consciousness. Logic began with the unity of consciousness as self-equivalent. Metaphysics begins with the *principle* of self-equivalence (and shows that this must be a self-mediation).

Logic ceases at the point where relationship ceases and where its members fall asunder as beings on their own account. For cognition as reflection into itself comes to be its own first moment; it unfolds

---

1. Since the two discussions are so vividly different, it seems unlikely that any useful parallel can be established between the moments or phases of the two texts at this level of the argument. Where Logic passes over into Metaphysics, the phenomenology of spirit becomes the explicit *Bildung* of the *Weltgeist*.

as what is passive and self-subsistent beside cognition (as another moment, which has its reflection into itself); it is the other of itself; and as itself it is connection with another. This differentiated cognition, as it connects with another, posits this other itself as an other itself; it is no longer an other for us, but rather for itself; that is, it negates itself. For the unity of reflection is what remains constant in the moments of cognition; and the otherness of its own self is for cognition itself. In other words, otherness is its moment; it itself is ideal₂ on its own account. This is for us: that the object of cognition is the whole cognition. This is for cognition, as formal: that in the object cognition is something negated, something other. Its otherness has only its own negative meaning; the object [is] only determined as this other; within it [the other] itself is only negated. The in-itself of metaphysics is this form of cognition: what is negative for cognition. The course of metaphysics—that is, the coming to itself of cognition out of its other or the cognition that becomes cognition—is that this undifferentiated other (something differentiated for the cognition) determines itself only as its negation, whereby cognition becomes that which is solely positive, or the true in-itself.

As the universal for which there is an other, cognition is at first simply connected with this other; it is the undifferentiated space of this other, and its movement as reflection into itself is this: this other moves within it as simple connection; it comes and disappears. In the space of cognition an other is posited and it returns into itself again, so that this other sublates itself. As at the same time differentiated vis-à-vis what thus comes and disappears, cognition is itself this its negative connection. Since the other is the in-itself—that is, it is the essential—the differentiated connection of cognition is thus only superficial; over against it stands the in-itself, and its movement is still on its own account. As above, there are only two passives, two self-subsistent beings, hence two movements on their own account, which [127] just thereby are indifferent to each other. But as movements these are immediately in one pure indifference [*Indifferenz*], in *one* universality, in *one* space; and this is determined immediately as negative unity, as infinity, because it is the unity of these movements, which are themselves differentiated vis-à-vis one another. It is the essence of their differentiation [*Differenz*], their absolute differentiation, or infinity. For the negative reflection, [that is] the comes-and-disappears,[2] or this uniquely linear movement, is connected with its passive self-equivalency, or equally with the movement of cognition as one that bends this linear moving into a circle. Since that necessity is determined through this cognition, the linear othering must reflect itself into itself, or its connection must become self-equivalent. And in that cognition thus [makes][3] that first movement disappear (just as its passive, unopened connection with itself coincides with its circular movement), so everything in it is closed. And the in-itself of the passive is still only something negative; cognition is absolutely negative unity of movement, sublating the other. It is absolute "I," cognition as negative *one*, hence at once another potency and its first moment.

Since it is the sublating of the differentiated connection of logic, cognition snatches away the moments from the idea (from the dialectical advance and sublating), posits them determinately as undifferentiated or as self-subsistent, and denies with respect to them [*von ihnen*] this self-sublating. They are moments of knowledge, and as such essentially on their own account, since they were hitherto undifferentiated in general (that is, indifferent as to whether they were undifferentiated or differentiated). For cognition itself is this negation of itself, or the being *per se* of the other—that is, of the other formerly posited as differentiated, as ideal$_2$, or moment. As what passes into metaphysics, cognition is just the sublating of logic as dialectic or idealism.

Directed this way initially, cognition posits the moments of its reflection determinately as being-in-itself, not as possibly disappearing but rather determinately as remaining. Cognition amounts to the moment of absolute principles.[128]

1 / Cognition as System of First Principles

As reflection that has become simple, cognition is self-equivalence that persists even in oppostion; a universality that negatively posits itself determinately as universality, is universality on its own account. The universality of the logic was an unpolemical one; in this one now, the ideal$_2$ is posited, thereby snatched away again from becoming sub-

---

2. *Trans.*: *Das kommt und verschwindet*, because of the neuter article, cannot modify the feminine *Reflexion*.

3. *Trans.*: Ehrenberg and Link reads "and while cognition, that is, that first movement [must] disappear . . . ."

lated, and indeed posited as excluding the becoming-sublated. What disappears and comes in cognition is simply and solely something relative, something in connection; but this negative unity, the other[ness], is sublated; in itself it is thereby on its own account. The content of cognition as thus persisting is nothing but the universal determinacy, the moments of cognition itself, which, as not to be sublated, express the absolute being and essence of all things. Cognition, as self-equivalent reflecting, reflects the whole logic (this advance into itself), posits it equal to itself, sublates the othering of the moments, and posits them as a system of absolute being *per se*, so that from being something differentiated, what is opposed becomes only something diverse, whose [elements][4] subsist indifferently next to one another. Until now it has been a moment of our procedure to take each result or each determinacy in general as something positive at first and then to sublate it. That positive taking counted as one side whereby nothing was yet decided about the determinacy; in general it was a thought, something that belongs to us. Here in cognition this positive is posited on its own account, and the determinacy is cut off from its two sides: backwards, from that of which it was the result, and forwards, from that of which it passed over to an other. The in-itself of cognition has indeed sublated the singular. In universality substantiality has passed away; but in cognition (or in its becoming) through thorough division, subject, or the negative *one*, has passed away. The determinacies, to whom the subject imparts being *per se*, are what is known, [are] posited as what is essentially taken from the becoming sublated, and therefore [are] moments of the subject itself in that it is this not-to-be-sublated universal.

The positive side of the previous discussion was not only a being posited [in] thought. [129] Rather, by virtue of its being posited in thought it was also the content or the determinacies themselves, universals; and the logic began with unity itself as the self-equivalent. Logic did [not] vindicate itself on this score; that happens here for the first time, since the in-itself here posits itself as a self-equivalence, [an in-itself] in which all moments are abolished and which emerges from this abolition. That unity at the beginning is a result, but that it is a result was not at all asserted with respect to it; it was a subjective

4. *Trans.*: The verb is singular here, presupposing "something diverse" as subject. By introducing a plural subject we have had to alter the number of the verb.

result, from which it was to be surmised that much must have preceded it in order to begin with it. Here in the absolute return to itself [the unity] is as this result. Insofar as it was not posited as a result, [the unity] was an arbitrary beginning that had absolutely many [others] next to it; it was a contingent first. Here it turns out to be an absolute first, or that which, after it realizes itself, has opposed to itself in fact the absolutely many, or as connection, has opposed to itself the absolutely many connections—that is, relationship. Having come back to itself, it has preserved itself, but as one that has thus come back to itself, that has annihilated the possibility of the many, of the other, and that is an in-itself, which as cognition (that is, as this movement and reflection) has sublated itself. The advance from this unity was precisely its not having been cognized, or this: that it was the possibility of the other. It was the movement of reflection that sublates itself, that leaves only the moments as diverse, being self-subsistent in their determinacy and indeed "in themselves" (in the sense that "in itself" has in cognition) as what are above [and] beyond sublation. According to their form, the moments have been up to now just such universals; they are cognized as they proceed from what is absolutely simple. That is, their form was that of cognition, of the sublatedness of multiplicity, even though according to their content they themselves were determinate. For example, causes and what follows after are determinate, but not universal in the way of an animal, which is followed by gender; rather, they are the universals of knowledge, with respect to which all determinacy is abolished. [Their determinacy is] the sort that they have in the antithesis, as result; [it is] the necessary determinacy, that is, the one that they only acquire just in this cycle. Their previous form as [object of] cognition is now what is essential to them; or [they are] self-equivalent, and self-subsistent in such a way that cognition, as self-moving reflection with respect to them, is abolished. They are the in-itself of cognition; it is cognition itself for which they are essential.

Thus the unity or the self-equivalent goes with the abolition of all diversity and is in itself, so that next to it there is an other. Unity is present as what is thus determinate, apart from which [130] there is another and which, in its connection with another, remains indifferent in it and unchanged. Similarly, the many that is opposed to it is thus on its own account, [hence] abolished; as opposed on its own account it is opposed to itself and becomes fixed as this $+$ or $-$. There is no third in which it would sublate itself. Thus, finally, the connection of both, the third, is likewise in itself, and what is determinate is present only as thus connected with its other, and as being in this connection.

A / PRINCIPLE OF IDENTITY OR OF CONTRADICTION

True propositions do not change and vanish like conscious selves. But in order to be cognitively significant, they must relate two distinct terms. Thus a cognitive identity involves a formal contradiction. The tree is not just tree but an *oak*—and that entails a multitude of differences between it and other trees.

This multitude can all be spelled out as determinate differences: the oak is deciduous (not evergreen); its leaves are not like maple leaves, and so on. And this mass of truths is the same identical truth as "The tree is an oak."

The unity of a truth is thus the ground of all the other truths it contains. This ground is rational consciousness. Thus in the principle of ground, cognition "comes to itself." But here, too, finite cognition "goes to the ground" (perishes), so that it is aware of the contrast between itself and the imperishable truth. We must pass to the "metaphysics of objectivity" because of this contrast.

The self equivalent is such, with indifference vis-à-vis every determinacy. $A = A$, let A signify what you will. The determinacy is posited in this self-equivalence; but in such a way that the self-equivalence is not affected by the determinacy and has completely abolished the otherness of the determinacy, which is now on its own account. Determinacy as quality, or for that matter as universal and as subject, is posited on its own account in the form of being, but in such a way that its essence—[which is] to be determinate—is; and in such a way that it is not to be withdrawn in general from becoming other [*Anderswerden*], but only from a determinate otherness [*Anderssein*]. For that very reason it cannot save itself from being sublated, since it is in general open to becoming sublated. But here, on the other hand, absolute self-equivalence is posited: a negation of reflection in general, or of transition into another. It is not the determinacy A that is in itself but the fact that it is self-equivalent; this is what is in itself. And the determinacy is withdrawn from otherness only because it is in fact abolished as this determinacy, only because it is wholly ideal$_2$; in other words, it is posited as something cognized. It is self-equivalent, so that $A = A$ expresses a diversity (that is, two A's), and this diversity, this other[ness], immediately is not. The two A's *ought* not just to be equivalent; it is not a case of A = B: B ought also to be an A. But A = A; that is, it is the same A that is on both sides. They do not have an inequality in virtue of their place, as in judgment, merely through being left or right when written, or earlier or later when spoken. These are distinctions that fall away immediately in that one [can]not say which is right or left, etc.; [131] it is not as [if] one were on the right and another on the left; each is the one and the other.

Here self-equivalence has become a principle, and it is this principle that expresses absolute equality, the in-itself,[5] for in this way it is displayed as self-equivalence reflected into itself, but one that has brought about reflection into itself, so that its semblance is there as opposition to it; but this is also in fact wholly sublated, pure semblance.

This principle of equivalence, a posited equivalence that is in itself, is thus withdrawn from dialectic; the equivalence cannot be sublated, since it has completely sublated all sublating, and indeed every connection with another. The determinacy A in which it is expressed is indifferent throughout; and this determinacy that is distinct in itself—materialized, as it were—is posited purely in the interest of expression. But this necessity of taking in some determinacy or other (indifferent though it be towards itself but just for that reason not as sublated) in order to express the completion of reflection into itself, or the semblance of opposition within itself—this is just where the not-being-in-itself of this self-equivalence is immediately expressed. The opposition is completely sublated, and precisely for that reason the determinacy is posited as not in itself. But it is the determinacy in fact that is posited in the form of self-equivalence, as having been in itself. A = A; if we abstract from A, the whole principle is sublated; if we posit it, then self-equivalence is predicated of it as a determinacy; but this predicating immediately dissolves into nothing. "The tree is tree" is the nullity of the cognition of the tree. As determinacy the tree is not something reflected into itself but quite the contrary; yet it is posited so. What strictly has no being in itself is posited as having it. The feeling of this contradiction (that the identity principle sublates itself) expresses itself in this way: that nothing at all is said in such a statement. "The tree is . . . "—we expect that something will be said about it, something that expresses it as maintaining itself in a determinacy, as remaining identical in the determinacy of the predicate. But "The tree is tree" simply does not even express the in-itself of the tree, in

5. *Trans.*: CE transforms the noun *An sich* into an adverb, *an sich*.

that it does not set it forth as something reflected into itself. The
expression of its opposition, into which it has gone and out of which
it has recovered itself, would be necessary for that. It [would need to
be] displayed out of that opposition, and indeed, the opposition being
posited with respect to it, it [would need to] reflect itself. [132] The
principle A = A falls apart into two "insofars," two sides that are mutually indifferent in it, each one being quite alien and contingent vis-à-vis
the other. The determinacy is contingent for the self-equivalence to
the extent that to have the latter we must abstract from the former,
and vice versa. The two are in fact connected with each other, and
when posited as one, each sublates the other. Hence, although the
self-equivalent and the determinacy are united, they are not united
in such a way that the latter should be subsumed under the former
and rendered ideal$_2$; on the contrary, the determinacy is quite indifferent to the self-equivalent. So in this way there is in fact only a
connection of the absolutely many, but of the many posited as something unconnected, as something self-subsisting. There has in fact to
be connection, however, determination of the one through the other.

B / FIRST PRINCIPLE OF THE EXCLUSION OF A THIRD

The many posited on its own account, as the self-equivalent and the
determinacy, is not opposed to and connected with a third but connected with itself and simply opposed one to the other (and hence
also connected). The one is not what the other is; otherwise, they have
no determinate character. The many as something reflected into itself
(or having being in itself) is posited as excluding what is opposed to
it, the unity in which it becomes ideal$_2$; it is not something opposed
as a many but rather as a sublated many that is not opposed. Thus it
does not exclude this third, its becoming-sublated.

The many, as cognized, reflected into itself, ceases to have indifference (the being-external-to-it of distinction and of connection with
another) and has it [the being-external] in itself. It is not another
generally but another in itself and is thus only determined by its
opposite. The many as such is self-equivalent and in this way set
against unity, but precisely thereby not distinguished from it, since
unity is self-equivalence. Here, however, the many is not many in
general, self-equivalent, but rather as it is in itself, apart from this
equivalence—something reflected into itself. The many as it is in itself
is thus strictly [133] not the indifferent determinacy next to which

there are others. Thus the many has so far been dealt with only in connection with its opposite—which might appear just as contingent as beginning with unity. But just as it emerged that the in-itself is reflectedness into itself (the state where distinction has been abolished—that is, unity) and that philosophy deals with the in-itself, or the absolute, so the in-itself is immediately unity, and what is first in philosophy. Similarly, the many enters immediately, through opposition to unity; but whether they only are in connection with one another is a matter of indifference for it *qua* many. The mutually indifferent many posited themselves in connection with unity and *qua one* with it, as self-sublating; and this connection appeared as a consideration alien to the many. But here it is posited that the many in itself is, in fact, only as the opposite; it is only in its connection with the other. And it is this differentiation in particular to which non-philosophic thought must first rise out of its intuiting; from the indifference of the many it must emerge to this point where the many is in itself simply and solely in connection with the opposite.

These opposites are, then, unity and the many itself. At first the many appeared as opposed to unity; and just for that reason unity itself is an opposite, included in the many, *one* of the many. The many ceases to be an indifferent many for this reason alone, because its many *are posited* as determined in this way: on one side, the not-many or the one; on the other side, the not-one or the many. Herewith the many divides into a many that is a many, and a many that is no many. That is how the many is with respect to itself.

This many, as it is in itself, excludes every third. For the third would be the unity of the two opposites of the many; but this unity is itself one of its members. Thus its exclusion of the third does not mean that there might still be something else outside it; rather, there is no other outside it. There is in it every other; there is in it[6] the other of its own self; it has unity, the contrary of itself, as one of its members. What it excludes is not something indifferent, for then that would not be something excluded. What is excluded is what is negated by it, but precisely thereby it is posited with respect to it. What is thus excluded, what it negates, is nothing but unity itself; for the other of its own self is [134] precisely what it excludes in order to be what it is. What is excluded from the many is just that which the many is not and which the many holds off from itself in order to be. It is therefore

6. *Trans.*: *Es ist an ihm selbst* in both cases.

the other of the many; but the many is the other of its own self, and
so it is what is thus excluded from itself.

   Positing itself thus (as it is in itself) both as a many that is a many
and as a many that is no many—[positing itself] as what it excludes
from itself in order to be, or, in other words, not as itself at all but
rather as the contrary of itself—the many is that which sublates itself.
It is in itself in fact the nothing of itself. It is not the nothing, for it
is itself again. As the many that is unity, it is nullified; as the many
that is itself, it is itself self-equivalent. Hence it is neither itself nor
the contrary of itself, and just as much itself as the contrary of itself.
These two are not diverse ways of viewing it that are external to it or
that it is indifferent to; they are not a distinguishing and a sublating
of the distinction, which might not be posited with respect to it. Rather
it is this in fact with respect to itself—in itself the absolute contradiction, or infinity posited in one, or as an indivisible, self-equivalent
unity. Thus it is, in fact, not the many as an either / or—the many
that just divides into opposed terms—but the third for these terms,
or the absolute immediate unity of them both, and a simple inward
self-destroying, the absolute concept, which is, with respect to itself,
the contrary both of the determinacy and of the sublated determinacy.
The *in-itself* is thus neither the first nor the second first principle in
the way they expressed themselves; rather, they are in themselves the
third.[7]

C / PRINCIPLE OF GROUND

The determinate is, then, simply the other of itself, or *one* with its
contrary; and this unity alone is its in-itself or its *ground*: as [135] much
that into which it returns as that from which it departs; that is, that
wherein it sublates itself, and that which it is, as a self-equivalent
determinacy. The being of the determinacy is its being posited as
something self-equivalent; and in connection with its reflection this is
its point of departure. As this self-equivalent determinacy it becomes
its contrary. In other words, it displays itself as that which it is, as a
many; it returns into itself; and it is thus the unity of itself, and its
opposed determinacy. This unity is its ground; the ground is the unity
itself as self-equivalent determinacy. "The determinacy has a ground"

7. *In the margin*: All singulars would contradict themselves.

means two things: determinacy is posited within itself as in a unity of itself and its contrary; as this determinate one, determinacy has this unity for its ground, a ground that divides into them (that is, into determinacy and its own contrary)[8] or engenders them. Their being engendered out of their ground is nothing other than that the ground confronts itself, makes itself into one side and stands opposite itself as its own contrary. Determinacy as indifferent is called "ground"— ground of itself, insofar as it appears in the differentiation. And again it is the ground as this unity of the determinacy posited differentially[9]— [as this unity of] it as that against which it is differentiated, or as the opposite of itself; hence it is that in which it sublates itself.

Herewith the ground shows itself as the reflection of cognition itself, as the self-enclosed simple. Cognition has in this way come to itself, in that it has reached the ground; it finds itself as the in-itself. [Previously] it was in relation to [*für*] the in-itself;[10] [now] it is the in-itself of [*für*] the in-itself, since the ground is for the in-itself.

Cognition was the circular movement of the return into itself, and thus the in-itself. *Qua* this in-itself it sublates itself, as that in which the posited is changed; it is the self-equivalent in which something other than it, as something self-equivalent, is connected only with itself. Its content is the determinacy that is in itself, posited according to the first principle as a self-equivalent determinacy. For cognition it is initially the formal in-itself, or it posits itself as its first moment; and indeed according to the determinacy of this first moment [it posits itself] in a simple form. The necessity of once again becoming itself out of its having become—in which case a start is made with itself in the form of the first power[11]—lies in cognition's coming to a point as reflection while it is circumference as movement. In its movement positive self-equivalence is, as it were, its [136] universal space; but it is at the same time negative unity, the *one* of the point, that in which the distinguishing of its moments sublates itself, a unity as its negative connection in which cognition is sublated. This unity is its moment

---

8. *Trans.*: Hegel first wrote "a ground that divides into itself and its contrary." In making the addition he perhaps forgot to change the gender of "its" modifying "contrary." If he had changed it, the text would read "into determinacy and its contrary."

9. *Trans.*: Following ms. CE: "as of one posited differentially."

10. *Trans.*: Following ms. CE emends: "it was the in-itself for [us]." The editors refer to CE 126, ll. 11–19.

11. *Trans.*: *Potenz*. Compare Schelling and Cartesian geometry.

and is opposed to it in its motion, which simply is connected with it; and this *one* is the one that appears as content of cognition and what comes to be the ground.

This realization of cognition is its second becoming; in the first it becomes the other that it is; in the second it becomes so for itself. The content that comes to ground is the becoming of cognition within itself—that is, its becoming for itself. However, this ground is indeed cognition, insofar as cognition[12] is for cognition; but in its reflection into itself (or in that it is ground), this its content as negative unity (or indeed itself, though as *one*) is at the same time within this determinacy. The content as self-equivalent determinacy becomes an other than itself in that as ground it has come to be totality; but this becoming other is now completely determined in that this cycle is its own. Thus it retains the determinacy that it has outwardly as something opposed to cognition, or as that wherein cognition negates itself. It is in itself, and as ground it becomes reflection into itself; but it still remains in itself as negated cognition. Cognition has not yet re-cognized this other cognition as itself. The ground *is* a cognition, but as something cognized, as something still affected with antithesis vis-à-vis cognition; this differentiation is not yet sublated. That is to say, it *is* sublated, but cognition has not yet sublated it.

Still to be determined is how ground or cognition (which for us are the same) display themselves for their part, in as much as they [are] still not *one*[13] for themselves but posit themselves in opposition. This being encumbered with a differentiation, in that they are the total reflection into themselves, lies in the moments of this reflection being posited for one another, each still external to the other, or mutually indifferent. We come back to the same determination that was initially made, with the difference that in ground these moments are, of course, equally indifferent, but that ground is the content of cognition; hence [it is] the sort of cognition that has indifferent moments [that] is this totality of formal cognition, indeed the moment of formal cognition. The other moments are this very totality [137] in the determinacy of the moments, and mutually indifferent. The difference in the way the ground is posited is that the ground is for cognition and in cognition. Because of this it not only is with respect to cognition; but

---

12. *Trans.*: The ms: *dasselbe*. CE reads *derselbe*, "ground."
13. *Trans.*: Hegel inserted in the margin "They are substances, souls," then struck it out.

there is posited the necessity that the ground make its way through reflection. It is on its own account, but at the same time a first moment, a determinate content of cognition. It is not possible to stay there, but its way is laid out before it—the ground must realize itself. In the progress up to this point, what is displayed as result or totality of a sphere was totality; and it became again its first power by means of a consideration that was initially applied to it from the outside, as it were: it was undetermined whether this totality might not be the last that would not first have to realize [itself] in this way through reflection into itself. Here, by contrast, the ground is immediately torn away from its being-in-itself and from the opposition against its movement, because in cognition it is posited as the point that arises from cognition in its movement. As a result the path is not first displayed by the going but [is] outlined beforehand; just as the necessity to travel it is posited in its having already been embarked upon in fact.

The ground, thus determined as reflection into itself, as cognition in itself, and at the same time connected with cognition, corresponds to that moment in the unreflective Logic that was called the relation of being and that is now posited as being in and of itself, self-enclosed, and held back from disappearing in the dialectic. The path that it travels in cognition is indeed its own dialectic; but this side of the path is what is not yet posited for cognition. To begin with, in other words, nothing is posited but its connection with cognition: cognition is at the same time the movement of reflection; but ground is in this connection posited as in itself—that is, although self-moving, yet indifferent towards the movement and unchangable through it. By contrast, the relation of being is posited as undifferentiated, or liable just as much to be changed as to remain indifferent. Here, by contrast, this relationship is posited as being in itself, as such reflected into itself. The relation of being passes over into the repose of universality. The ground, however, is in itself the universal that has negative *ones* (or substances that [are] in relation) ideally$_2$, as contained within it, but in such a way that in their ideality they [are] at the same time also on their own account. In other words, the ground as their ideality is negated with respect to itself, since it is its own first moment—that is, ideal$_2$, sublated. As ground it is their ideality; they are only as posited in it, and in their being-posited in it (not simply insofar as they are for it) they are at the same time on their own account as well. The ground is their arising and vanishing within it; and it is [138] indifferent towards them just as it is towards its own alteration. Their

arising and vanishing within it is indifferent to their being-in-them-
selves; and their being-in-the-ground is indifferent to their own unreflected movement. This determinacy of the ground's indifference
is posited, in that the ground itself is in cognition connected with
cognition; as the self-subsistent (or as that wherein the reflecting movement of cognition negates itself) the movement of the moments over
against one another in the ground and against it as their unity has
this indifference. The ground is content of cognition, and indeed as
its first self-equivalent moment; and the determinacy of cognition is
this determinacy of being indifferent: not as a being-indifferent that
could also become non-indifferent, [that] could divide itself into itself
and into its contrary, but rather [one] that excludes its contrary and
thus in its determinacy would be in itself.

The ground, the totality insofar as it is reflected out of cognition's
moments to be its content thus posited as first power (although the
ground ought to be in itself and is so posited), looks towards the path
on which it becomes other, and out of this becoming-other becomes
other again. This path is its realization, wherein it will give itself its
real totality, a totality whose moments the whole ground itself is.

B / Metaphysics of Objectivity

This is the theory of the intelligible reality that the eternity of cognition
presupposes. On the side of consciousness the ground of cognition is the
soul, the Cartesian *res cogitans*. But this is not simply conceivable in abstraction
from the realm of truth that it knows. Rather, its independence is its own
abstracting of itself and positing of itself as independent. The intelligibility
of this activity is still dependent on the context of consciousness within which
it takes place. So immortality becomes a metaphysical problem. In its actual
experience the soul is nothing but a window on the world—a monad.

The world is a community of other selves, and its independence is identical
with their freedom (of which cognition is the primitive form). Truth is the
objective structure of their freedom, the structure that all must freely recognize. Freedom and necessity are one world, not two; and there is no need
for the establishment of harmony by a higher power. As one world, the
monads must necessarily be a harmony. Each is "passive" in its self-defining
activity of perceiving the world of the others; and "active" in its reshaping of
the world it perceives. Thus the cognition of "the world" is the condition of
free activity in this higher sense; and active freedom is essentially communal
in character. Sexual differentiation and recognition is the natural anticipation
of this active freedom, but its proper exposition belongs to the metaphysics

of subjectivity. The natural identity of the genus (restored in the offspring) is the real immortality of the soul. In the real order only the *Gattung* is immortal. The family lifeline is the real monad.

In the "highest essence" God emerges as the necessary ground of our cognition of all this. "In God we live and move and have our being." When we think, we *must* think for the community, or for "the genus." God is not to be conceived substantially (as in Spinoza, or in the bodily immortality of the natural species). As the highest essence God is a subject above and beyond the antithetic unity of soul and body. But now the final problem is to reconcile this absolute subjectivity with the finitude of the world of rational monads. Notice the influence of Boehme on Hegel's image of finitude as a metaphysical darkness, or evil, that is a necessary moment for the self-creation of the divine light (CE 153–54).[14]

In the way it has been determined as being-in-itself, the ground is the same as cognition insofar as cognition has a content, or insofar as it determines the content in such a way that the content is in cognition and cognition is differentiated vis-à-vis the content. At the same time it negates itself in its determination of the content; or it lets it be on its own account. Just like cognition, the ground determined in this way is something self-equivalent that, being indeed negative unity according to its essence, sublates the moments. But as absolute reflection it sublates itself as well; whether in the determining of the moments or in their being-ideal, it posits them at the same time as self-subsistent, thus as a synthesis whose moments are on their own account absolutely separated: reflection, and reflection as negated— a synthesis that is indifferent oneness [139] of reciprocal action, each just as much the active as the other, and the passive as well, the determinacy in the form of the determinate concept.

This ground or cognition is what is called the *soul*.

I / THE SOUL

Since ground has been sufficiently explicated and since the soul is precisely the ground as first moment of its realization, to that extent the soul has therefore been determined. The undifferentiation of the soul, or its unity, has been cognized as absolute unity in virtue of its

14. Compare the meditation in the *Wastebook* (Rosenkranz, *Hegels Leben*, pp. 547–48; trans. M. Hoffheimer in *Clio* 12 [1983] 405–7) and the discussion of evil in the *Phenomenology* (*Gesammelte Werke*, IX, 412–14; trans. Miller, paras. 776–77, pp. 468–70.)

being reflection into itself. As such it is determinate; and just as absolutely is it the sublatedness of its determinateness. Its determinateness—that is, that it is posited as something sublated—is[15] the soul itself; for it is so only because, as ground in its simplicity of reflection, the soul comes to be just the determinacy of this simplicity and its own first moment—which for the soul thereby comes to be its content, inherently [*an sich*] outside of it. In that this content is the ground coming to be the first moment (the ground being, however, the totality of the moments as absolute reflection), so it is what is differentiated vis-à-vis that content, connected negatively with it as sublating it. As this differentiated unity, opposed to the first unity, which is connected with itself, the ground is only in that opposition, and therefore something determinate. The unity appears as something passive, upon which that first moment operates. But this is precisely something determinate—and indeed, through its opposite, through the negative unity. It is something posited through the unity; they reciprocally determine each other. And what is third, or synthetic, is the content of cognition, whose factors, however, as falling outside each other, are posited on their own account, each negated in the other, existing in itself, so that only this synthesis is in the soul. There is only[16] this negative or synthetic connection as content of cognition (in the manner this content is posited, originating as from what are independent from each other), and in this incomplete connection there is the soul in the moment of differentiation. [140] Therefore the soul must reflect itself into itself, sublate this connection, and in this return-into-itself must posit itself as simple, indifferent. It thus sublates its content just as it sublates its connection with the content. However, since it is this negation only as ground—though even as ground it has in general an opposition, a determinacy in itself, to which it is nevertheless indifferent—its absolute reflection into itself is the return to the indifference of the determinateness vis-à-vis the other, which other, just as much as it, is in itself. Reflection is the falling apart of the content, or the separation of its two sides. Since the soul as what is thus separated is also[17] as something determinate—namely, that of indifference—it is reflected into itself through the other; and the disappearing

15. *Trans.*: Following ms. CE reads "is [for] the soul itself."

16. *Trans.*: Following ms. CE reads "only [since]," with the main clause starting on p. 140: "therefore the soul . . . "

17. *Trans.*: Following ms. CE reads "has also [come to be] something determinate."

of the content is just as much a free movement of the soul itself, independent of the soul.

As this negative *one* that excludes itself and in this exclusion is self-equivalent, the soul is substance, which, however, is not merely the differentiation of the accidents that would be only posited within it as connected with each other and in their positedness would have their possibility outside themselves. Rather, their possibility is posited with respect to themselves; in other words, they are posited as ideal$_2$, sublated. And the substance is rather subject, in which the determinacy is not an actual but a particular determinacy—that is, withdrawn from its connection with its opposite. This subject, however, is not at all something universal and self-equivalent in general, but rather what is displayed as such, as differentiating its self-equivalence: both taking itself and being itself taken back from it—in other words, reflecting itself. It is determinacy only as having an indifferent determinacy vis-à-vis the other in itself, in such a way, however, that its alternation is equally present as an accident, and in this alternation it yet retains the character of an indifferent determinacy. The soul is therefore the *one* of substantiality and subjectivity, and neither genuine substance nor genuine subject: not the former, because of the indifference of the accidents; not the latter, because of the differentiation, the alternation of determinacies. Through their indifference and the indeterminateness of the subject through them, these accidents at one and the same time are [a] themselves substances, [b] as such in their alternation idealizing themselves on their own account, and [c] synthetic in the connection with the subject. The soul is the whole circle, and its peripheral movement, which is at one and the same time connected with the soul as middle point [141] and extended indefinitely as a straight line—extended indefinitely because, to the extent that the soul is the middle point, to that extent the periphery is opposed to it and on its own account.

As what reflects itself into itself, making itself into its first moment and becoming its own content, the soul is the ground of this content, or of itself as of a moment. The second moment, opposed to the first, is just the ground itself, which is differentially connected with itself as its first moment; and the reflection into itself is the sublating: of the soul as its content, of it as something passive, and of it as something differentiated therefrom. This sublating is so constituted, however, that the passive in it ceases to be something determined through the differentiated soul and comes to be in itself again. Both of them, the soul as this differentiated soul and the soul as its content, fall asunder once more, each as a separate self-subsistent in-itself. For even though the soul as ground is just the same as cognition, yet ground and cognition are posited as opposed to each other, and the soul has this determinacy on its own account. And for this reason its reflection into itself is what is thus formal, in the sense that reflection only sublates the soul as its content (in other words, the form of the first moment) and sublates itself as its unity differentiated from the content. The reflection into itself, however, is not this original determinacy that it has: as cognition, which would be opposed to the ground, or as ground, which would be opposed to the cognition. On the contrary, reflection occurs within this determinacy; and the completed reflection of the soul (or its coming-to-be-totality) is itself only a falling asunder vis-à-vis another in-itself, or the negation of itself, and the position separated therefrom. Its totality is only the formal taking back into itself of the determinacy, so that the indifference that is its form retains a content that is determinate. The indifference [is] only something common to it and an other; and the pure in-itself is divided into diverse [in-themselves], which, within the movement of reflection, have their unity only in the middle as a synthetic unity, only in the second moment (that of the differentiated soul), not in the totality.

This determinacy lies in the essence of the soul; and the requirement of sublating it lies immediately in the fact that the essence is a determinacy. This requirement is expressed in the attempts to assert and to prove the immortality of the soul. The determinacy is to be sublated, however, only to the extent that the cognition or ground is sublated as posited under the determinacy that one is opposed to the other, or to the extent that cognition or ground is sublated as soul.

The soul as indifferent, having another in-itself indifferently beside it [142] (or as in the movement of reflection, which in its determining is itself determined), is immediately a plurality of things that are in themselves, self-reflected into themselves, connected among themselves in a superficial way—a chain of syntheses. Their in-itself is what is not coming forth, for their being in their reciprocal indifference comes to be immediately a becoming-determinate on their part through each other, since one is the content of the other. Each is on its own account a negated cognition; but just for that reason [each is] something determinate and connected with the other as with its cognition. In other words, it is something passive, which, as passivity, is immediately the first moment of reflecting. To the extent that it is on its own account, the soul itself is in fact through its determinacy only this passive moment; and neither as reflected into itself (that is, as thus passive) nor as what is differentiated from such a passive [entity] is it the absolute in-itself. In fact there is posited a multiple reflecting into itself that, as self-equivalent, is the first moment of another; as self-moving, is differentiated from any such other.

B / THE WORLD

The soul presupposes the world and itself as in the world. For its determinacy is nothing else but this: that originally, in its being-in-itself, it is the moment of an other just as much as the other is in turn its moment too. The world would be nothing else but the reciprocal action of the synthetic series collapsing into complete rest. It holds itself apart and in motion, however, inasmuch as the [members] that connect with one another in this way are not only in this connection with others, but in truth also in connection with themselves, since they return back from the others into themselves, and in their necessity they are free. For their freedom is their being cognition or ground. Since something other than themselves is in them a moment, they are in this way necessary; but the connection they have with this momentary [other] is its ideality. They sublate their differentiation, and are free on their own account: they fall apart, indifferent to the other. As was shown with respect to the soul, however, this freedom is a formal₂ one; for it only has to do with the [143] sublation of the formal antithesis in which the soul remains just that original determinateness that is the moment of another, in that it is on its own account, and that is therefore determined in its very freedom. What in fact holds the many apart, however, is this formal freedom—as self-isolating, as one of the opposites, not as the universal of reciprocal action, in which nothing that stands in reciprocity is posited as self-subsistent—[that is, as] tearing away at determinacy. For in this connection or in the unity with the other, this freedom is in fact also not in the connection; it draws back from it instead.

This coincidence of freedom and necessity is not a semblance that would have to receive its corrective through the sublation of the one or the other. Just as little do they proceed side by side, indifferent to one another; nor are they diverse aspects of one and the same thing, which, just for this reason, would be other than they, and they outside it, indifferent to it. Instead, this coincidence is a necessary moment in the realization of cognition. Freedom cannot [be] sublated, for otherwise all movement generally, and every antithesis arising only through movement, would immediately be sublated. No more can necessity, for the latter is what is sublated by freedom for it to be. They are not two systems that remain unaffected as they interweave, that would be together without connection, as it were (in the way we think of space and time), such that one could say of neither that it is and the other not, yet that in their being united would be absolutely without influence upon one another. Each is rather the moment of the other. Freedom is that which is passive, connected with itself— which, just in being so, is moment vis-à-vis another; and this connection is its necessity, which, once more as reflection into itself, passes over immediately into freedom, into connection with itself. Both are moments of one and the same whole—not, however, ways of considering it from which it could abstract.

Previously, in ground or cognition, this whole was the *one* that, having turned into content, was then connected with it differentially, as with something by which it was determined and which it determined, for its part, just as much. This content disappeared, however; for the *one* went back into itself, and thereby turned into content once more. And so what is now posited is that in fact this content, the in-itself, is itself what is reflected into itself and is self-reflecting; and that hence it is related within itself in the same way as only the soul was posited as relating to it—like the soul itself entering upon the [144] line of this kind of self-relating. But the soul is not in a particular relation vis-à-vis the other with which it is connected. This other is rather just as much an in-itself that reflects into itself; it itself determines its determinacy through another, sublates the determinacy thereby, and posits it ideally$_2$. In other words, this other is just as much a representing monad as the soul is. Inasmuch as it reflects into itself, preserving itself undifferentiated in its being determined through an other, the monad is self-subsistent totality for which the other is something negated in it. And the distinction can only be one of degree, a matter of the greater or lesser freedom with which the monad remains indifferent on many sides. For the distinction with respect to the monad itself is this alternation between the form in which the monad is a content, something passive, and [the form] in which it is differentiated unity. The disappearing of the monad within the dynamic [*thätigen*] chain (which at every point spreads out in all directions) consists in its appearing more in the form of that enveloped, undisclosed, passive content, and as something differentiated in a narrower expanse, in a more restricted sphere, and in relation to fewer things. Since each is in itself, reflects itself into itself, and expels itself from others, this expelling is posited with respect to each as well. It is something absolutely determinate; and the graduated transition is infinitely divided within itself. As absolutely determined, negative *one*, it is a "this." But this singularity goes aground in its own totality. For at the same time the soul, or the monad in general, receives another significance in the world-process; in other words, the opposition of freedom and necessity, which previously displayed itself as moment of one and the same thing, must itself divide this concatenation of monads in another way.

For the world-process displayed itself in such a way that the same thing was at one time content, something passive vis-à-vis another; and at another time active vis-à-vis another that was passive. And this same [thing] returns into itself from its differentiation, and is thus itself in the form of something that is connected with itself. What comes back to itself in this way preserves itself as an in-itself, posited, as reflected, for it becomes totality. But in totality it becomes also another; as totality of its determinacy it confronts itself as moments, in which it is just as much a simple negative *one* as it is differentiated unity. It does not enter into the antithesis as determinacy in general, itself already posited as moment; rather, it is moment only for us. It enters as subject, as a negative *one*, as one reflected into itself; and in its determinacy it is itself absolute determinacy, [145] negative unity, which in its being determined through another posits itself as not determined [and] the determinacy as sublated in itself—that is, [posits itself] as a "this": something simple in its infinitely complex determinacy. This bad infinity is posited immediately as absolute infinity, as *one*, as a point. Negatively connected in this way with the opposite, it is what is active. Vis-à-vis another, what is passive and connected with itself is equally a "this"; vis-à-vis what is active, however, it is only something that connects with itself. Reflecting itself into itself from this its determinacy, what is active sublates itself as a "this," and as a totality [comes to be] universal. From the *definitum* it comes to be its definition; and the process of its self-preservation is much more the demise of its singularity and the realization of the genus. The monad that is a reflection into itself is so only as a "this." It is the other moment; but this other is in itself too. In other words, it is on its own account in the form of the first moment; so far as it is so, however,

it is passive. It reflects itself into itself as simple, or as soul, and preserves itself; this reflection in general is that of the soul. It preserves
itself, however, also as a second moment, or as a "this"; and it is an
in-itself, active vis-à-vis another. That first self-preservation is the ideal
one, where the other disappears in the monad. This second one is
that of the nullification of the other, not of its relative disappearing.
But this other self-preservation, as the other moment, is just for that
reason immediately the contrary of itself as well. It is the liberation
from itself and the sublating of itself as a "this."

In the world the soul comes to be monad. To that extent there is
only an absolute multiplicity of monads that represent the world to
themselves and, indifferently connected with themselves, remain in
this differentiation of representation. Monad it is, but only monad;
in other words, as this connectedness with itself, as a moment, it is so
only vis-à-vis the differentiated moment.[18] But this differentiated moment is the development of the soul itself, which negates itself as its
own ground. As something simple it changes itself into the ground
that is outside its existence. This its existence (or the fact that it changes
itself into ground) is its being absolute determinacy, negative unity,
as reflection connecting itself with itself, or as formal cognition. As
absolute reflection, its freedom within itself is immediately its excluding the other from itself, and a connection of [things] that absolutely
are [*absolutseyender*]. The former self-preservation of the soul ends
with the freedom that is immediately this differentiating of freedom,
[that is,] of negative unity vis-à-vis itself [146] in the form of monad—
vis-à-vis itself as something negated in freedom, which vis-à-vis freedom is something passive. Cognition changes itself into an absolute
cognition as *one*, and the world is thereby posited. The sublating of
this differentiation vis-à-vis something absolutely in itself or passive,
which to us is on its own account, is the sublation of this *one* itself.
And thereby [it is] the totality as a universal—totality that, however,
precisely in that it is simply this connection in itself, itself appears
again as first moment under the determinacy of equivalence.

The world as this process of the genus sets freedom up as a higher
sphere that turns against the world's lower ones. Previously freedom
was in general what is undifferentiated as reflection into itself; and

18. *Trans.*: Lasson reads this text as "Monad it is, but only vis-à-vis the differentiated
moment; in other words as this connectedness with itself, as a moment, it is only so."

the first moment, or the monad, was in itself just as much something free as the second moment, and as totality, which is itself what is simple in the first moment and falls back into the determinacy of this first moment. But the former reflection, as the formal in-itself or its concept (which freedom previously was), is now the higher freedom of totality of which the monad and what is active are themselves moments. This totality, the genus, is henceforth the in-itself and ranks above its falling back into the form of the first moment, as remaining self-equivalent in the first moment. Its falling back is much rather its own stretching out into the two moments of what is passive (or the monad) and what is active. As the in-itself of the whole, it is the essence of these moments, which is doubled in them; and as their genus, it is their universal. And the process—that is, the self-preservative process of the genus—is like the coming to be of the genus, precisely the self-preservative process of the singular.

Opposite the differentiated in-itself stands another, in general as something passive. Its preservation is the annihilation of the in-itself, but at the same time its own annihilation—that is, its coming to be the genus that, to be sure (as the absolute reflection of itself), displays this other that stands opposite the differentiated unity. It displays it as the kind of thing that returns out of absolute totality into the determinacy of the first moment; that is, [it shows] that this passive [thing] is in fact genus only in the form of the first moment. Sublating itself in its self-preservation, what is active becomes in this infinity its own contrary; and maintaining itself in its contrary, it stands by itself as opposed to itself. Instead of having negated itself in its contrary, it is, rather, positive. The other in-itself is not its own negation; but in the other it cognizes itself. The genus tears itself apart into the differentiation of the sexes—from cognition into recognition. The singularity that passes away in the process of the genus is ideal$_2$, but posited as something ideal$_2$; [it is] ideal$_2$ in another.[147] On the other hand, [once] posited, what is ideal$_2$ is on its own account. Singularity has come to the point where the first moment itself is a cognizing, [that is,] a self-preserving, a connecting of itself with itself, and therein a self-sublating, such that its being itself is something other than itself. The reflection of singularity into itself is the genus that has come to be; but singularity preserves itself throughout this its sublating, and finds itself in another. The genus is not only the universal, but also the infinite. In the totality the singular has changed itself into the whole process; and in it the whole process comes apart as a duplicated process. It is only this process of the totality that, in its totality, comes to be the first moment.

The moments of the genus are the existing singularities. It itself as absolute reflection is only as this cycle of its moments, precipitating and dissolving into themselves. Since as determinacy of universal in-difference it stands over against them as moments, it is itself rather their one[ness]; yet it is equally the not-determinately universal, or the indifferent that is not opposed, and their ideality, or equally their being. It is the free, which, elevated above the moments of the cycle, is alone what is self-equivalent. The being of these moments is only now an *existing*; all previous being was so merely in a determinacy that was not complete reflection into itself. Here for the first time is genuine reality posited, for the genus is absolute reflection into itself, and as such also changes itself into its moments of reflection insofar as it is something other whenever this reflection, opposed to these, is a moment.[19]

Previously it was a matter of indifference whether we considered the soul as cognition or as ground (only with the limitation that it be as the determinacy of an opposition). In existence, however, this in-difference is sublated and the two are posited as connected with one another. The ground is over against cognition and is the universal as reflecting itself into itself; or [it is] absolute reflection posited as uni-versal in itself and not opposed. Cognition is the same genus but is so as a moment of reflecting itself into itself; its reflecting into itself is its self-preservation, which is directed against nothing but the genus, the universal. The self-preservation is reflection into itself appearing as simple; that from which it is differentiated [148] was in general something self-subsistent that, having been synthesized and deter-mined, disappeared again. Only its concept was posited; once reflec-tion is realized, then this other is for it what is strictly passive, nothing other than the genus, the whole of the moment itself that confronts it as moment and that is something self-subsistent, something con-nected with itself. Positing singularity self-negated within it, this ne-gation sublates itself and thus preserves itself; with respect to it, it takes its essence up into itself, as it were, for the first time.

The distinctions of reflection within itself thus come to pass in the

---

19. *Trans.*: The French translation of Souche-Dagues has "insofar as it is something other than this [or], opposed to these, is a moment."

following way. Cognition and ground are one, but for us. And so cognition is soul, undifferentiated, on its own account; its differentiation is an indifferent coming and disappearing of an in-itself vis-à-vis which [it] is equally in itself. In the world-process this diverse in-itself becomes differentiated within itself [*gegeneinander*] in existence; the self-preserving singular has passed over into the genus; and the world-process is the process of the genus, which, remaining a whole in its moments, posits them differentiated over against each other [*gegeneinander*] and exists in them.

As its concept, cognition is soul; the latter, as this determinacy of the concept, is itself a singular that, thus reflecting itself into itself, becomes genus [*Gattung*]. Realizing itself, this in turn is bifurcation into genders, existence of natural things and preservation of the species [*Gattung*]; as this, freedom confronts its process. It is the ever self-equivalent content of the cycle of cognition, or of the process of the genus; and real cognition has stepped forth from formal cognition. The monads as existing things express only one and the same universal. Their multiplicity as much as the determinacy of their movement is what is strictly contingent;[20] and what is existing in connection with singularity [is] in fact what is only possible. In the genus this [21] is sublated and its self-preservation is rather its sublating. Singularity exists in that it, without coming to be genus, returns into itself, since the genus is rather what is in the form of being connected with itself (or what is passive, against which singularity turns and which it sublates) and is free. Conversely, the genus is that in which singularity sublates itself; *genus* is the differentiating unity in which the singularities are moments that themselves come to be genus. Both freedoms—that of singularity and that of genus—are [149] opposed to each other and so are both necessities—the one in which the genus only is a passive, the connection with itself only as moment, and the other in which conversely the self-preserving singularity comes to be genus just as the latter falls back into being moment. Because of this falling back, the genus is not absolute ground, not absolutely undifferentiated in itself; it is thus indeed completely closed within itself in that its last is again its first. In this immediate overturning, however, it is itself not posited as freedom; but its liberation becomes rather only passivity. It is the cycle that changes itself into the cycle; that is,

20. *Trans.*: Hegel has no punctuation here.
21. *Trans.*: "This" could refer either to "singularity" or to "multiplicity."

the cycle moves itself as its moments but is not absolutely free. Indeed, it is only in the form of necessity—that is to say, as throwing itself over from one side to another through a middle that, to be sure, is the genus as universal or rather communal. Yet as such [it] does not step forth with the annihilation of its being moment; rather, it is posited only in the form of existence; and the genus itself is nothing but fulfilled soul, which would be self-equivalent reflection, indifferent throughout to the alternation and the passing over. Cognition as reflection posited in an absolutely simple way, or simplicity, is not yet posited. The soul was of course this simple, but its content was the indeterminate. Now there is this content or fulfilment; as the moments of the cycle, the content is the total reflection itself, but it is also only the content. In fact, therefore, this content is also only in the form of opposed terms. It is only the genus as a passive moment that preserves itself as singularity opposed to the genus *qua* something alien, devouring the genus within itself, and thereby springing over to the differentiation of the genus. Unlike the first, this genus does not stand opposed to the differentiation as something alien but as something equivalent to it, something that finds itself in the other as the latter finds itself in it. But [it does so] in such a way that they express the genus not *per se* but only as their undifferentiatedness. And since they express this, it is itself again that first opposed moment.

If the self-preservation is only this coming and disappearing of something alien in cognition, then in the process of the genus as well the preservation of the genus is itself only the coming and disappearing of the singularities positing themselves as themselves outside themselves. It is not cognition as absolute reflection into itself, or this as simple.

As the universal, however, the genus must [be] as that which is the same in this form [150] of existence; in other words, it in its existence and it as the self-equivalent must be equal to each other. And in fact in this existence of the genus, the genus alone is what is in itself. What is existing [is] the self-sublating negative; and the genus is itself this negative unity. The simple, self-equivalent reflecting-itself-into-itself (which just thereby is something absolutely reflected) and the negative unity[22] in the mode of divided genus, as necessity, is strictly *one*; what appears other than this unity is purely something ideal$_2$, not subsisting in itself.

---

22. *Trans.*: Grammatically the pronoun could refer to "genus."

Genus is the ground of existing singularities, as also of their connection; or rather [it is] their connection itself. Yet not only this, but the connection is in fact the absolute unity; for what is connected, the singularities, are not in themselves, but strictly self-sublating with respect to each other.

c / THE HIGHEST ESSENCE[23]

As we have shown, there is in the process of the genus, as of the existence of the world, totality itself only in its antitheses and in their unity, the empty middle of going over. There is in fact never anything but the two sides of the transition; they are posited as being in themselves, yet indeed characterized by their antithesis—in other words, moving themselves to disappear into the opposite.

The essence of this movement is necessary. For the way it is posited as process, there is in it only the appearing of the antithesis between the self-preservation of the singularity and that of the genus. The passing over, the unity of both, is an "inner" that does not step forth; that is, it is what is not posited for this alternation but only what is posited by us, or the "outer." For the self-preserving individual, however, this is, as cognizing or as unity of itself and its opposite, its nonbeing or its disappearing. Thereby there is for it too this contradiction. And since it finds itself as something other in the genus, then immediately opposed is this: having its essence only as connection with another and not in itself, and on the contrary preserving its reflection into itself as itself. The unity of both is [151] outside the self-preserving individual because the individual is only the subject of this contradiction. For this unity of the contradiction (which it is) is its being *per se*. It is this unity that, as formal reflection, steps aside, sublates itself in the self-equivalent positive of the genus, and has this sublating and this self-equivalent outside itself—or as "inner," as its ground, from which it is yet distinguished.

The connection of the self-preservation with the genus has the aspect that each singular is strictly contingent for the other in that, as self-preserving, each is on its own account and indifferent for the other. They are equally contingent for the genus, since the latter is in itself; and the determinacy that is in the self-preservation (whereby the individual [is] something unique [*singuläres*], something absolutely

23. *Trans.*: Alternate translation: "the Supreme Being."

determinate in both senses—pure point and point of an infinite aggregate of lines intersecting in it) is not for the genus. Rather for this as universal what is unique is indeed only with the determinacy of universality,[24] or as particular that has gone back into itself, having bent together into the circle of its reflection that aggregate of lines extending through it into infinity.

Yet this indifference of the singulars for each other and for the genus sublates itself, for in fact they [are] for each other generally—*one* is only with the determinacy of connection with the other and equally as singular under the genus, since the points of its lines are just such an in-itself. As point it falls on the line, which is on its own account a higher reflection into itself—namely, just the genus; the alien, which stands opposed to what is self-preserving—and it is itself an alien thing of this kind—is in itself nothing other than the genus itself for what is self-preserving. The singular is necessary vis-à-vis the singular, [and] equally vis-à-vis the genus. For this genus is vis-à-vis itself as first moment, and in this as formal reflection, as not reflected. In other words, it is itself in its moments not only particular, but unique.

However, this necessity is the bad sort in which the connection is not as such or in itself, but only with respect to the opposites. Yet it is altogether in itself, and the opposites are in the absolute necessity. For their bad necessity is in fact the absolute one. That bad indifference, like the bad necessity, are nothing in themselves; and the [152] singular is present only in the absolute indifference and necessity of the genus, which is its essence, the essence of the essence, not only according to determinacy in general (metaphysical necessity) but according to its absolute determinacy as a singular.

If [a] the process of self-preservation (as that in which the absolutely determinate posits itself as self-equivalent, posits the many determinacies as ideal$_2$ within it and remains itself, undifferentiated in their sublating) we call "thought"; [and] if, however, [b] the process of the genus in which the singular itself is only within the universal, indeed something ideal$_2$, negative, [we call] "quantum," whose essence is the

----

24. *Trans.*: Following Lasson we have changed the punctuation and inserted "is." This does justice to the word order. The ms reads " . . . the determinacy that is in the self-preservation (whereby the individual is something unique, something absolutely determinate in both senses—pure point and point of an infinite aggregate of lines intersecting in it—not for the genus but rather for this as universal) is what is unique, though only with the determinacy of universality. . . ."

self-equivalent, the singular only as negation and the latter as connected with the self-equivalent as delimitation (whereby, however, the
universal in fact, like space, is not delimited by the determinacies
posited in it—that is there is no point where space would not be)—if
we [now] call this universal "being" or "extension" as that in virtue of
which alone something possible is, then, since both [conditions] are
one, thinking, and extension or being are strictly *one*.

Since the genus, or the universal, is not as some determinate genus
or other but as the absolute genus, which is reflection into itself,
moments of which it itself is, it is hence the highest essence of all,
which is not itself a moment and a stepping over into the determinate
existence of something else, but rather absolute existence itself; not
something necessary, but necessity itself; not the empty universality
that is common, but the ideality of that to which it only would have
been common, hence the essence of the genus or its substance.

Whatever superficial connection with the singular is given to what
is thus in itself, the connection is in itself null and void. If this singular
is posited as being in itself, then it has a side of indifference vis-à-vis
the highest essence, and the latter has a reality outside it. Its being as
the in-itself is yet posited in another way, namely, as an extension that
would not be one with being, something determined through an alien
[thing] whose determining, not being inherently ideal$_2$ or sublated,
would be negation. Extension or being in the highest essence is, however, immediately one with singularity—that is, negation. Since the
division in it is only as a sublatedness, this singularity is strictly simple;
and the multiplicity distinguished in the singularity is the genus, the
simplicity of [153] reflection itself. If a being *per se* is to be ascribed
to the many, it becomes quite simply equal to itself; and its distinction
is its being in the other—that is, its sublating; it is only the nothing,
which is the simplicity of being and indistinguishable from it. Thus
the determinacies of quantity of the pure universal are only this negative; and the negative is in itself simple and is the universal itself.
There can be posited no external determinacy not equal to the universal; that is, this [universal] can be posited, not with respect to an
extension diverse from being, which extension would be externally
determined. What thus determines externally is the nothing—completely simple, and hence itself being.

This highest essence has the antithesis of what preserves itself
(thinking) and of being (extension) simply and solely as an attribute,
as moment, as something ideal$_2$ within itself, not as substance [or as]

what is in itself. On the contrary, it is rather its being in itself, and the differences belong only to the ideality, to the nothing in itself.

The highest essence, thus equal to itself in that which appears to be unequal, is the absolute ground of this unequal. For this is in itself nothing but just the highest essentiality itself; and [that] whereby it is on its own account, separated from it, is pure negation. To be in itself it can only strive to sublate this—that is, its being *per se*—and can surrender its sphere of self-preservation in which it is set over against something alien—and it does indeed catch sight of itself in the process of the genus, but only as something other than itself—a sphere of self-preservation that is only the negativity of the highest essence. The highest essence is equal to itself thus: that it is what is strictly reflected into itself; that there is not this movement or reflecting within it, but rather in its emanation in appearance as multiplicity it is absolutely the same.

It is *proven* that the highest essence is the one and only, the in-itself. It is something infinitely extroverted; it has infinitely created, yet its creation, to the extent that in it the singular as individual is separated, is in fact only negation. What is thus negated has only to preserve the contradiction in itself and preserve itself as negation; yet since it is only negation it is to revert, as self-preserving, into non-existence and into the highest essence.

To this there stands opposed, in its self-equivalence, simply negation as the evil principle that builds itself up within itself. In its pure clarity this [154] darkness is not present; for darkness is the nothing for the light, and the clarity is to the light strictly as self-equivalent. Yet equally the light is not without darkness, as darkness is not [without light]. The highest essence has created the world, which for the essence is of ether-bright transparency and clarity; yet the world on its own is dark.

It is proven that only the highest essence is in itself; yet this being *per se* of the world stands strictly opposed to this necessity. Its being is a non-being; yet this "non-being *is*" is itself over against that absolute being. It dissolves away, vanishes within it. Yet that it so vanishes presupposes that it has been, or it retains its being *per se*. And this being *per se* and the absolute essence remain divided. The proof goes back to the latter, but it does not proceed from it. Rather, it begins with an inconceivable point of departure—namely, that of existence—which must freely sublate itself. But if it only must do so, then it has not been; and it has not been; it is not. This itself is only the result of a proof, which was preceded by the movement of the proof and the point of departure of the proof but not by its *construction*. The emanation of singularity out of the highest essence is an empty thought; for that whereby it would be filled would be only an inequality, of which the absolute unity of the genus is not capable.

Yet this highest essence is self-equivalent in that it is itself absolute negation, and this in an absolutely simple way. It has to do with nothing but displaying just this negation as what is simple. And it only [is] this simple as an absolutely simple reflection into itself—as "I" or as intelligence.

c / **Metaphysics of Subjectivity**

As we move from objectivity to subjectivity it is worth noting that what Hegel says in the *Science of Logic* about the relation of his new logic to the older metaphysics applies fairly comprehensively to his own "old metaphysics." It is "the *objective* logic" that "takes the place of the metaphysics of former times."[25] What he calls here "the metaphysics of subjectivity" has some affinities with the higher reaches of the *Subjective Logic* of 1816. But most of the topics of *that* logic have no place in the Metaphysics of 1804. They are left behind in the finite realm of the logical relationship of thought. The metaphysics of objectivity arrives at the concept of the highest *essence*; and it is in the context of essence that the metaphysics of subjectivity evolves. (In terms of the *Phenomenology of Spirit* we have now reached chapter 8.)

God is not a substance but an essence: the essence of subjectivity. The absolute self is the ultimate *ground* of reality. The final phase of the Metaphysics is thus a reinterpretation of Kant and Fichte, just as the penultimate phase was a reinterpretation of Descartes, Spinoza, and Leibniz. God is the self who is a community of selves. But this is just the logical structure of real self as our argument has revealed it. The single human organism cannot join the end to the beginning. It dies and leaves a new cycle to unroll. Rational consciousness, by contrast, is true resurrection.

The rational self knows its identity with the community of selves. It thinks for the genus (that is, for *homo sapiens* in his world as an eternal community). It knows its own natural self as an empirical datum among the rest, but this self is only a sublated moment. The consciousness of determinacy is only the

25. *Gesammelte Werke*, xi, 32; *Hegel's Science of Logic*, trans. Miller, p. 63.

consciousness of the world as an *Anstoss* to which the self is passive. Where now is the objective immortality of this self? In the objectivity of what it knows and in the general validity of that knowledge.

This rational self has active impulses. It is a will. Here, too, absolute singularity is infinity. The rational will for the genus is the true infinite of absolute spirit.

As the absolute genus, the absolute essence is what is self-equivalent in the moments of existence; and existence is the negative. As negative the essence disappears within being; indeed, it is equivalent to being; but in order for it to disappear, it is necessary that it be opposed to being and that in its opposition only this its sublation should itself be what is self-equivalent.

This negative is nothing else than infinity, but here it is what is fulfilled, or absolutely infinite. The two moments of simple connection in their [155] realization—unity or being (determined as quantum, for which negation is something strictly external) and infinity, which [is] just this sublation into itself—are here posited as fulfilled. Unity was so posited earlier, as having returned out of the totality of the antithesis; infinity is so posited now as returning therefrom. The [moments] whose infinity is the I are themselves infinite, reflections into themselves; they are not simple circles but such as themselves have circles as their moments, and are the circles of these circles. Indeed, self-preservation is already something reflected into itself, absolute singularity that remains self-equivalent in the unequal, and reverts into itself out of its own determinateness. Vis-à-vis singularity the alien [moment] is the universal; and singularity, combined with it, is something synthetic, something particular from which it ascends to the universal once again. Singularity interlocking with the universal through the synthetic unity of the particular is itself this movement of ascending, which, *qua* universal, is immediately singular once more in that as a universal it has opposed singularity to particularity as to what is synthetic. It posits them both ideally$_2$: the universal as opposed to the substance, and the singular as opposed to the determinate concept. It is negative unity or singularity, having thus returned to its starting-point. The universal that stands opposed to the singular is the singular itself, and vice versa: what is alien in this reflection is that [universal and singular] have each of them this determination vis-à-vis the other, while their unity is only for us. In the world—that is, in the process of the genus—the process sublates itself for what is itself self-reflexive;

as this whole cycle the self-reflexive is opposed to itself—two self-preserving [processes] that are now therefore no longer something in principle alien for one another, since that primary reflection does not fall back simply into singularity but in such a way that it fall backs as the totality that has come to be. In this guise it has its very singularity within it sublated as the one moment and as something merely ideal, in itself. Consequently, while the totality is singularity once more, singularity is also something sublated; and hence its opposite is not something alien but something equivalent to it. This oppositeness is only a sublated one for the first singularity, something transparent, through which it catches sight of its self and is cognitive. For it does not see therein something reflected but something reflecting itself, the motion that is its own essence.

Both of them are the absolute self-equivalence of reflection; and the singular, connected with itself as with an other—though for it the otherness is also merely [156] form—itself passes over into the genus, or into what is self-equivalent. The return to the first moment is not for that moment. Inasmuch as it is singular, it is only so *qua* self-preserving; it cannot hold out through this passage. It perishes therein; and this transition is the having-come-into-being of another singular— of a singular because it is a first moment necessary of itself and is opposed to the singular that is pushed into a higher sphere. That the singular cannot descend, cannot turn itself into the first moment, is because even existence is enclosed in this sphere and the transition into another is the cessation of existence. Yet the turning back to the first [moment] is only for the absolute universal of the sphere. For the singular, however, it is its vanishing, and its having been turned back is the arising of another, a vanishing and arising that is equally contingent for both of them as such and is only the absolute necessity of the universal.

The universal, as the highest essence, or as the genus, is the state of self-equivalence along the path of singularity, which alone is the reflection of existence, or absolute existence. For us, accordingly, it is what is equivalent in self-preservation, or what is opposed as genus to the self-preserving singular. For the singular, the alien [moment] is its still not being something reflected of itself, or its being affected with an absolute determinacy, since the sublatedness of the determinacy within the totality lies behind it; that is, it exists for an other. But this singular, having here arrived at the absolute nothingness of determinacy, is no more; the other emerging from its womb, therefore, stands forth immediately, born completely free and indifferent. Since the essence of its indifference, however, is just that it has come forth from negation, or is its *being* reflected (for there is no indifference otherwise than in being reflected), it is in fact connected with what was negated, even though, *qua* singular, it is indifferent to it (that is, it is connected with it as with something absolutely alien, having being in itself). For the singular it is not that this alien [moment] is an in-itself, simply what is sublated, or the self-oppositing genus. For us the indifferent antithesis, which remains in self-preservation, and the antithesis of the genus (in the sexes) is the same. The first is the second posited as ideal₂; the alien quality in self-preservation is the sublated equality of the sexes, and vice versa.

The highest essence is this equivalent that returns as universal into the first potency, or into [157] the beginning. However, it does not return to the beginning *qua* singularity but only *qua* universal, since the singularity posited therein is other than that which has come to be universal.

But just the singularity that has become universality is not only what is self-equivalent in the moments of existence, but their negative unity. It is absolute singularity, absolute determinacy, infinity. The singular's having-come-to-be the universal is the sublatedness of singularity. But this simplicity is not the nothingness of singularity, so that it would have singularity over against it. On the contrary, it is immediately one with singularity. For us, the singular of self-preservation has its coming-to-be in the coming-to-be of the concept of cognition. At this point, in its first potency, when returning into its beginning, it does so as an other, not as the first singular but as a singular that has become universal.

This absolute unity of singularity and universality, the I, consists in the fact that singularity, in that it is this I, is now as opposite immediately simple, or that the opposite only is for it as something sublated. In its opposition, and in connection with this, [it is] something universal and self-equivalent that has annulled *all* indifference of determinacy and all half-connection. Self-preservation, returning out of the simple totality, is not an indifference in which an indifferent alien [moment] that has only the form of universality enters. Because singularity becomes at the same time what is differentiated, this [alien element] opposes to itself, as synthesis of both, the fact that the indifferent is within it; and it sublates this opposition in such a way that

both [opposites] become unconnected and indifferent once more. Instead, the determinate opposite is for the singularity itself only *qua*
universal; thus in its own determinacy [it is] immediately something
sublated. For the singular, the genus is precisely what is alien in the
self-preservation.

1 / THE THEORETICAL I, OR CONSCIOUSNESS

The singularity, which is not this mere determinacy but is absolute
reflection in every dimension and in all its moments instead, is (*qua*
infinity) [158] simple; that is, its movement in its moments is just this
transparent universal, sublated in its oppositeness. In the soul the
determinate is something alien and something to be sublated by abstraction from it—that is, through its disappearing. But in the I, *qua*
self-subsistent or alien, the determinate is immediately something ideal₂;
it is something indifferent in itself, in connection with the I, since
formerly it was something differentiated vis-à-vis the soul, something
alien that posits in the I something other than the I.

The monad represents the world to itself; and the boundary of its
presentation, the point where it stops, is its contrary, [or] what is alien
to it. The universal representing is not bounded by this boundary;
for of course the boundary is nothing positive at all but is strictly
negative in itself. This negative status, however, was not for the monad,
for which on the contrary the boundary is something positive, since
the essence of the monad is singularity, the negating of an other, or
exclusion. For the I this other is not a nothing by virtue of abstracting
from it, since abstracting only lets something else take its place; instead, the other in its otherness is immediately something equal to the
I—that is, something sublated as other. It is something recapitulated
in itself, or a many as something self-equivalent, even as the many
was sublated right at the beginning of philosophy. This it is now not
for us; rather, the "us" for whom it is so is now the object of our own
consideration.

In the monad there was this reciprocity of both [terms]: through
what was posited in it as alien, the monad was in itself the synthesis
of that in which an effect occurs; and conversely the monad posited
once more in the alien [moment] something alien to it and made it
into a synthesis of this kind, sundered itself as thus synthetic from
itself as the indifferent, took itself back into itself, and thus sublated

what is alien[26] in that it disappeared. The I, by contrast, is in its own self, and is *for* itself the universal; the indifference or the being *per se* of the alien [moment] is nothing other than the form of universality. But this form belongs to the I; and the alien [moment], so far as it thus exists on its own account, is itself determined through the I. There is simply and solely the second synthesis (the determinateness of the alien [moment] through the I), not the first one (the determinateness of the I through the alien [moment]); and there is in fact nothing alien posited in the I. The reflection of the I into itself is no longer that formal or negative one in which the genus is for the I not genus, not universal, but something else. Instead, the beginning of the genus is just the genus reflected into itself, the I as genus; and singularity is this [issuing forth] from itself[27] of the genus into the first and the other moment of the I. This issuing forth [159] is the absolute concept, or infinity as simple negation that is the contrary of itself; and this contrary, being the contrary in itself (that is, the contrary of its own self again, other in itself, or the other of itself), is sublated in itself as other. [This is] the infinity of the I, as the contrary of infinity, and equally the contrary of this contrary. And the other is just for that reason ideal$_2$; it is the contrary of its own self. The antithesis only exists as one reflected into itself, as sublated, or as the being nullified of everything alien.

The I, being in this way an inwardly reflected genus, or absolutely universal, in its singularity, has the alien [moment] simply and solely as a universal vis-à-vis itself. But for this reason this opposite is in fact only sublated; it is not something opposed. For there to be an antithesis with respect to it, what is designated as universal (the ideal$_2$) must at once be something determinate, or something opposed to the I; and [it must] have a side from which it is not determined through the I— that is, [that] is not equal to it. For [it must be] precisely not as I but as something that has come to be an I, or as a universal that throughout its universality carries being by virtue of its inherent opposition. In essence the I is nothing but absolutely universal singularity, in that the singularity has returned out of the world, only as something reflected. The genus, as singularity, is precisely thereby a determinate negation of the determinate, and is itself determined. The I as infinite, which turns into the contrary of itself, becomes so as something orig-

26. *Trans.*: The German pronoun could be referring to "what is synthetic."
27. *Trans.*: CE reads "self [making]"; Lasson reads "self [sublating]."

inally determinate—that is, as an [I] that is a determinate infinity. Despite reflection and negation, it is a part of the world, a part posited in negated form, but thereby a determinate negative. Thus the I confronts nothing alien in its self-preservation—a self-preservation that does not preserve itself vis-à-vis what is alien—since it would originally have preserved a determinacy that now it would also have to sublate. Rather, since it is on its own account and preserves itself, the determinacy is prior to the opposition that enters in self-preservation; it is a determinacy that consciousness brings with it, so to speak. The process of this self-preservation is simpler than the first; there is not in it the doubled, reciprocal determining. The synthesis is [not] of the kind in which the alien would at first be the essential, the in-itself, something that would posit itself in the I as what is passive, and [of the kind in which] in this I an otherness would thus not arise through the I itself. Rather, the process begins at once with the fact that in the antithesis the essentiality is not altered and overturned but immediately is the I, as the infinite, what is essential. The antithesis itself begins with the inequality of something essential [160] and something inessential; as the essential, the I has the other only as something passive, determining it. The determinacy of the I is not, as it were, engendered before its eyes. Rather, the determinacy cannot be conceived by it, is unconscious; and the antithesis in the self-preservation is thereby wholly immanent within the I. In other words, the I is only *its* infinity, in which is the antithesis. What is added to this antithesis from that original determinacy is not something alien to the I; that is, the connection of the determinacy with the I is not a synthetic but rather an absolute unity, one that gathers itself together in the totality of the self-realizing genus but one that, although quite pure unity as totality, is thereby something determinate in that it would be derived from singularity, or has sublated something singular. The highest essence, as this which sublates something singular within itself, is itself singular, and thus steps into existence again; because it [is] absolute essence, this negative singular must itself sublate itself. As what is equal to itself in the two processes of self-preservation and genus, the highest essence is only something formally$_2$ equal; in its totality, [it] has come to be the real equal in such a way that it is differentiated vis-à-vis the former inequality (to which it formerly was indifferent) and sublates it. But the determinacy is thereby itself only synthesis, or what was posited as sublated; and thus the highest essence turns back into its beginning as the I, is in this return its own first moment, or something determinate, and is so in that it is absolutely determinate—that is, it has taken up the determinacy into its essence.

Therefore this determinacy appears for consciousness as an original one; for it is not only in the antithesis or in the determinacy to which the I is opposed, but it is ground, what is common to both. Hence it appears at first as an infinite impact, which is basically in the inner absolute essence of the I itself; and its very reflection is for the I not a sublating of that determinacy, but the determinacy that is in this cycle. In other words, for the I itself, the determinacy is a formal one. The self-preservation of the I is only something directed against it, or against its consciousness. For that first circle of self-preservation, posited in the I as in the soul, still has for it only the one side of what is synthetic, that of the determinateness of something alien through the I, or the fact that it is in itself something sublated. And its reflection into itself is not the sublating of this synthetic [combination] and letting it fall apart, but the sublating of the illusion that in what is [161] thus synthetic, there is in fact an alien component. This reflection is only the sublating of the illusion that the I is something synthetic, and brings the I forth as something simple, as original determinacy in its essence. Thus what is opposed is for the I just the formal reflection; or its return is its [coming] to consciousness—[that is,] that what is opposed is its own self. The opposite is only an illusion—that is, a nothing within itself; or it is formal reflection—that is, the cycle that in fact contains nothing alien within itself, and only appears itself as something alien.

For the I it is just the self-preservation of the soul that is the object; for it is the reflection in which what is alien is only transitory. As object of the I, what is alien is the reflection turned back into itself, the entire formal circle outside which is the determinacy—in other words, the reflection that does not just come forth in the circle but remains what is internal, *one* with the essence of the I. The self-preservation of the I is precisely this removing of what is alien from that circle, so that [the circle] remains only the universal [and] only the universality pertains to the object of the I as such. In this way the I indicates to itself what is thus alien, and does not allow it to disappear from itself; it posits itself as something sublated, but posits this alien as *one* with its essence; and it posits its own essence as this determinacy. Thus the object is what is self-equivalent in the genus itself; and its in-itself is not the negation of the I within it but rather just this self-equivalent, or the circle of reflection. The sublating of what is alien is not a pushing out but a taking back into itself; and the antithesis and its taking back is something wholly contained in the I.

The I as determining, or the I for which the alien comes forth only as what is determined by it (as something in itself universal, not [as] something singular or determining), is in the self-preservation of the I the moment of differentiation, the moment of reflection, of self-equivalence come to itself. It is the taking of the determinacy back into the essence of the I, the recognizing (as its own determinacy) and the alien (as just something equivalent to itself). But these two, as sides of the I, now go asunder in this way: its being united with the self-equivalence of the alien, and its being united with its determinacy; the former, free I and the latter, originally determined I are the two moments of the antithesis. They are so for us as the self-equivalent genus, and as determinacy of the existence out of which it raises itself. But for the I itself they are, only in that the I, as infinite, splits itself into the unequal self-preservation [162] and the self-equivalence of the I, and has equated the former as pure reflection to itself, just as [it has equated it to itself] as determinacy. But in so doing it has undertaken a further division of another sort.

The turning from the first to the second division is the same turning of the process that, when first coming to be genus, splits itself this way: the transition of the self-preserving singular into the genus, and the transition into the absolute genus. [It is] the process of the self-realizing concept, which thus emerging out of itself is only in bad reality, collects itself out of this into the concept, and becomes absolute reality. The sublated first division, or the becoming self-conscious, is this: the I appears originally determined and just as originally divided; it recognizes the determinacy that is in the division as its own, sublates it, and indeed posits at first the formal$_2$ division or the infinite reflection as itself, as freedom; it posits the determinacy also as its own. The I can no longer pass over into the formal$_2$ sublating, into the negative in general; [it] cannot allow the opposite to disappear. For it is real$_2$; it is something universal; but it is at the same time [through]out[28] only something synthetically, not purely, universal. For the I has determined itself only as universal, for us as what is self-equivalent in existence, [and] not as that which is this equivalence on its own account.

---

28. *Trans.*: The ms: *aus*; CE emends to *auch* ("also"). We follow Lasson in reading [*durch*]*aus* ("throughout").

Through the reflection of this potency into itself, the I has come to itself in the opposite as a universal, but not yet as a particular. Of course the determinacy falls in the particular—it is this very particular; but the former reflection, its absolute self-discovered freedom, is only through separation. It is not as a whole reflected within itself. It takes the formal [moment] of separation to be its own infinity, but it posits the determinacy only in a simple unreflected manner as *one* with it. In the opposition the determinacy has not become the other of itself, but as original determinacy has remained self-equivalent.

To the universal self-discovering I, which has severed its infinity from its particularity, stands opposed this particular as the I itself; the process of self-preservation as formal passes through itself over into that of reality. The I is simple, universal reflection, which has severed the reflection from itself and has posited it as *one* with itself; simple reflection, reflected into itself.[29] The I, as something determinately reflected into itself, [163] immediately confronts this simple reflection connecting only with itself. The I itself is what is reflected into itself; it is just this reality, but in such a way that the reality is essentially determined as singularity. Since the former simple reflection is at the same time the universal side of this I as something singular, it has immediately turned against this its conflict, and is differentially active against it.

II / THE PRACTICAL I

If the theoretical I has found itself to be formal reflection, though reflection that is absolute, reflected into itself, then as practical the I must find itself as absolutely fulfilled reflection.

Formal, absolute reflection, which has found itself and has become something simple, equivalent, finds itself facing itself as singularity, as determinacy, which is its very essence. The I must sublate this determinacy, this antithesis. On the side of determinacy as well it must turn into something self-equivalent and simple and take back into itself the whole system of conditions—in other words, the ideal origin of itself. For this determinacy, here under consideration, is already in itself the negatively posited of the species itself, or of absolute essence as something existing.

This determinacy, considered to be nothing, is *qua* determinacy not

29. *Trans.*: Following ms. CE inserts [*sind*] ("are").

to be sublated; for its sublating would always be a determining of determinacy by the I, and the product would be strictly nothing but a synthesis, which in itself would have essentially the nature (determined ever anew) of something alien. And in the manner of the monad, if the determining of the I is directed only against something alien, it is nothing if there is not something alien. And its negating is equally well only an abstraction, as an other must step into its place.

The I is not a determinacy in general but rather a determinacy that is equivalent to its essence, or the absolute determinacy, [that is] the genus's existence posited as sublated. It is the absolute determinacy, the whole of the absolute universal's othering of itself. Determinacy has elevated itself to absolute determinacy by being the universal determinacy, even as singularity. [164] The determinate I is so, simply *qua* theoretical. To the extent that it opposes itself as determinate to its absolute reflection, it has not ceased to be something theoretical— that is, to posit determinacy not as its own or original; rather, determinacy is still for the I not yet the I itself. Taking determinacy back into itself, [re]cognizing it as original, means nothing other than positing it as sublated in and of itself. In singularity, determinacy has elevated itself altogether to absolute determinacy. The genus, as what is negatively posited in antithesis or existence, is itself infinity; to posit here, still as negative, this which has been negatively posited means nothing but [re]cognizing that negatively posited singularity is no determinacy—that is, that the absolute singularity is infinity, which is the same simple that the universal is. A singular I belongs wholly to the hypothesis of the world-process, in which many singular Is (or equally a plurality of Is that are in themselves, reflected into themselves, alternately passive and active) make their entrance. In the realized genus this existence sublates itself; and at that stage the I (which would posit the determinacy as deriving from the genus, as being indifferently separated in this way) would fall back under itself. In being separate vis-à-vis the universal I, determinacy is simply a differentiated one, since the I has, as it were, taken all being-in-itself back into itself. The I is the circle of its own circle and of the other's— that is, of the in-itself of the opposite; and for this in-itself there remains nothing left over. This determinacy that falls back into the I is infinity itself, or precisely the inherently sublated relation of what exists in the genus. Hence this infinity is immediately just the unity of both reflections: that which the I finds, and that which the I itself is—in other words, that which just finds itself, and just is only in that it finds itself. That the I is, only as a finding of itself—not separately, somehow prior to its having found itself, but rather that the I [is] this finding of itself—this is its absolute infinity. And the antithesis of the practical I lies solely in its being for itself what had not yet found itself. The determinacy embedded in the I is nothing other than the infinite itself, posited as something equivalent to itself, connecting only with itself. In its singularity, I is simply a universal; its original determinacy is its absolute singularity, or its infinity—a determinacy sublated with respect to it, [165] which merely as determinate I is the semblance that the practical I sublates. Just as the theoretical I is the cognition that what is opposed to it is *a* universal, so the practical I [is the cognition] that in the deed[30] this opposite is *the* universal proper, and the determinacy is absolute determinacy. The I, *qua* theoretical, is spirit in general; *qua* realized, practical I—for which determinacy is itself absolute determinacy or infinity—it is absolute spirit.

III / ABSOLUTE SPIRIT

The doctrine of absolute spirit is what gives a novel—though hardly unexpected—turn to the interpretation of Kant and Fichte. Just as Hegel used the dogmatic rationalism of the older tradition to found the speculative realism of his philosophy of nature, so he uses the postulational moralism of Kant and Fichte as the scaffold for his objective idealism. Logic ended with a formal review. Metaphysics ends with the real application of that review. The subject that thinks and wills rationally is neither a postulated Ego nor a bad infinite progress towards an ideal community. It is the community that is the real self of the rational consciousness here and now, the self of the ethical substance, the " 'I' that is 'We', and 'We' that is 'I' ":[31] "the longing for immortality is a reversion of the spirit into a baser sphere."

Absolute spirit comes to be *for itself* (or really) only at the climax of the Philosophy of Spirit (and of the system itself) in art, religion, and philosophy. At this stage it has come to be for us as thinkers, or for itself as pure thought. This formal reality is the concept of the *ether*. The ether is the *energy* that is absolutely conserved, the continuum at the basis of all experience. Hegel conceives pure thinking as the self-comprehension of the ether because in this way he can close the circle of experience. Spirit and nature are the subjective and objective aspects of the ether, which is their logical ground-

---

30. *Trans.*: *In der That* could be translated "in fact."
31. See *Phenomenology*, trans. Miller, para. 177, p. 110.

concept or absolute identity. Here he calls the ether "absolute matter," but in the Philosophy of Nature we learn that it is also "the Idea of God." Absolute spirit is here said to be "the Idea of the highest essence"; and it closes not just the Metaphysics but the Logic and Metaphysics into a speculative circle because it is "once more its own first moment, simple connection in general" (CE 176, lines 24–26). Thus Hegel was implicitly bound to absorb his critical logic into one unified speculative science in the end.

Here the progression that has been going on comes to a halt: the progression by which the concept in its reality turns into an other, and thereby, as totality itself, or as something reflected within itself, passes over into another sphere. Totality is [now] absolute totality; for all determinacy has been sublated, or is absolute universality proper. *Qua* being-in-itself (in that it is what is enclosed within itself) cognition is realized in absolute spirit. The idea of cognition is the following: the side of the definition (which expresses singularity, existence, and in which there is the many as something indifferent, each [one of the many] abstracting from its contrary) is one with the other side, which is universality and has within it in the form of a simple determinacy that developed singularity. Cognition is formal because its reflection into itself is complete only to the extent that singularity in general is also the contrary of itself, [that is,] universality. But this singularity is a determinate singularity that excludes a determinate other from itself. As pure singularity it is point, simple, yet for that reason opposed to its multiplicity of determinacies, which are, in that they exclude their opposite qualities. This singularity is the unity of these qualities. Yet although it is the singularity of negative *one*, it is so only in connection with the excluded other, not in connection with the determinacies connected with singularity. It is not the negative unity of the determinacies, but it is rather only a whole, an indifferent universality that does not affect the determinacies negatively, since it [166] could be this only through its opposites, which are however excluded. Singularity is therefore negative only in a quantitative manner; in other words, it is externally restricted. And the positive negating of its restriction is not singularity itself, but something else; at the same time this negating is equally a new positing in singularity of restrictions that are *in it* and *for it* equally indifferent. This singularity—posited in its determinacies as a simple one, in such a way that they are all gathered up into it as the universal's particularity—is nonetheless only a determinate, not an absolute, particularity. The universal indeed contains within itself, as self-dividing, the whole totality of particularities, though these are at the same time indifferent to each other. Proof is this dividing up of the universal, its constructing; the universal divides, not as definition does, into pure determinacies to which the universality (*qua* point) is opposed, but rather into parts that themselves have in them the nature of the whole [*das Ganzen*]. In the proof, this their being *per se* is completed [*ergänzt*] through their connection with one another, so that the universal displays itself as much *qua* their universal, as *qua* their negative, unity, and is as much a singular as a universal, being now singular, however, in the genuine sense of negative *one* in connection with the opposed determinacies contained in it. This concept of cognition is the formal returning into itself. The universal is divided within itself—the determination is not an external one—the universal is not a quantum; rather, quanta are contained in it. But this indifference of determinacies vis-à-vis one another—as having the nature of the whole within themselves, as determined and on their own account—at the same time sublates itself. The movement of proof shows that they are in fact differentiated with respect to one another, are only in the connection, and are thus ideal$_2$; and [it shows] that the first division is not an arbitrary, external one, but determined exclusively through negative unity; in other words, it has in itself nothing but the connection with one another of what appear indifferent. The result is that the singularization of the whole is in fact absolute singularity, and the determinacy that appears in it is absolute determinacy, since the determinacies all fall into that whole, which is thus their unity, the one in which they are equally sublated. *Qua* first moment, the whole appears passive, connected only with itself, equivalent to itself, and its separation appears to be something to which it is indifferent, as absolutely contingent, and which, as something alien, it simply does not affect. The meaning of the division is here something wholly concealed, unexpressed. The hidden connection that the parts have to one another as they emerge sublates [167] their indifference to one another; and they show themselves to be simply and solely a relation, or to be moments that as unity are related to plurality in such a way that the two are simply equivalent. What before was an indifferent relation becomes a genuine relation; and what before was outside the universal, something alien to it, now becomes a relation to itself. What were the parts relate [now] to the parts as a whole; and because they are parts of *one* whole, parts that relate to the parts as a whole, they are sublated in their determinacy, this being their contrary (in that the part is the whole quite ideally, and the others sundered from the whole are themselves equivalent to it); and the whole is absolute singularity. Their negation is singularity itself, and is with respect to itself without [any] excluding connection with something alien; and the being *per se* of what appear as parts, [namely,] existence, so far as their being is itself only the differentiating connection, coincides completely with their ideality. That existence of the whole, as a whole opposed to its division, is a relation to itself. *It* is the unity of this antithesis as moments—of the universal and of the particular, which are equivalent to each other: the universal expresses the whole as a moment of the whole; the particular expresses that same whole as a division, which is equally a moment of the whole. The result: this division has returned completely into itself; for it is merely[32] not a plurality of self-subsisting beings but a plurality of moments. These being differentiated, they are only their connection; and this connection is the whole. The turning point of this reflection lies in the fact that what is divided, simply and solely *qua* differentiated division, shows itself to be differentiated connection and passes over into relation—that is, into the being of the parts *qua* moments. That first division is itself therefore only through this second relation; in other words, the relation is nothing contingent but rather what appears in the proof as necessity. The necessary content is the determination of the construction, with the result that it only constructs itself so far as it is differentiated unity, the way the unity appears first of all in the proof.

This cognition is rounded out in itself; the singular is enclosed with the universal. However, even the whole, which thus moves within itself, is still a determinate content vis-à-vis cognition. It is only this movement of cognition that is absolute in itself; but the moments of its movement are not in the same way this cognition itself. Cognition is thus formal; and singularity in cognition is at once an absolute singularity and something turned outward; it has a side from which it is a quantitative determinacy. The indifferent dividing becomes one that is not [168] indifferent; but what is self-equivalent in the division is not that which determines the division. In other words, it has not yet begun from the insight that the indifferent dividing in fact is nothing but a dividing into an indifferent dividing and into a differentiated dividing. These *two* moments of the process of cognition are

---

32. *Trans.*: We follow ms. CE: "it is not merely a plurality."

themselves not yet posited as unity, as what is first, or as the absolute content. Only if this takes place is the initial dividing directly through the whole itself. In other words, cognition itself is not just what is so divided as content that cognition, *qua* self-dividing, would be immediately the necessity of the content's being able to be broken up into no other commensurable names than these. Only in the proof does the necessity of the construction show itself. The construction must in itself be the division of the proof; thus results cognition as a whole, posited as the in-itself.

This idea of the in-itself is realized in metaphysics, since cognition becomes its own content: or the circle of reflection, as this movement, as the in-itself, is now what goes through its circle. Formal cognition, as the circle that is distinct from what constitutes the cycle, is on its own account shut up in itself [and] indifferent towards the determinacy of its content. It is a monad or even an idea that is not affected by its determinacy but is determinate in that there are many of them. And there are many of them because, connecting only with themselves as [being] in themselves, they are passive. They possess determinacy as something external; determinacy did not stand over against them as something absolute. For since negative unity and the universal as moments (so to speak) are only at the one time in the idea, the coming apart is a dividing, since it is not the unity of both moments—in other words, the whole circle that still stands opposed to itself. Otherwise there would be nothing remaining on the other side; there would in fact be no crossing over.

Cognition is the idea of the in-itself, or the idea in general. This monad is the determinacy of what is undifferentiated; for this reason it is so directed towards itself that it negates what is external—it abstracts from it. Outwardly its determinacy has only this negative side. It is thus the relation of substantiality, complete in itself; and its realization is in keeping with it, except that in the former entirely ideal₂ relations what stands in connection is essentially only how they are when connected, whereas here what in the realization emerges into an external connection is not [169] essentially how it emerges when connected, but essentially the self-enclosed circle of cognition. Just as the relation of being is realized in the universal, so the monad is realized in the highest essence, in an absolute self-equivalency in which cognition, as opposed, doubled cognition, has remained for its part an absolute simple unity. The highest essence, as what is absolutely universal (that is, [whose] sublated [moments] within it are the wholes of the in-itself, of reflection), is their *being* self-equivalent, their sublated*ness*. It is the *one* moment of absolute essence to be absolute unity and simplicity. Since the being *per se* of the monads or ideas is an indifferent multiplicity, it can do nothing but sublate itself in their movement vis-à-vis one another. For to the extent that the monads are exclusive, their determinacy takes on the character that they are essentially on their own account, and that for them their essence is being *per se*—that is, that they only have the consciousness of the relation. In themselves and with respect to us they come later. However, at first the relation is what is posited ideally₂ *in* the monad; that is, the monad is the positive and negative unity of the relation: the monad is in it and is at the same time indifferent to it. This, then, is what sublates itself in the world-process, in the process of the genus: that for the monad the being *per se* of the monad, as of something determined—this determinacy that accompanies formal cognition—disappears. For the monad there is in this disappearing through its realization only the negativity of what is essential to it, its being *per se* (the self-equivalent universality). For us [there is] this universal as idea, as negative unity of a relation of existing ideas—the real, abiding genus. [It is] an infinity for which the determinacy of the monad is not one turned outwards, as it is for the monad in its self-preservation or in its idea, but one turned [against the] monad, against cognition itself. And in the indifference of both, the determinacy of both perishes. The self-preservation of the monad is its negating of another; this other is cognition, even as it is; and in this other cognition, its negating becomes something sublated as well. The self-preservation of the monad [sub]lates itself for the monad to the extent that its negating of another sublates itself. "Negating of another sublates itself" means that the other becomes for the monad the monad itself. The negative is not the negating of another, but the negating of the monad as something essentially singular. The negative is for the monad a beyond of absolute universality. [170]

The moment of the process of self-preservation is the sublating of the externality of determinacy and the [monad's] coming to be genus. The other moment is the sublating of the merely negative of sublated externality and is the being of determinacy (as of something equivalent to the monad) and a being for the monad. [It is] at the same time, however, a sublating for the monad of the essentiality of determinacy in general—that is, the coming to be of absolute being *per se*. At first determinacy becomes something not other than the monad; deter-

minacy itself becomes cognition; and so[33] for the monad it comes about
that determinacy [is] equivalent to the monad, and by that very fact
the essentiality of the monad too [is] sublated for it. At first the determinacy becomes equivalent to the monad for us, then for itself.
Thus the monad, as a negative *one* that is excluding only as determinacy, *qua* something external, is sublated for the determinacy itself;
and for the monad there is only the essential being as something
external, as an absolute beyond. For us, in fact, this external [thing]
is something internal to the monad. In other words, the monad coincides with its determinacy as something original to it. For the monad,
its beyond is the highest essence, and the monad is sublated as singularity. But in fact the highest essence is the genus, in which, however, the singularity is just a sublated one, one that is not annihilated
but has gone through the null-point of infinity. Yet for the monad
[the singularity is] one that is annihilated. Its self-preservation is only
a longing that sets out to save singularity by way of that null [and] by
the stripping off of determinacy, to preserve singularity as immortal,
as absolute singularity.

Since the monad views what is opposed [to it] as itself, singularity
is in fact sublated as external or quantitative determinacy, and is
absolute or pure singularity, something simple, self-equivalent. But it
[is] not yet so with respect to the monad; for the monad, singularity
only annihilates itself. Since, however, singularity is not in fact annihilated, this annihilating is only an "ought." Singularity, as absolute
[and] simple, is the I. For the I the determinacy is posited not as an
external one, having being in itself, but only as one that is to annihilate
itself. Moreover, on its own account the I is only the idea. *Qua* idea
the monad has confronted itself in this determinacy; or it is for the
determinacy[34] as something that is ideal$_2$ in itself [but] is not yet so
for the I. The monad has indeed penetrated to the idea of the in-
itself, just as *qua* monad it has penetrated to relation. [171]

Thus the I has completely excluded the in-itself of determinacy;
the monad is simply and solely in connection with the I; that is, it is
its original determinacy. The monad is a universal, something sublated
in itself as determinacy; but once again only something that is to have
been annihilated, no longer the synthesis of an in-itself and of a
determinateness by means of the I but of something determined solely

33. *Trans.*: We follow Lasson, reading *alsdann*; ms: *alsdenn*.
34. *Trans.*: Following ms. CE: "it is on its own account."

by means of the I. However, the I is itself this determined [thing]; it is both the synthesis of universality and determinacy as well as what is opposed to the I. The other is equivalent to the I; but both are in themselves the non-equivalent. Singularity has disappeared in the universal only in the sense that it would be no longer an external one. Yet it is still the same chain or line—but only as a diverse one, sublated by the monad. The monad is itself determinate monad. However, the monad that severs itself from itself in this way becomes free. Insofar as determinacy is cognized as the absolute determinacy of the idea itself, it is nothing other than infinity, and the practical monad cognizes itself essentially to be infinite. As a result the in-itself is this: that the monad *qua* singular confronts itself *qua* universal, and posits its singularity as absolute. The theoretical I discovers itself to be the highest essence, as that into which its realization had [already] gone over for us—that is, as that which the I had posited as its absolute beyond. It discovers itself to be the absolutely self-equivalent, which has emerged out of the disappearing of all determinacy. It discovers its opposite within itself to be for that reason itself, to be the in-itself; that is, as the closed circle of reflection it discovers the closed circle of reflection. It finds itself; it is spirit, or rational. The longing for immortality and the beyond of the highest essence is a reversion of the spirit into a baser sphere, since the spirit with respect to itself is immortal and the highest essence.

This spirit, however, is itself formal spirit—highest essence, but not absolute essence or absolute spirit. For there is for spirit only the one side of the its-self opposed to it; and the very discovery of itself is only by way of separation. The highest essence does not find itself as something existing; on the contrary, it finds existence as something negating, or finds itself in its freedom confined within inconceivable limitations. Now it finds what is unequal, determinacy, to be the beyond, just as before it found self-equivalency to be so.

This determinacy, however, is for us nothing else but infinity, or the determinacy that is directed in genus no longer against something external but against itself. *Qua* original, the determinacy is for the I— that is, as a determinacy that would lie beyond the freedom of the I, that would be one with the I as with something simple, self-identical and self-connecting. Since it is self-connected, however, this [172] determinacy, as the determinacy of the process of genus, is itself nothing but that absolutely simple of reflection, which the I has discovered itself to be.

The I as simple reflection that has found itself is opposed to, and turned against, determinacy as its determinacy in order to sublate it. It is turned against itself, not in the determinacy of being against an individual or something singular, but as an original, universal determinacy, determinacy in itself, or in fact it is turned against the universal itself. The self-preservation of the I is the preservation of itself *qua* reflection that has discovered itself, or of itself *qua* negated singularity, and [that] is genus for itself. What is opposed to formal spirit is the same singularity that is in genus: infinity. And the practical I that is self-preserving is no longer connected with itself *qua* singular [*singuläres*], but with itself *qua* genus. It preserves itself as what has found itself—the universal. What it negates in order to preserve itself is its-self *qua* singular. The singularity of the practical I has disappeared within universality. To turn itself against determinacy is only a deception arising from its wanting to be practical; for what it is turned against is its-self and, as it has discovered itself to be, its-self is simple infinity. What it turns itself against is simpleness itself—that is, the nothing, the self-connected, the passive.

The I that has found itself, or spirit, is the unity of both reflections, which connects with itself: the first reflection is what preserves itself but has become universal; the other is that of genus, or the universal reflection that has within itself absolute singularity. This spirit is complete in itself; and this is what makes it still practical for us—and for itself. [Spirit is practical] for itself because, as the unity of both these reflections having come to itself, it has its self-alienation outside itself and wants to preserve itself against it. [Spirit is practical] for us because it has, to be sure, cognized itself as self-equivalent. However, neither the non-equivalent as itself, nor yet infinity as such has cognized what infinity is. Spirit is infinite for us, but not yet for itself. For itself spirit is only self-equivalent. It intuits itself, but not infinity; it does not intuit itself as the other.

Formal spirit is on its own account formal in that it opposes to itself as something simple the infinity of reflection, infinity in itself, or its pure concept. For its reality is not the relation or the process of the genus, for the formal spirit posits as equal to itself what is real in this, or the self-equivalent. But spirit [173] opposes to itself infinity outside itself; for infinity is this: that spirit has sublated itself as existing, as a fixed point. It is what is thus sublated that is spirit's object, but strictly as something sublated; that spirit has found itself consists in the fact that it has sublated itself. There is for it something purely negative, against which it is practical; this is its nothingness. It is directed not against its existence but against the nothingness of existence. Its existence is to have discovered itself as spirit, and what it fights against as spirit is nothingness. Because it is spirit, its self-preservation is its absolute connecting with itself as something discovered, or an its-self that spirit [re]cognizes itself to be. Its negating is directed against its not having found itself, its being not-spirit, its being something alien to itself. But that which is to itself something alien is the contrary of itself, is what sublates itself in itself. It is nothingness; in other words, it is the absolute contrary of itself; and as this contrary of itself it is the contrary again, absolute unrest. It is the absolute concept, infinity. Spirit, thus preserving itself as something that has found itself, is directed against nothingness, or infinity; its self-equivalence [is directed] against this absolute non-equivalence. But nothingness, infinity, or absolute non-equivalence is just the absolutely simple, what is absolutely returned into itself, simply and solely self-connecting and it is the same as spirit is. Spirit discovers the other as such, as absolutely other, as self-sublating, as itself. In other words, it does not only intuit itself as itself, but [it] also [intuits] the other-as-such as itself. It is equal *to itself* and equal to the other; the other is that which sublates itself and is equal to itself. This unity is the absolute spirit. It cannot be asked how the infinite would come to be finite or emerge from it, and what meaningless expressions of this sort amount to. For the self-equivalent [re]cognizes the infinite as an equal (and it itself as something self-equivalent, as infinite, or as something coming out of the other to itself), as being only in that it, the other, comes to itself; and this other is just as much its-self as its-self is the other. Since spirit thus [re]cognizes infinity, it thereby comprehends itself, for its comprehending consists in this: that it posits itself as connected with another. It comprehends itself, for it posits itself connected with the other—that is, it itself as the other of itself, as infinite, and thus equivalent to itself.

Thus the absolute cycle of absolute spirit. What has discovered itself to be self-equivalent intuits itself as the kind of thing that is non-equivalent to itself, is the other to itself; [174] it is infinite. And this infinity is its-self for the other is the contrary of itself; it is the self-equivalent. This is spirit, which thus intuits itself in the non-equivalent.

In absolute spirit construction and proof are absolutely *one*. The dividing within construction is just what displays itself as *one* in the proof; in the proof, however, it is the self-equivalent unity and the infinity that posits itself as *one*, and these two are moreover the only parts of the construction. The construction itself is as such necessary; for it is one with the proof. In other words, spirit in itself is this: that it discovers itself as spirit; and that in which it discovers itself, or rather that which it finds itself to be, is infinity. Spirit is only as this self-discovering; and this latter is the necessity of its division into itself and into the other of itself, which is the self-subsistent absolute other— that is, the other with respect to spirit, or the infinite.

Absolute spirit is simple infinity, or infinity connecting with itself. As infinite, this simple essence is immediately the other, or the contrary of itself; as simple, as connected with itself, it is determinate; it is the passive; and the self-equivalent confronts this its other. "The self-equivalent is something other" means that it posits itself as something connected with an other; and *qua* that first it is this other as self-equivalent. But this other, or passive, is infinite, the contrary of itself; it is what is in the other. Similarly, the active is the contrary itself; it is what is in the self-equivalent. Hence the otherness, the connection of self-equivalent spirit as preserving itself and negating the other—namely, what connects with itself—is immediately the other of itself, or what has come back to itself.[35] Its negating the other is immediately the being of the other; for the negating of the other is a connecting with itself, and the other is precisely this connecting with itself.

Absolute spirit is the self-equivalent that connects only with itself; for spirit as such, just this connection with itself, is the passive, since the spiritual is this: that it finds itself in the other of itself. But the self-equivalent is not what finds itself as the other of itself. That is why self-equivalent spirit is precisely this very other that spirit finds as itself. The connection of spirit with itself, as this other, is however immediately [175] the contrary of itself as well, or that which spirit finds as itself. This connection of spirit with itself, which with respect to itself is at the same time the other of itself, is the *infinite*. It is nothing other than what was called the first part of logic, or the logic of understanding. Unity or self-equivalence becomes for itself the absolutely other; unity comes to be the many, and the whole as the self-equivalent, indifferent unity of unity and multiplicity comes to be infinity. This infinity [is] the unity of something that, as infinity

---

35. *Trans.*: The ms: *zurükgekommen*. CE emends by adding *-seyn*; we have simply added an -e.

strictly in its being *per se* (and it is posited on its own account as the other of the unity, at the same time only in connection with its opposite), is itself as such a unity or as relation, is just something other and herewith doubled, because the relation is equally marked with the character of otherness in general. The division of the infinite, as well as the being of its parts, is just for this reason nothing indifferent either, but is what sublates itself in itself; and only thereby does it [come] to pass that what is posited is in itself the absolutely other than that as which it [is] posited. This its otherness is its passing over into a being otherwise; and the posited infinity connecting with itself is at the same time with respect to itself the movement within itself of becoming an other; and the uninhibited connecting with itself is in the contrary, infinite within itself.

The infinite, as the system of simple connection that becomes the contrary of the connection, or infinity, and divides itself into the two opposed infinites or relations, has within this its constructing passed over to the self-equivalent, to the circle of the return into itself. The whole inner movement of this system emerges as what is in itself; what is moved, however, is the ideal$_2$, or is posited only as sublated. Cognition is the in-itself of infinity, the absolutely equivalent in absolute non-equivalence, the unity of simple connection and infinity, which fell apart in infinity and are indeed its two absolute arms or moments. As a result, the second as the non-equivalent is infinity once more, just as the simple connection is only the first moment. Cognition as the in-itself is spirit connecting with the other or with infinity. Viewed from the side of infinity, spirit [is present] in the way that it, as self-connected, is an other to itself; or from its side, in the way that it comes to itself out of its otherness, out of infinity. Again only the infinity and cognition constitute the antithesis—that is, the antithesis with respect to itself or [176] [the one that] is posited. Infinity, or otherness, is on its own account only at this point; cognition itself and its content fall apart even for cognition, whereas previously infinity divided itself only for us, while for itself it fell apart indifferently. The infinite is essentially connected in its moments—for the infinite it was not thus connected; essentiality was internal to it, or unposited. Only cognition is both: it is the essential connection of moments, posited infinity; and for it the infinite, as the holding apart of the moments, is an indifferent content. Up to now this indifference was *for* us; that is, we were the indifferent unity, the contiguity or succession, as well as their movement. In its becoming, the infinite became our object; its becoming-other was for us also something other than the movement of cognition.[36] Thus the movement of cognition, the positing as different, as moment, is here posited as connected with an indifferent content. This antithesis, existing for the first time in cognition, is the moment of infinity, as connection with itself (which becomes an other *for itself*, in the differentiation),[37] or in connection with spirit (which in itself comes to itself out of the infinite, as out of other[ness], but which as coming to itself out of the other has this other as its antithesis). Metaphysics is the moment of spirit that has found itself, is in itself, and finds itself in its other. What is opposite to cognition becomes itself cognition; the content of spirit becomes itself spirit; and thus has spirit in its other[ness] found itself for itself. The infinite, which for us was in itself in its essence, is so for spirit itself; and spirit, which has thus found itself as itself in its other[ness], is therein only connected with itself, not with an other. In other words, spirit is again its first moment, the simple connection in general, or connection in its reality, infinity.

This [infinite] is the *idea* of the absolute essence; it is only as absolute spirit. It is this: that out of its connection with itself it becomes another for itself. The connection with itself is the infinite for spirit—that is, for this very connection; for us—that is, for cognition, or for spirit coming to itself—the infinite is the other[ness]; and spirit, which in this way is spirit and finds itself in the infinite, is connected only with itself, or it is equivalent to itself. It is again its first moment and has returned completely into itself.

But this return too is still an othering of itself; this whole [177] idea of spirit is only idea, or the idea is first moment to itself. For spirit as this movement of return into itself has found itself in the in-itself, in the content of cognition, and is only spirit as this unity in its other[ness]; thus it is only absolute spirit. But it is *itself* not absolute spirit, or has not [re]cognized itself as absolute spirit. It is this for us, not for itself; metaphysics is its coming to be, and is spirit as idea. Spirit *is* absolute spirit, positing the other as itself, infinity returning into itself. But this return is again simple connection or infinity itself; at its highest peak it thus falls back again into its first, into its beginning, which again is only this beginning—is the infinity that splits itself into simple

36. *Trans.*: Possible alternate reading: "its becoming other, as the movement of cognition, was. . . . "

37. *Trans.*: Following ms. CE inserts [*übergeht*]: "which goes over into differentiation."

connection and infinity as something opposed, not infinity as it has now come to be, as an infinity [re]cognized by spirit as itself, but again only as other[ness]. But this other[ness] [re]cognized by spirit is hereby of this sort: the other[ness] is itself spirit's self-discovery forged together out of its infinity, a unity that can be dissolved. This return that is exhibited as spirit is all by itself the other[ness], the finding itself, as well as itself in the other[ness]. The cycle that is spirit is the self that runs through this cycle; and it does so in the shape of spirit that in its moments never forgets itself and would not be in them as absolute spirit on its own account. Spirit, as it has been exhibited, is therefore only idea, because it is only a simple cycle, because it is not in all moments of the cycle (not in infinity only as other[ness] nor in the reflection of cognition as connecting with itself)[38] [but because it is] only spirit that is itself coming to be spirit. [It is so] when spirit that has found itself is again on its own account, not when this spirit, having found itself, is another to itself, not when it comes to itself and has found itself as one that spirit has confronting itself even *qua* spirit (which returns to itself from this fall of infinity as victor over a spirit, and is just as eternally returned). This totality of the return is for the first time in itself, and no longer goes over into the other. Spirit is the absolute; and the absolute as its idea is realized absolutely, only in that the moments of spirit itself are this spirit; but then there is no more going beyond it.

The idea of spirit, or spirit that intuits itself in other[ness] as itself, is immediately again spirit connecting with itself as absolute spirit. In other words, it is absolute spirit as infinity and, for its self-cognizing (or the becoming itself out of *its* other[ness]), the other of itself. It is *nature*; [178] the simple absolute spirit connecting with itself is *ether*, absolute *matter*. Spirit, having found itself in its other, is self-enclosed and living nature. As spirit that is at the same time connecting with itself, nature is other[ness], spirit as infinite, and the coming to be of absolute spirit. Nature is the first moment of self-realizing spirit.

A Note on the System of 1804

The Metaphysics—and with it our translation—ends on the first or second page of the fifty-fifth sheet. Hegel's manuscript continues without a break under

---

38. *Trans.*: The French translation of Souche-Dagues reads: "(not in infinity only as other[ness] or as connecting with itself) in the reflection of cognition it is only spirit. . . ."

the new heading Naturphilosophie. This is broken off only at sheet 102 (which is less than half full and comes to a halt near the top of a page when the argument has just reached the concept of "organism"—*das Organische*).

In the Philosophy of Nature Hegel traces the evolution of the "ether" (which he calls "the Idea of God" but says is *not* "the living God") from its primary positing as light and darkness, through the dynamic space-time equilibrium of the solar system, to the physical equilibrium of the earth-process, which sets the stage for organic life. He takes motion to be as primitive as rest, and like Heraclitus he interprets all physical stability as a tension of opposites or as a more complex cycle of tensions.

The perpetual-motion machine in the heavens Hegel regards as the open display of the true nature of body. But he no longer uses the language of "intuition" and "concept" that he employed in the *System of Ethical Life* in 1802. Instead, when he reaches the earth-process—which is the frame of all natural consciousness—he calls it "absolute cognition." He makes it quite clear that this cognition does not exist "for the earth." It is mankind as a rational genus that is the conscious subject of this absolute cognition.

From his "metaphysics of objectivity" we can see how the theory of the living organism was projected in Hegel's mind as the movement from absolute cognition to self-cognition. But he abandoned his phenomenology of the absolute spirit at this stage, so we have to turn to the manuscripts of 1803–4 to fill the material gap. In fact the Philosophy of Nature is in rather a disorderly state in these earlier drafts because Hegel has not yet managed to articulate it properly as the realization of cognition. But enough survives from the fragmentary Philosophy of Spirit[39] to show how the natural human consciousness becomes the quest for absolute knowledge, from which logic starts.

Unfortunately, we have no developed account of the theory of absolute spirit in Hegel's own words. We have to depend on the reports of Rosenkranz[40] (in which the manuscripts of different years are often mingled together). But the general conception of the absolute triad of art, religion, and philosophy is clear; and the concept of systematic philosophy as a circle that closes upon its own beginning is a constant in Hegel's theoretical program from 1802 to the very end of his life.[41]

39. See Harris and Knox, trans. and eds., *System of Ethical Life and First Philosophy of Spirit*.

40. The relevant reports are translated in the appendixes to ibid.

41. For a fuller discussion of the system that this Logic and Metaphysics is designed to introduce, see Harris, *Night Thoughts*, chaps. 5 to 7; for the theory of absolute spirit see also chap. 4.

Glossary

das Andere	the other
das Anders	the other[ness]
Andersseyn	otherness
Anderswerden	becoming other, othering
an ihr (ihm) selbst	with respect to it, in it
an sich	in itself, inherently
dans An sich	the in-itself
An sich seyn	being-in-itself
an und für sich	in and of itself
aufheben	sublate
aüssern	utter, express
Bedeutung	significance, meaning
begreifen	comprehend, conceive
das Besondere	the particular
bestehen	subsist
Bestimmtheit	determinacy
Bestimmtseyn	determinateness
Bestimmung	determination
bewirken	effect (verb)
beziehen	connect
Beziehung	connection
darstellen	set forth, display
different	differentiated
Differenz	differentiation

Ein, Eine	as noun: one; as adjective with capital: *one*
Einheit	unity
Eins	*one*, one[ness]
Einsseyn	oneness
Einswerden	becoming one, unification
Einzelne	singular
entgegensetzen	oppose
entzweien	split
sich erhalten	preserve itself
erkennen	[re]cognize, cognize
Erkennen	cognition
für sich	on its own account
für sich seyend	self-subsistent
für sich seyn	being *per se*
Gedankending	*ens rationis*
Gegensatz	antithesis
Gegentheil	contrary
gleich	equal, equivalent
Glied	term, member
Idee	idea
indifferent	indifferent, undifferentiated
Indifferenz	indifference, neutrality
in sich reflektiert	reflected into itself, self-reflexive
Menge	aggregate
Sache	Thing
schlecht	bad
theilen	divide
trennen	separate
Übergang	transition
übergehen	pass over, go over
Übergehen	passing over, transition
Unterschied	distinction, difference

verbinden	bind up, bond
Verbindung	bonding, combination
Verhältnis	relation, ratio, relationship
verhalten	relate
verschieden	diverse
Verschiedenheit	diversity
Vertheilung	dividing up
Vorstellung	presentation
Wahrhaft	true
Wirken	acting
wirkend	effective
zusammenschliessen	interlock

Works Cited

Cerf, W., and Harris, H. S., trans. and eds. *G. W. F. Hegel, Faith and Knowledge*. Albany: SUNY Press, 1977.

Chiereghin, F., et al., trans. and eds. *Logica e metafisica di Jena*. Trento: Quaderni di verifiche, 1982.

Di Giovanni, G., and Harris, H. S., trans. *Between Kant and Hegel: Texts in the Development of Post-Kantian Idealism*. Albany: SUNY Press, 1985.

Fichte, J. G. *Grundlage der gesammten Wissenschaftslehre*. Leipzig: Gabler, 1794.

– *Sämtliche Werke*. Ed. R. Lauth and H. Gliwitzky. Stuttgart-Bad Canstatt: Fromann, 1964–.

Harris, H. S. *Hegel's Development I: Toward the Sunlight (1770–1801)*. Oxford: Clarendon, 1972.

– *Hegel's Development II: Night Thoughts (Jena 1801–1806)*. Oxford: Clarendon, 1983.

Harris, H. S., and Cerf, W., trans. and eds. *G. W. F. Hegel, The Difference between Fichte's and Schelling's System of Philosophy*. Albany: SUNY Press, 1977.

Harris, H. S., and Knox, T. M., trans. and eds. *G. W. F. Hegel, System of Ethical Life and First Philosophy of Spirit*. Albany: SUNY Press, 1979.

Hartkopf, W. *Kontinuität und Diskontinuität in Hegels Jenaer Anfängen*. Königstein: Forum Academicum, 1979.

Heath, P., trans. *F. W. J. Schelling, System of Transcendental Idealism*. Charlottesville: University of Virginia Press, 1978.

Heath, P., and Lachs, J., trans. *J. G. Fichte, Science of Knowledge*. New York: Appleton-Century-Crofts, 1970.

Hegel, G. W. F. *Briefe von und an Hegel*. Ed. J. Hoffmeister and R. Flechsig. 4 vols. Hamburg: Meiner, 1961.

– *Dokumente zu Hegels Entwicklung*. Ed. J. Hoffmeister. Stuttgart: Fromann, 1936.

— *Gesammelte Werke.* Ed. Rheinisch-Westfälischen Akademie der Wissenschaften. Hamburg: Meiner, 1968– (CE).
— *Hegels erstes System.* Ed. H. Ehrenberg and H. Link. Heidelberg, 1915.
— *Hegel's Science of Logic.* Trans. A. V. Miller. London: Allen and Unwin, 1969; New York: Humanities, 1969.
— *Jenenser Logik, Metaphysik und Naturphilosophie.* Ed. G. Lasson. Leipzig, 1923.
— *Lectures on the History of Philosophy.* Trans. E. S. Haldane and F. H. Simpson. 3 vols. London: Routledge and Kegan Paul, 1892.
— *Logic.* Trans. W. Wallace from *Encyclopaedia of the Philosophical Sciences.* 2nd edn. Oxford: Clarendon, 1892.
— *Phenomenology of Spirit.* Trans. A. V. Miller. Oxford: Clarendon, 1977.
— *Werke.* Ed. E. Moldenhauer and K. M. Michel. 20 vols. Frankfurt: Suhrkamp, 1970–71 (*Theorie Werkausgabe*).
Hegel-Studien. Ed. F. Nicolin and O. Pöggeler. Bonn: Bouvier, 1961–.
Heinrichs, J. *Die Logik der "Phänomenologie des Geistes."* Bonn: Bouvier, 1974.
Kant, I. *Critik der reinen Vernunft.* Riga, 1788.
— *Critique of Pure Reason.* Trans. N. Kemp Smith. London: Macmillan, 1933.
Kimmerle, H. "Dokumente zu Hegels Jenaer Dozententätigkeit." *Hegel-Studien* 4 (1967): 21–100.
— "Zur Chronologie von Hegels Jenaer Schriften." *Hegel-Studien* 4 (1967): 125–76.
Knox, T. M., trans., and Acton, H. B., eds. *G. W. F. Hegel, Natural Law.* Philadelphia: University of Pennsylvania Press, 1975.
Nicolin, G., ed. *Hegel in Berichten seiner Zeitgenossen.* Hamburg: Meiner, 1970.
Rosen, Michael. *Hegel's Dialectic and Its Criticism.* Cambridge: Cambridge University Press, 1982.
Rosenkranz, K. *Georg Wilhelm Friedrich Hegels Leben.* Berlin, 1844.
Schelling, F. W .J. *Sämmtliche Werke.* Ed. K. F. A. Schelling. 14 vols. Stuttgart and Augsburg: Cotta, 1856–61.
Souche-Dagues, D., trans. *G. W. F. Hegel, Logique et Métaphysique (Iéna 1804–1805).* Paris: Gallimard, 1980.
Stirling, J. H. *The Secret of Hegel.* Edinburgh: Oliver and Boyd, 1865.
Trede, J. H. "Hegels frühe Logik (1801–1803/4). Versuch einer systematischen Rekonstruktion." *Hegel-Studien* 7 (1972): 123–68.

Index

Italic numbers refer to H. S. Harris's commentary.